RICHARD COBDEN
AND FOREIGN POLICY

GEORGE · ALLEN
PUBLISHERS · LONDON
& UNWIN · LIMITED
RUSKIN · HOUSE

RICHARD COBDEN
AND FOREIGN POLICY

A CRITICAL EXPOSITION, WITH SPECIAL
REFERENCE TO OUR DAY AND
ITS PROBLEMS

BY

WILLIAM HARBUTT DAWSON

AUTHOR OF "THE GERMAN EMPIRE, 1867–1914"
"THE EVOLUTION OF MODERN GERMANY"
"PROBLEMS OF THE PEACE," ETC., ETC.

LONDON: GEORGE ALLEN & UNWIN LTD.
RUSKIN HOUSE, 40 MUSEUM STREET, W.C.1

First published in 1926

Printed in Great Britain by
Unwin Brothers, Ltd., Woking

" What is true requires but time to establish it in men's minds. Time and truth against all the world ! But you must have time, and that time which destroys everything else only establishes truth."

RICHARD COBDEN, Speech at Manchester,
October 19, 1843.

PREFACE

THIS book has been written as a tribute to a great Englishman, and with the hope that it may throw light upon some of the difficult problems which to-day confront British statesmanship in the domain of foreign relations and policy. Criticizing in the House of Commons Mr. Gladstone's Reform Bill of 1866, Disraeli said : " Ignorance never settles a question. Questions must be settled by knowledge, and it is not the vexation of an opposition, from whichever side of the House it may come, that prevents this Bill from advancing. *It is that we none of us see our way.*" Do not these last words accurately describe the present position of most people who occupy themselves with international politics ? And is not much of the prevailing perplexity due to want of knowledge and, what is worse, positive unwillingness to face the hard, naked facts of the situation and accept the conclusions to which they point ?

It is my belief that no statesman of modern times is better able than Richard Cobden to give to our statesmanship and to public opinion the help and guidance of which they so sorely stand in need to-day, and for the lack of which they are largely floundering, and will continue to flounder, in doubt, despondency, irresolution, and the pessimism which is ever the grave of faith and all earnest endeavour. Granting that some of Cobden's opinions on foreign and imperial policy have been invalidated by events which neither he nor any of his contemporaries could have foreseen, yet his teaching, in the main, is still sound, and it seems to show, as no other, a possible way—if not the only one—out of the morass into which our statesmanship blindly stumbled at the beginning of the century, and from which as yet it has failed to extricate itself.

Just half a century ago Lord Salisbury wrote :

"The commonest error in politics is sticking to the carcasses of dead policies. When a mast falls overboard you do not try to save a rope here and a spar there, in memory of their former utility ; you cut away the hamper altogether. And it should be the same with a policy. But it is not so. We cling to the shred of an old policy after it has been torn to pieces, and to the shadow of the shred after the rag itself has been torn away. And therefore it is that we are now in perplexity."

That is the exact position to-day. In the mass we persist in regarding ourselves as still bound to the unhappy past ; we are still trying to compromise with that past, when the only hope of safety lies in boldly renouncing it and making a fresh start in altogether new ways.

Cobden's doctrine of foreign policy has the supreme merit that it translates the reader into an atmosphere utterly dissimilar from that in which Europe has lived a feverish and unhealthy life for well-nigh a generation. It is also in the highest degree stimulating. His entire conception of international relations is a challenge. He disturbs your tranquillity ; he forces you to think and keeps you thinking, now with him, now against him ; he looks beyond tradition and convention, and calls for stark facts ; he rejects the pompous claims of authority and emphasizes personal responsibility and the duty and dignity of private judgment ; he bids you demand of your most cherished opinions that they shall prove and justify themselves.

Not the least of his claims to revived interest is the fact that he emphasized, as few English political leaders have done, the place of conscience in national policy. The present is a time of unrest, lassitude, and apathy, and the prevailing mentality might be expressed by the words " Nothing matters." To Cobden everything in public life mattered : to him justice, honour, faith mattered greatly, and national righteousness mattered tremendously. No statesman was less an opportunist than he ; none was ever more in earnest, more free from sophistry and equivocation, more upright and forthright in public word and act. Knowing his principles, everyone, friend and foe alike, knew what on any public issue Richard Cobden would say and do. The mere study of a character and a public career so steadfast, wholesome, and clean as his is a moral tonic, and of moral tonics the present age cannot as yet have too many.

It will be seen that the exposition of Cobden's teaching here offered is frankly yet impartially critical, and an endeavour has been made to apply it, where application seemed pertinent, to present international conditions and problems. That method of treatment was inevitable, since an admirer of Cobden would be unworthy of his theme who hesitated to avow freely the conclusions to which inquiry and reflexion had led him, however much some of these conclusions might go counter to current preconceptions.

W. H. D.

HEADINGTON, OXFORD,
    September, 1926.

CONTENTS

RICHARD COBDEN
AND FOREIGN POLICY

CHAPTER I

THE MAN

" Politics were the one commanding interest of his life. But . . . what Cobden talked about and cared about was real politics, not the game of party. Politics in his sense meant the large workings of policy, not the manœuvres of Members of Parliament."—LORD MORLEY, *Life of Cobden*, ii. 478.

" An intense love of justice, a singleness of aim, a habit of judging men fairly and estimating them favourably, an absence of the suspicion that so often forms the base of our public life—these elements and all other such elements were to be found in the character of Cobden abundantly supplied." —MR. GLADSTONE.

TO add to the biographies of Richard Cobden is not the purpose of this book. Lord Morley's *Life*, written with so much skill, grace, and sympathy nearly forty years ago, still justifiably holds the field ; for the picture therein presented of this outstanding figure in the modern political life of our country has lost nothing of vividness and fidelity in the interval.

Rather it is my aim to expound Cobden's doctrine of foreign policy, with a view to disclosing its bearing upon later international episodes and the difficult tasks which to-day beset British statesmanship in relation to foreign affairs. For it is this part of his political thought that gives to Cobden his unique position amongst statesmen of the mid-Victorian period ; and it may be that future generations of his countrymen, as much habituated to peace, let us hope, as his and our generations have been to war, will recall his unselfish work in that domain with increasing admiration and gratitude.

A historical survey like this will naturally suggest comparisons and contrasts with events and tendencies of the present age, and therein may be found its principal value. Speaking of our own country, may it not be said with truth that something went radically wrong with British statesmanship in the early years of this century, when the Government in power committed the nation light-heartedly to liabilities of whose grave character and indefinite extent it would appear at the time to have had no clear idea ; and again during the feverish months of 1919, when, after a devastating and exhausting war, the destinies of Europe were being decided in Paris— a place the least suited in the whole world at that time for the transaction of business of such delicacy, calling for quiet thought, cool decision, and entire freedom from disturbing influences.

It fell to me to pass some weeks in that city at a critical stage of the peace deliberations, for the purpose of being consulted on certain territorial questions, and after a few days' experience of the all-enveloping miasmal, hate-laden atmosphere, the thought, " Why here ? What good can come of it all ? " never left me for a moment. In the course of a memorable conversation with him, President Wilson spoke of the " prevailing madness," and the words in no way exaggerated the temper of Paris and of France at that time. How far psychical reactions influenced the men, or some of them, who negotiated the peace settlements in such unfriendly surroundings might be an interesting subject of speculation. The world knows to its cost that the outcome was a series of forced treaties of peace—Turkey, by an unexampled irony, being the only enemy State which was able to defy its arbitrary judges—each of which, whatever the intention, is, in effect, a direct provocation to future war.

What the representatives of other nations did and were determined to do at that time and place does not alter the fact that many of the decisions arrived at, and of the measures adopted, marked a disastrous and infinitely deplorable deflexion from the best traditions of British foreign policy. The nation's signature, seal, and authority were attached to territorial arrangements which, while they have upset much in many parts of the world, have settled little permanently, with the result that to-day, eight years after the end of the Great War, Europe faces a future darkened by the menace of even worse disaster.

Most indubitably European statesmanship, and not least our own, went wrong in 1905, 1914, and still more in 1919.

But a fact which it is still more important to take to heart is that it had been going wrong long before the century began, and every year more wrong, owing to its vain attempts to build peace upon the rotten foundations of alliances and counter-alliances, ever larger armies and navies, the chicanery of scheming war-mongers, and the shifts of secret diplomacy, instead of on the broad and solid basis of amity and open faith between nations.

In the existing critical condition of European relations perhaps no more useful service can be rendered to public opinion by any student of affairs, who stands outside' the sterilizing influence of party controversy, than to call to mind the forgotten principles of national and international well-being for which Cobden contended. For the greater part of his public life his entire thought and endeavour were concentrated upon the one question—how can the nations of Europe be united in the bonds of concord and peace ? No Englishman of the nineteenth century recognized more clearly the fundamental principles which must govern foreign policy and relations if war is to be outlawed and its curse to be finally lifted from mankind. Not as yet universally accepted, these principles will need to be reiterated and reinforced again and again until they have become part of the normal mentality not only of his countrymen but of mankind. Their victory would be the salvation of civilization, their permanent failure would be its ruin.

It is true that some of Cobden's practical conclusions may require modification and readjustment to-day, owing to changed conditions and the emergence of new problems, caused in part at least by disregard of his teaching and warnings ; yet in its broad aspects his political doctrine of foreign policy still stands unshaken.

In order to understand this doctrine aright and to do justice to it, it is necessary to know something about the man and to view his teaching in relation to the political events and movements of his time. Cobden was born in 1804, at a farmhouse known as Dunford, in the Sussex hamlet of Hey-shott, near Midhurst, at the foot of the South Downs, which overlook to the northward the green, well-wooded, and far-stretching weald and to the south fall down in graceful undula-

tions to the sea. It is worth recalling that the year of his
birth was that in which Napoleon was proclaimed Emperor,
and that the succeeding three years witnessed his decisive
triumph over the allied monarchies of Eastern Europe and
the dismemberment of Prussia. The later representative
and spokesman, for some time at least, of the manufacturing
industry and of commerce was really a son of the soil, for his
father and many Cobdens before him were yeomen whose
names may be traced in the records of their county as far
back as the fourteenth century. A supposed ancestor of
the later antagonist of large navies and armies, one Thomas
Cobden, of Midhurst, contributed the then very substantial
sum of twenty-five pounds to the fund raised for resisting the
Spanish Armada. Cobden had in mind his ancestral connexion with the land when on one occasion, in paying a
tribute to the better qualities of the old English aristocracy,
he said :

> "You gentlemen of England, the high aristocracy of England,
> your fathers led my forefathers ; you may lead us again, if you choose ;
> but though—longer than any other aristocracy—you have kept your
> power while the battlefield and the hunting field were the tests of manly
> vigour, you have not done as the *noblesse* of France, or the *hidalgos* of
> Madrid, have done ; you have been Englishmen, not wanting in courage
> on any call."—(March 13, 1845.)

Misery hung like a pall upon workaday England at the
beginning of last century. Only the owners and cultivators
of corn land escaped for a time the general impoverishment ;
and the heaviest weight of suffering fell as usual upon the
"bottom dog," the labourer. With the close of the wars
the artificial prosperity which had hitherto kept the heart of
the sorely ailing body politic beating came to an abrupt end,
and agriculture, too, fell upon evil days. Under the pressure
of adverse conditions the Cobden household went under.
A man of the highest character, its head was greatly lacking
in strength, judgment, and practical sense. As he had failed
to profit by favourable opportunities when they came his
way, so he failed to evade disaster when the farmers' run of
good luck ended. Already he had experienced more than an
average share of the jolts and jars of oscillating fortune ;

now came utter collapse, entailing the sale and relinquishment of the ancestral farm and removal to the neighbouring Hampshire.

Hence it came about that Richard Cobden, the fourth of a family of eleven children, and the second of five brothers, was thrown early in life upon his own resources. After undergoing a miscellaneous course of instruction of an attenuated kind, first at a dame's school at home and later at a cheap boarding-school of the notorious " academy " order away in Yorkshire, he was turned out as a finished product, and bidden to face the world, at the age of fifteen years. For a time he worked as a clerk in the warehouse of an uncle in London, learning French by stealth, and both eagerly reading books and as eagerly buying them when his scanty means allowed.

An impetus to ambition came when his exacting relative advanced him at the age of twenty-one to the dignity of a commercial traveller for the " house." One of his journeys took him to Ireland, and the letters which he wrote home, recounting the painful impressions made upon him by the poverty, degradation, and ignorance of the peasantry, show at work a mind not only singularly active and observant, but sympathetic to the misfortunes of his fellow-men. Duty also took him periodically to Manchester ; and in 1828 he set up in business with two other young men as a seller of calico prints for manufacturers of that town. So well did the enterprise prosper that three years later the partners began to print their own fabrics, engaging for the purpose an old factory in the Lancashire village of Sabden, near Blackburn. Of this trade Manchester was the recognized centre, and a Manchester man, for practical purposes, Cobden now became.

He might seem to have been born to succeed, in spite of the fact that undue optimism and dependence upon others, due to preoccupation with public affairs, eventually brought upon him serious losses. The note of high enthusiasm, of triumph and mastery, resounds in a letter written in 1832 to his elder brother, intimate, and _protégé_, Frederick, a business failure like his father, in the hope of spurring him to greater energy and self-confidence :

" I wish that I could impart to you a little of that Bonapartian feeling with which I am imbued—a feeling that spurs me on with the conviction that all the obstacles of fortune with which I am impeded will (nay, shall) yield, if assailed with energy . . . I want to see you able to pitch your voice in a higher key, especially when you are espousing your own interests, and above all never to see you yield or become passive and indifferent when your cause is just, and only wants to be spiritually supported to be sure of a triumph.   But all this must proceed from within, and can be only the fruits of a larger growth of spirit." [1]

Easy-going brother Frederick lagged behind to the last, but by this time, at the age of twenty-eight, Richard had succeeded so well that he was able to buy for three thousand guineas a large house in a fashionable part of Manchester, valued by expert opinion at twice the amount. " All the world is talking of the bargain here," he wrote to his brother, with a " John Halifax, Gentleman," cock-a-hoop, " and there being but one opinion or criterion of a man's ability—the making of money—I am already thought a clever fellow."

Cobden's whole life was a sustained process of self-education, not perhaps in the merely bookish way, but in a wider and deeper sense. While he was struggling under the cares and worries entailed by the conduct of a new business which he was establishing in Manchester (1832), he was able to find time for the study of Latin and mathematics as a home occupation for the winter evenings. His biographer speaks of his " moderate knowledge rapidly acquired." There is abundant evidence in his utterances that he must have dipped often, if diffusely rather than deeply, into the literature of his country, and that modern history had for him an absorbing interest. Perhaps he read less for reading's or learning's sake than in order to equip himself for his special public work ; for intellectually everything was grist that came to his mill. One of his friends and political associates said that he spoke and wrote always " to the top of his knowledge,"

---

[1] Cobden had a feminine fondness for underlining purple patches in his letters and writings. In quotations from these I have usually (as in this instance) taken the liberty of ignoring that method of emphasis. Further, in omitting portions of quotations for the sake of brevity and coherence (which, of course, has only been done where the context is immaterial), I have departed from the somewhat pedantic rule of citation which requires omissions to be indicated by a series of dots.

and the impression given by his speeches and writings alike is that of a man of remarkably alert mind, and with an exceptional mastery of his own practical subjects, who possessed the rare faculty of rapidly mobilizing his knowledge, whatever the cause or principle which he happened at the moment to be either defending or assailing, and concentrating it upon the weakest points of his opponents' front.

Not a few great statesmen have had small beginnings. Bismarck's first speech as an unknown deputy in the local Diet of his native province of Pomerania was on " the excessive consumption of tallow in the Workhouse." Cobden's introduction to public life was likewise a modest one, and gave no indication of the arena in which he was soon to appear as a controversialist and no promise whatever of the European influence which awaited him. His first civic work related to the improvement of elementary education in his factory village of Sabden, and was done in 1836, at an age when some of the most famous of English orators and statesmen had already won their spurs. His first recorded public speech was made in Manchester about the same time, and was on the subject of municipal government; on that occasion he broke down, and the chairman of the meeting had to apologize for him.

Before this, however, he had made his first bow to the general public as the writer of a pamphlet entitled *England, Ireland, and America*, hiding his face behind the veil of anonymity, for he was described on the title page as " A Manchester Manufacturer." The pamphlet drew from the London *Times* the encouraging compliment that it contained " some sound views of the true foreign policy of England, and some just and forcible reflexions on the causes which keep us in the rear of improvement." Three editions at the respectable price of 3s. 6d. were speedily called for, and within a year a fifth and popular edition was published. As a piece of literary work the essay affords an admirable example of Cobden's style and methods of craftsmanship—his diligence as a collector and sifter of facts and evidence, his respect for accuracy of statement, his eagerness to view controversial questions from different standpoints, freedom from the dulness and heaviness which so often—and sometimes deservedly— discredit literary productions written with a purpose. Altogether six substantial pamphlets from his ready pen appeared between 1835 and 1862, most of them owing much of their value to independent and first-hand investigations into the political, social, and commercial life of foreign countries.

During that period he was an unwearied traveller, going abroad in part for business reasons, in part for health and pleasure, but most of all for information and profit. In his youth the " grand tour " was still the fashionable finish to the educational outfit of wealthy young Englishmen. Not long ago I read the disinterred record of such a " grand tour," which took the coming head of a " county family " to all the leading capitals of Europe early in last century. It contained much gossip and comment upon Courts and diplomatists, with lively descriptions of social figures and functions, but little that could help the reader to envisage the Continent itself, its peoples, their minds, habits, and manner of life, as they were a century ago. Cobden travelled in order to study foreign nations and know them better, and his inquiries took him beyond the *habitués* of Courts and salons to the men who were doing the world's work, in legislatures and Ministerial offices, in factories and warehouses, and other spheres of practical life.

In these journeyings he was the antithesis of the Little Pedlingtonian, who cannot live a week away from home unless he carries with him the bottled atmosphere of his petty circle. Leaving behind his accustomed tables of mental currency, weights, and measures, he judged foreign ideas and institutions by native standards, therein showing a rare mastery of the art of travel. So it was that he brought home rich trophies in the form of authentic first-hand knowledge of many lands and peoples when such knowledge was rare even in the political circles where it was most needed ; and the better to keep his facts up to date, he established friendly relations with ruling statesmen and leaders of public opinion. He belonged also to a generation which both wrote long letters and kept diaries, and these records of his wanderings are full of illuminative reflexions. And everything of value that he experienced he gave back sooner or later as opportunity offered. If Ulysses was part of all he had seen, all that Cobden saw, heard, and learned abroad went to his equipment as a public man.

His first foreign journey was to France in 1833, but it took him no farther than Paris. In the following year he visited France and Switzerland, and was delighted with all he saw in the Alpine republic. A year later he undertook a more ambitious enterprise when, gratifying a wish of long standing, he visited the United States, passing five weeks in the country in June and July—just the duration of the voyage out. The visit marked a critical stage in his mental growth and his development as a student of public affairs. Not only did it widen his horizon in a way that travel in slower-going Continental countries might never have done, but it opened his eyes to the immensity of America's resources in natural wealth and intelligent manhood, and convinced him that the great rival which England had to contend with, if not to fear, lay across neither the Channel nor the North Sea, but the Atlantic. The eagerness, vitality, and energy of the Americans were just the qualities likely to impress Cobden at that time, when he was himself wooing fortune with a passionate devotion. Of the country's boundless possibilities he wrote enthusiastically in letters to his elder brother, the recipient of much of his early impressions of travel. It was a country " on the soil of which I fondly hope will be realized some of those dreams of human exaltation, if not of perfection, with which I love to console myself." And looking westward from the last northern summit of the Alleghanies, he made the bold forecast, " Here will one day be the headquarters of agricultural and manufacturing industry ; here will one day centre the civilization, the wealth, the power of the entire world."

Yet he was not blind to the blots on American civilization. The institution of slavery in particular moved his indignation. He had no sooner landed than he was discussing the eternal problem. " Here " (in Ohio), he wrote home, " I found, as in every other company, the slavery blot viewed as an indelible stain upon, and a curse to, the country. All agreed in the hopelessness of any remedy that had been proposed " ; and when, after visiting the Southern States, he passed into the free atmosphere of Pennsylvania it was with a hearty " Thank God, I am no longer in the country of slaves ! " It will be seen later how valuable his knowledge of the slave question proved when he was championing the North in the Civil War.

He records that when the first pamphlet appeared his publisher told him that "nobody ought to print a pamphlet unless he had some other object in view besides publication," and he adds that he had, in fact, "another object in distant and dim perspective." What was this still dormant design? His biographer suggests that he was already contemplating a parliamentary career. It is probable enough that the thought had occurred to him, yet, if his own words can be relied on, membership of the House of Commons had as yet no great attraction for him. In the General Election of 1837 he did, indeed, offer himself as a candidate for the representation of Stockport, though he does not appear to have been much awed by the prospect either of success or failure. "The worthy folks may do as they please," he wrote in Coriolanus vein at the time; "they can make me M.P. by their favour, but they cannot mar my happiness if they reject me." But the Coriolanus way does not win parliamentary contests, and Cobden's independence may account in part for his rejection at the polling booth, though it is clear that when the final tussle came he threw into it all proper energy.

It is at least likely that he was already contemplating his later crusade against his country's costly armaments and the continual interferences of its Governments in Continental affairs which made them necessary. For what was the argument of *England, Ireland, and America*? We find in this writing the earliest public avowal of his fundamental doctrine that all reform and improvement must begin at home, that no nation is justified in interfering in its neighbours' concerns, and that England in particular has no title to pose as a sort of universal saviour of society—an assumption more commonly and more arrogantly assumed in his day than in ours, yet even now never far from the consciousness of any true-born Briton.

Politicians and writers of his day were championing Turkey against Russia. Cobden suggested that not these countries, but down-trodden, impoverished, and ill-educated Ireland and the great Republic which was forging ahead across the ocean ought to claim their attention, and that only when the English nation kept aloof from Continental meddling would it be able to count on security and peace abroad, and so reduce the oppressive weight of military and naval expenditure which was crushing it.

The second pamphlet appeared in the summer of 1836. It was entitled simply *Russia*, and the " Manchester Manufacturer " again preferred to remain unknown to the world at large. The subject was one which he had closely studied, but what led him to put his ideas to paper was the fact that an insidious agitation against Russia as a disturber of European peace had been set on foot. Just before circumstantial stories of an intended Russian invasion of our shores—stories which anticipated the later French invasion scares—had been industriously circulated. Referring to this mythical conspiracy in a speech made at Manchester two years later, he said :

" I am rather identified with and interested in that invasion of Russia. It was that which made me an author ; it was that which made me a public man. . . . They (' the public newspapers ') then told me that the Russians would be coming over here some foggy day and that they would land at Yarmouth. If it had not been for that insanity I should never have turned author, never have written pamphlets, but must have been a thrifty, painstaking calico printer to this day."

In the second pamphlet the morals enforced in the first were repeated even more vigorously. Now he formally challenged the accepted principles of British foreign policy. He contended that the time had come for a reorientation of foreign relations " in conformity with the changes that have taken place over the entire globe." Asking the question, " Can the States system which was applicable to the international affairs of Europe a century ago be suitable to the circumstances of to-day ? " he answered it negatively ; and again taking the Russo-Turkish question and England's relation thereto as a test, he dared to assail the awe-inspiring doctrine of the balance of power, and again roundly condemned every kind of intervention in foreign affairs.

Like its predecessor the pamphlet had a great and immediate success. Remembering that Cobden had had no training in letters, and had never before, as far as is known, fostered ambitions in that direction, these first writings are remarkable productions, and afford striking proof that the paramount qualification of a successful publicist is that he shall have a definite message to deliver and be under the compulsion to utter it. Morley speaks of the pamphlets as forming " a great landmark in the history of politics in England." With their appearance Cobden, no longer to be hidden behind the veil of anonymity, became recognized as one of the shrewdest, most trenchant, and best informed political writers of the day. Other pamphlets and public letters followed, though he never became, in his own phrase, " author-mad."

By this time there had come to him the irresistible call to active public service which makes havoc of the happiness of so many lives, selfish and unselfish alike, and brings complete satisfaction to so few—perhaps to none. Each year this call grew in urgency, and found a readier response, until political work became his one absorbing thought, and the aim and purpose of his life. He, too, paid a heavy penalty for his unsparing devotion to national affairs, and at times moments of doubt came when he asked himself the terrible question whether it were worth while.

In the meantime his business had continued to prosper, insomuch that we find him, after four years of successful manufacturing and merchanting on his own account, looking forward to the time when he would be able to devote exclusive attention to the larger interests which he had entered into his life. In 1838, when still only thirty-four years old, he wrote to his brother Frederick, whom he had indiscreetly installed in the management of his business affairs, " All my exertions will be with an eye to make myself independent of all business claims on my time and anxieties," and he calculated that, with the help of his brothers as partners, five years more of sustained effort would enable him to become " a willing exile " from the factory and commerce. Fate, by a strange irony, decreed that the reasonable expectations of this man of immense energy and will-power should be completely disappointed, owing in part to the incompetence of others, in part to his own proneness to over-confidence.

When seeking to represent Stockport in Parliament, he professed that he would have preferred to wait two years longer before undergoing that experience ; and actually four years passed before he again tried his fortunes at the hustings. He employed the interval well. He spent the winter of 1836–37 in the east of Europe, journeying first to Egypt by way of Lisbon, Cadiz, and Gibraltar, then visiting Constantinople, Smyrna, some of the Greek islands, and Athens. His journals show how diligently he spent his time in studying Turkish conditions, political, commercial, financial, and social, with results which gave special value to his later discussions of the Eastern Question.

All that he saw of Greece and the Greeks excited his admiration, and the judgments which he formed were not modified by a second visit, made nearly twenty years later. He was convinced that Greece, whose independence Turkey had already formally recognized, would outlive the unnatural limitations which an opportunist diplomacy had imposed upon her, first by the Treaty of London of 1827 and then by the Treaty of Adrianople of 1829, and his confidence in her future was unbounded. He wrote to his brother, " All the East will be Greek, and Constantinople, no matter under what nominal sovereignty it may fall, will by the force of the indomitable genius of the Greeks become, in fact, the capital of that people." That view he never relinquished.

In the autumn of 1838 he spent a month in Germany. There he made a nearer acquaintance with a rising industrial community which was making vigorous efforts to gain an entrance into the markets of the world, and the moral which he took home was that if Germany was to be fought successfully in industry it must be with her own weapons of science, organized skill, application, industry, and frugality.

It is significant of the severe test of fitness for parliamentary work which Cobden applied to himself that before he entered the House of Commons he had enlarged his knowledge of foreign affairs by visits to most of the important European countries, as well as America, Egypt, and Asia Minor. Visits to Russia and North Africa were yet to come. Not the least advantage of these foreign travels was that they opened his eyes to a multitude of antiquated laws, customs, and institutions which were holding back his own country and handicapping it in the race for material and moral primacy in the world—

laws which prevented the free exchange of land and obstructed the development of coal mines ; the prejudice against railways entertained by land-owners, great and small, who were allowed to place their personal convenience and amenities before the public need for improved transport facilities ; the lukewarmness and often open hostility shown towards education by selfish people, themselves educated, who held enlightenment to be a dangerous weapon to put in the hands of the masses of the people ; obsolete customs tariffs which restricted commerce and made dear the food of the toiling millions ; and Press laws and paper duties which made books and newspapers so expensive that only rich people were able to buy them.

By the year 1839 the historical anti-Corn Law movement was well under way. Though primarily a domestic matter, it must be mentioned here for obvious reasons. For it was this cause which took Cobden into active political life, and to it the earliest of his recorded political speeches were devoted. The famous League was preceded by an Anti-Corn Law Association formed in London in 1836, but most of the leading men behind this organization were theorists, strong in faith yet weak in works, and while they talked much the practical results were small.

Free food was a special concern of the industrial towns, and it was fitting that the agitation which gave this boon to the masses of the people had its birth in Manchester. The Chamber of Commerce there took up the question at a meeting held in December 1838. Cobden was present, and while the older members favoured the old-fashioned device of a petition to the Government, asking for some modification of the existing duties, he called for total and immediate repeal. For many of the cautious wise-heads this bold proposal was too rash, too abrupt, too sudden, and the meeting was adjourned for a week to allow of calm reflexion. Cobden used the time for busy action, and at the next meeting he produced, ready drafted, a memorial embodying his ideas, and had the satisfaction of seeing it adopted. The struggle for an untaxed loaf was sharp and short, for after only seven years of fighting (1839 to 1846) complete success crowned the most resolute assault ever made in this country upon an immensely powerful vested interest, still strongly entrenched behind a legislature largely representative of its own opinions and prejudices and under its control. Fox once said that " Middlesex and York-shire together make all England." On this occasion it was Lancashire's association with York hire that converted public opinion.

It was this agitation which brought Cobden and John Bright together in an intimate and loyal comradeship which, long after its immediate object had been gained, was con-tinued in the service of other great public causes.[1] The historical meeting took place in 1841, when Cobden again stood for Stockport. This time likewise he accepted nomination reluctantly and only in the interest of the League and on the pressure of his colleagues. The great issue of the election was free food *versus* taxed food. The repealers carried the North by storm ; and Cobden was one of the majority which made Sir Robert Peel Prime Minister for the second time, so sounding the death knell of the Corn Laws. In May of the previous year he had married.

Next to Free Trade the most constant subjects of his speeches in the House of Commons were armaments and the expenditure on them, International Sea Law, the danger of the continual British interventions in Continental affairs, arbitration, and the immeasurable folly and wrongfulness of war. Writing to his brother, reporting how his early speeches had been received, he remarked that " it is quite clear that I am looked upon as a Gothic invader, and the classicals will criticize me unmercifully." He did, in fact, receive hard knocks, just as he gave them, yet from the day he entered the House he was able to count on the respectful hearing which that assembly invariably gives to the man who adds to zeal knowledge, and to knowledge freshness and sincerity of utterance.

Such a man could not remain in the background, and it was not long before his practical speeches, always timely and to the point, free from rhetorical artifice yet all the more heavily weighted with telling facts and figures, convinced

[1] Cobden said on one occasion : " I have lived with Mr. Bright in the most transparent intimacy of mind that two human beings ever enjoyed together. I don't believe there is a view, I don't believe there is a thought, I don't believe there is an aspiration in the mind of either of us that the other is not acquainted with."—(Manchester, March 18, 1857.)

even his opponents that they had to do with a statesman of uncommon mould, who must be taken seriously. He cannot be said to have ever mastered the House as did his friend Bright, whose superiority as an orator he readily admitted, but his power as a parliamentary figure was exceptional. Though it was his fate to divide the House over issues which excited keen and at times bitter feeling, his earnestness, honesty, and force of conviction compelled recognition in every quarter, and when his career as a parliamentarian ended nearly a quarter of a century later his fame stood at its zenith.

He had not been in Parliament five years when he received from Lord John Russell the first of two offers of Ministerial office which fell to him. When in December 1845 Russell tried to form an anti-Corn Law administration he invited him, not very pressingly, to be Vice-President of the Board of Trade. Cobden declined the offer on the ground that he could do better work for Free Trade as a private member. Russell's attempts at Cabinet making failed on that occasion, but when a few months later he again tried and succeeded he did not renew his invitation, but, knowing that Cobden was about to go on another European tour, merely wrote to express the hope, sincerely or not, that he would join a Liberal administration at a later date.

Meanwhile, on January 28, 1846, had come Peel's announcement of a change of fiscal policy—" Peel is at last delivered, but I hardly know whether to call it a boy or a girl," wrote the repealer-in-chief at the time—and on June 28 following Cobden was able to flash home from the House the jubilant message : " Hurrah, hurrah ! The Corn Bill is law and now my work is done." Opinions have never ceased to differ as to the wisdom of the policy which the Leaguers were instrumental in introducing in this country, yet he would be the most churlish of partisans who pretended that the victory of Free Trade was not a great achievement.

Cobden's work had really only well begun, and in that fact lies for our purpose the full significance of the Free Trade movement, before which protective duties of every kind were soon to be swept away.[1] It is true that in the later stages

---

[1] The abolition of the corn duties was followed by the abolition of the sugar duties (1848), and of the Navigation Act (1849).

of the agitation against the Corn Laws he had contemplated retirement from parliamentary work as soon as success had been achieved. He had formed " a growing distaste for House of Commons life and a distaste for mere party political action " ; the long strain of ceaseless and almost superhuman effort was telling on his strength ; and his business interests were suffering owing to neglect. Even then it was only the consciousness of an imperious call to see the fight for free food through that kept him at a task which was undermining his health and emptying his pocket.

During the parliamentary session of 1844, disturbed by depressing business reports from his brother, he wrote, " I shall have a month or two for private business, and Heaven knows it is not before it is required. It is a dog's life I am leading, and I wish I could see my way out of the collar "— (August 8th.) In the following year only the timely help of friends staved off financial embarrassment and prevented his withdrawal from the anti-Corn Law crusade. He has left it on record that concentration on the crusade, to the disregard of his business affairs, entailed " the complete sacrifice of my private prospects in life," and that the victory of the cause found him " a poor man."

In a letter written to a friend about this time, he said :

" It has always been to me a spectacle worthy of reproach to see a man sacrificing the welfare of his own domestic circle to the cravings of a morbid desire for public notoriety. And God, who knows our hearts, will free me from any such unworthy motives. I was driven along a groove by accident, too fast and too far to retreat with honour, or without the risk of some loss to the country, but the happiest moment of my life will be that which releases me from the conflicting sense of rival duties, by restoring me again to private life."—(April 2, 1846.)

Like so many strong yet emotional men Cobden was subject to moods. Whatever have been his impressions of parliamentary life when he wrote these words, it is difficult to believe that he can have seriously entertained the idea of complete withdrawal into the background. Speaking at a meeting which decreed the dissolution of the League, he plainly hinted at other tasks ahead. " We are dispersing our elements," he said, " to be ready for any other good work, and it is nothing but good work which will be attempted by good Leaguers."—(July 2, 1846.)

Now more clearly and vividly the design envisaged eleven years before as still in a "distant and dim perspective" entered his field of vision. Long before this time he had conceived the idea of grafting the Free Trade question upon the peace movement. The conviction grew with him that the two causes belonged to one another and in the long run would stand or fall together. What was needed was to bring home to the reason and conscience of mankind the essential interdependence of nations, and he saw that if this end was to be attained the peace movement itself must follow international lines. "The efforts of the Peace Societies," he wrote in 1842, "however laudable, can never be successful so long as the nations maintain their present system of isolation."

In the course of his advocacy the cause of Free Trade had more and more taken for him a moral and idealistic aspect, to which the material advantages to be expected from unrestricted commercial intercourse, important though they were, had become subordinated. "When I advocated Free Trade," he said to a peace meeting held at Wrexham on November 14, 1850, "do you suppose that I did not see its relation to the present question, or that I advocated Free Trade merely because it would give us a little more occupation in this or that pursuit? No, I believed that Free Trade would unite mankind in the bonds of peace, and it was that, more than any pecuniary consideration, which sustained and actuated me, as my friends know, in that struggle." Never again was the conception of international peace and Free Trade as twin causes, or rather as soul and body of the one cause, absent from his mind.

The abolition of the corn duties having been enacted, the ardent combatant gave himself a short rest amongst the Welsh mountains, yet within a month he had entered on a new Continental tour in prosecution of the larger call which had come to him. Announcing his mission and its object, he wrote to Mr. Henry Ashworth (July 4, 1846):

"I will with God's assistance during the next twelvemonth visit all the large States of Europe, see the potentates and statesmen, and endeavour to enforce those truths which have been so irresistible at home. Why should I rust in inactivity ? If the public spirit of my countrymen affords me the means of travelling as their missionary [1] I will be the first Ambassador from the people of this country to the nations of the Continent. I am impelled to this step by an instinctive emotion such as never deceived me."

Travelling this time not alone but with his wife, Cobden began his unique tour a month later and remained abroad until October of the following year. He visited France, Spain, Italy, Germany, and Russia, halting in Paris, Madrid, Vienna, Rome, Berlin, St. Petersburg, and less important capitals and towns, interviewing reigning Sovereigns, viz. Louis Philippe of France, the Kings of Sardinia and the Two Sicilies, Frederick William IV. of Prussia, and the Pope—a reception by the Tsar of Russia, though virtually arranged in advance, does not appear to have taken place—and meeting many Ministers of State and notable statesmen, diplomatists, and publicists of the day, including, amongst Frenchmen, Guizot, Thiers, De Tocqueville, Bastiat, Léon Faucher, and Alexandre Dumas, with leading figures in the worlds of finance, industry, and commerce. His fame had preceded him, and he had everywhere the reception due to a great representative Englishman, being feasted, serenaded, addressed, entertained, interviewed, silver-medalled, and versified to an extent that would have turned a less sober head than his. In Italy alone he was the victim of over a dozen banquets, as well as of " private parties without end."

As usual the tour was used for serious study and inquiry, and he returned home with a well-stocked mind and full note-books. References in his journals show that he collected information on an amazing diversity of subjects—in France on the iron monopoly, customs tariffs, and forestry ; in Italy on rural labour, vineyard culture, the salt, gunpowder and tobacco *régies*, and Leghorn bonnets ; in Spain on official corruption ; in Austria on the iron and cotton industries and absolutist government ; in Germany on land ownership, rural life, the iron and textile industries, wheat growing, the Zollverein, and of course education ; in Russia on the natural resources, the vastness of the forests, the growing industry

---

[1] An allusion to the national testimonial then in course of subscription.

and commerce, serfdom, the backwardness of agricultural methods and implements, and the grave political problems which faced an aristocracy contented to tolerate an illiterate populace and a corrupt bureaucracy.

Of few of the men whom he met does he appear to have formed any very exalted estimate. In Paris neither the King nor his Ministers impressed him favourably. He tells of a long evening's talk with Louis Philippe at the Château d'Eu, and he remarks that " nothing so much struck me as his contempt for people through whom and for whom he professed to rule." He " formed the opinion that he is a clever actor, and perhaps that is all we can say of the ablest Sovereigns of this (France) or any other country." He speaks of Guizot as " an intellectual pedant and a moral prude, with no more knowledge of men and things than is possessed by professors who live among their pupils " ; and he describes Thiers as " a lively little man without dignity, and with nothing to impress you with a sense of power."

What he thought of French protective legislation at that time is drastically told in a vigorous letter addressed while he was still in France to his friend, M. Arles Dufour, a Free Trade silk manufacturer of Lyons, whom he urged to agitate until he had moved the Government to action. In the event, as will be shown, it was Cobden himself who undertook and partially accomplished in 1859–60 the work which he vainly urged upon the French Free Trade party at that time.

His visit to Spain synchronized with a royal episode (October 10) which later was magnified by Lord Palmerston into a European *affaire* and created serious friction between Great Britain and France—the marriages of the Queen and her sister the Infanta, the one to her cousin, Don Francisco d'Assiz, Duke of Cadiz, and the other to the French Duc de Montpensier. Cobden's party received complimentary tickets for the ceremony and attended. They also went to a bullfight for the sake of the experience, and to their disgust found it graced by the presence of the Spanish Primate.

He was in Rome at Carnival time and he contrasted the restraint and grace of the native masquers and merrymakers with the roystering antics of the English participants, who seemed to confuse the *fêtes* with election meetings, " shovelling " upon each other chalk confetti " with all the zeal and energy of navigators " (i.e. navvies). He feared that if a carnival were attempted at home " people would begin with sugar-plums, and go on to apples and oranges, then proceed to potatoes, and end probably with stones." In Rome he called upon the Pope (Pius IX, elected June 18, 1846), whom he judged to be " sincere, kind-hearted, and good," and " possessed of strong common sense and sound understanding." During the interview he daringly directed the Pontiff's attention to the brutality of the Spanish bull-fights and the impropriety of holding these exhibitions " in honour of saints and virgins on the *fête* days," and he was relieved to find that his protest was sympathetically received.

In Vienna he met Prince Metternich, who " entered into a long essay upon differences of race and the antagonisms of nationality in Europe. . . . Why did Italy still have favourable feelings towards France, notwithstanding the injuries she had received from the latter country ? Because the two nations were of the same race. Why were England and France so inveterately opposed ? Because upon their opposite coasts the Teutonic and Latin races came into close contact." He notes Metternich's bitterness towards Italy, and adds : " It struck me that his hatred of the Italians partook of the feeling described by Rochefoucauld when he says that we never forgive those whom we have injured."

The ageing Chancellor seemed to challenge his visitor to find any defect in the Austrian political system, and invited him to investigate the condition of the people. With singular optimism, and a higher opinion of statesmanship than he entertained later in life, Cobden remarks :

" He is probably the last of those State physicians who, looking only to the symptoms of a nation, content themselves with superficial remedies day by day, and never attempt to probe beneath the surface, to discover the source of the evils which afflict the social system. This order of statesmen will pass away with him because too much light has been shed upon the laboratory of Governments to allow them to impose upon mankind with the old formulas."

Prince Esterhazy, for twenty years Ambassador in London, whom he also met, appears to have talked to him to this effect, perhaps with his tongue in his cheek, for there is a record of his remark that " diplomacy upon the old system was now mere humbug, for that the world was much too well informed upon all that was going on in every country to allow ambassadors to mystify matters." Strenuously though he combated it, Cobden was fated to see this " old system " of diplomacy, humbug though it might be, continue in ascendancy until the end of his life.

Much of his time in Germany was passed in Hamburg, Lübeck, and Stettin, but in Berlin 180 Free Traders entertained him at a non-political dinner at which, nevertheless, in the German way, political speeches were made, the eating and talking lasting for the space of three hours. His verdict on King Frederick William IV of Prussia, though given at second-hand, accurately hit the mark : " He is said to be clever but impulsive, and not practical."

He crossed the frontier into Moscow in the company of a Polish Jew, a Russian subject, who gave him the encouraging assurance that while the Russian nobles were " barbarians " the Polish nobles were " civilized scamps " ; and, further, that " there is some respect for truth in the Russian, but none in the Pole." In illustration of his countrymen's tact abroad he tells, on the authority of a St. Petersburg Embassy *attaché*, how the English members of an Anglo-Russian commercial association failed to understand why their Russian colleagues should have resented the playing of the air " Rule, Britannia ! " at a meeting of that international organization.

Within a year of these travels a flood of revolutions overspread Western Europe. Thrones fell, kings and ministers fled their countries, and democracy triumphed for a season. Cobden had not foreseen this convulsion, but neither, with far less excuse, had the watchmen on the British diplomatic towers which have been built in all the capitals of Europe for the wider survey of events and the better enlightenment and guidance of statesmen at home.

The stirring events of that time found him immersed in personal matters. While he was abroad his Free Trade friends had wound up his shattered business, settled his private affairs, and made provision for his future needs. With part of the money (in amount between £75,000 and £80,000) raised in the form of a national testimonial he bought the paternal property at Dunford, where later he built for himself a larger house. It was characteristic of his contempt for mere tradition and custom and of his sense of equity, that as soon as he entered into occupation of the little estate he had all the hedgerow trees cut down, and authorized the tenants to grub up all fences and exterminate both rabbits and hares, and the labourers to set gins for the same despoilers of their allotments, bidding them to be sure to put them in their own pots. He also drained all land that needed such treatment, and finally reduced the rents in order to meet the fall in prices due to foreign competition.

Only the main incidents in Cobden's further parliamentary life need occupy us in this place. In the General Election of the autumn of 1847 he stood again for Stockport as a passive candidate, for he was still abroad, and he was returned both for that borough and also, without being consulted, for the West Riding. He acknowledged the compliment done him by the Yorkshire Liberals by becoming their member, and he represented that great industrial constituency during two Parliaments, Lord John Russell being Prime Minister in the first and Lord Derby succeeding him in 1852. In the meantime Peel was killed by a fall from horseback on June 29, 1850.

Long before his second tenure of the seat expired, however, the growing consciousness of a want of sympathy with the wire-pullers of the Liberal Party, on most capital issues other than Free Trade, convinced him that he was not in his right place. He had taken up new causes and had failed to find the response from his old friends and fellow-workers which he had expected. Foremost amongst these causes was the question of non-intervention. His experience abroad had increased his distrust of the Foreign Office and the policy of meddling and muddling with which, under the influence of Lord Palmerston, it had been identified for half a generation. To his West Riding constituents he wrote in 1850 :

" Without egotism I may perhaps say that few Englishmen have had better opportunities of learning the effect of our foreign policy upon other countries than myself. I travelled throughout Europe under the rare circumstance of having free access, at the same time, to the Courts and Ministers and to the popular leaders of the Continental

States. I came back convinced that the interference of our Foreign Office in the domestic affairs of other countries worked injuriously for the interests of those for whom my sympathies were attracted—I mean the people—by exciting exaggerated hopes, encouraging premature efforts, and teaching reliance upon extraneous aid, when they ought to be impressed with the necessity of self-dependence. I found, too, that the principle of intervention, which we sanctioned by our example, was carried on by other Governments in opposition to ours without scruple, and with at least equal success to ourselves."

Of the policy so impugned Lord Palmerston was the impersonation, and Cobden was now in the midst of a controversy with that high-handed statesman—the evil genius of British politics, as he honestly believed—which ended only with his life. Of one of the later and more formal oratorical duels between these two statesmen, the one no less combatant, honest, and convinced than the other, Sir M. E. Grant-Duff, who was a spectator, gave an account in an address to his constituents at the time. The occasion was a debate on foreign policy—on Cobden's side an attack on Lord Palmerston's methods—which took place on August 1, 1862. Cobden told the House at the outset how some of his friends had just warned him " not to be personal " and to " keep his temper," and he promised not to ignore this advice " more than he was obliged." He kept his word ; for direct personalities and temperamental excess were absent, yet the speech was a severe, even mordant, indictment of Palmerston as a statesman, and candour was not spared in the recital of his costly filibustering enterprises abroad, to the neglect of domestic questions of great importance for the nation.

" There they stood," runs the contemporary narrative, " unreconciled and irreconcilable—the representatives of two widely different epochs, and of two widely different types of English life. The one trained in the elegant but superficial culture which was usual amongst the young men of his position in life at the beginning of this century, full of pluck, full of intelligence, but disinclined, alike by the character of his mind and by the habits of official life, from indulging in political speculation, or pursuing long trains of thought ; yet yielding to no man in application, in the quickness of his judgment, in knowledge of a statesman's business, and in the power of enlisting the support of what has been so truly called ' that floating mass which in all countries and in all times has always decided all questions.' The other derived from

nature finer powers of mind, but many years passed away before he
could employ his great abilities in a field sufficiently wide for them,
and he has never had the official training which is perhaps absolutely
necessary to turn even the ablest politician into a statesman. There
he stood, an admirable representative of the best section of the class
to which he belongs, full of large and philanthropic hopes, and full of
confidence in his power to realize them, yet wanting in pliability of
mind and deficient in that early and systematic culture which prevents
a man becoming the slave of one idea." [1]

During the periods of seclusion, passed in his Sussex home,
which alternated with much platform work in Yorkshire
and other parts of the country on behalf of his favourite
causes, Free Trade, finance, parliamentary reform, education,
the reduction of armaments, and foreign policy generally,
Cobden found time to write more pamphlets—1792 *and* 1853
in Three Letters (1853), a defence of France against her distrustful English critics ; *How Wars are got up in India*
(1853), a scathing exposure of the origin of the Burmese war
of 1851–2 ; and *What Next—and Next* (1856), being words
of counsel on the best way of ending the Crimean War, in
which Great Britain became involved, again largely under
Palmerston's influence, in 1854.

In February 1857 he moved what was in effect a vote of
censure on Lord Palmerston's Government on account of its
proceedings in the notorious affair of the *Arrow* and the subsequent destructive bombardment of Canton, and on this being
carried Palmerston dissolved Parliament. In the ensuing
election Cobden stood for Huddersfield. Neither physically
nor intellectually was he in full fighting form, and for a time
he was tempted to withdraw from the contest. He felt
incapable of the effort of platform speaking : " his throat or
lungs failed him ; symptoms both at his head and heart
warned him against overstrain ; and he felt twenty years
older than when he began the anti-Corn Law agitation."
Once more, too, there was apathy amongst men of influence
who should have been his best supporters. Added to all
this, honour bade him divide his time between the furtherance

---

[1] *Elgin Speeches*, p. 25. It is fair to add that to the above passage, as
published, the speaker adds a note qualifying his qualifications, for he says,
" These words do not express my more matured opinion about Mr. Cobden,
but I learned to appreciate that remarkable man more justly than I did in
1862 at a somewhat later period.

of his own prospects and helping those of his friend Mr. Bright, who, laid aside by ill-health, was fighting a forlorn hope at Manchester. Both men went down in the general rout of the Prime Minister's assailants. Cobden did not relish the reverse, but what hurt and (as he said) " irritated " him acutely was the " atrocious treatment " of Bright by the constituency which he had served so faithfully.

Now for nearly two years he lived in retirement in the South, but, while part of his time was devoted to " mangolds and pigs," his pen continued as busy as usual. Palmerston's victory was short-lived, however, for in February of the following year he was defeated on the Conspiracy to Murder Bill and resigned. In the ensuing election the Tories came to power and Lord Derby's second administration was formed, with Disraeli at the Treasury. The new Ministry fell with its Reform Bill early in 1859, and Palmerston came back. The election took place in May, when Cobden was in America, but he was returned for Rochdale without a contest, and he continued to represent that constituency until his death. When at the end of June he landed at Liverpool he found awaiting him an invitation to take the Presidency of the Board of Trade, a fine act of generosity on Palmerston's part in view of the strained controversial relations of the two men. An office for which his qualifications were so many and so conspicuous can hardly fail to have tempted him, but he declined it, even after Palmerston had made a handsome attempt to persuade him to alter his decision.

Undoubtedly, on old-fashioned views of political probity forsaken by a later generation, Cobden's action was strictly correct. He had been attacking Palmerston for many years, and his opinions had undergone no change. Hence, as he wrote to his wife, " to take office now, without a single declaration of change of view regarding his public conduct, would be so monstrous a course that nothing on earth shall induce me to do it."—(June 30, 1859.) In conversation in London the new Prime Minister endeavoured to overcome his scruples, and clenched his appeal with a plausible argument : why would he not enter the " citadel of power " ? " You and your friends," he said, " complain of a secret diplomacy, and that wars are entered into without consulting the people. Now it is in the Cabinet alone that questions of foreign policy are settled. We never consult Parliament until after they are settled. If, therefore, you wish to have a voice in those questions you can only do so in the Cabinet."

Cobden at first found this argument " difficult to answer," but reflexion told him that even had he, as a member of the Cabinet, been behind the scenes, a diplomacy known to himself only officially would still have been " secret," and he would inevitably have been soon faced by the alternatives of resigna· tion or accepting the responsibility for acts of policy which he could not have honestly approved. Apart from such scruples, it is certain that the idea of sinking his individuality in the collective voice of an official block, however eminent its members, must have been obnoxious to his strong and resolute spirit.

The man who refused Ministerial office for conscience' sake was a nine days' wonder to the general, but it is doubtful whether any act in his political life gave Cobden greater satisfaction. Whatever of personal antipathy there was in his antagonism to Lord Palmerston may have been moderated by this episode, so creditable to both men, though his repugnance to nearly everything which Palmerston's foreign policy represented to his mind continued unabated. To the last decade of his life fell many pregnant episodes in foreign affairs, to be mentioned in appropriate relations in later chapters, which gave point to this deep-seated distrust of the masterful statesman, and upon all of these he had his say both in the House of Commons and in the hearing of the ardent working-class audiences which he was wont to address from time to time in the provinces. Such episodes were the Crimean War of 1854–6, the Italian war of 1859, the American Civil War of 1862–5, and the Prusso-Danish War of 1864 over the Elbe Duchies. Nor did any important questions of home politics come before the country without drawing from Cobden illuminating contributions to public discussion. In the meantime he attended Peace Conferences both at home and abroad, visited America for the second time (1859), was instrumental in concluding the French commercial treaty of 1860, and spent a winter in Algeria (1860–1).

The conclusion of the French treaty was one of the great

moments of his public life, and was a source of justifiable pride to him. It also raised him higher in public estimation, and for a time he was the hero of the political clubs. Although he had been fighting for years against political privilege as exercised by the aristocracy and landed classes, and against the mighty Panjandrum of English political life, Lord Palmerston, whose hold on the national attachment continued unweakened, he tells of his amused surprise that the treaty had made him a "respectable" citizen, fit to be looked at and even smiled on by Society. Yet no sooner had he put off the civil garb of the amateur diplomatist than he donned again the armour of political warfare, though conscious that by that token he would sacrifice his recovered "respectability" and would have to encounter the old unpopularity and abuse. This he did when there appeared early in 1862 the last of his pamphlets, viz. *The Three Panics; an Historical Episode.* It was an appeal for a policy of reconciliation and disarmament between Great Britain and France, and his argument required a renewed exposure of British policy towards the latter country under the Palmerston *régime.* Writing to the Rev. Henry Richard [1] (February 2) when the pamphlet was ready for publication, he said :

"I shall just be the same Ishmaelite I was after the Free Trade victory in 1847. Then I might have set up for a genteel politician, and everybody was disposed to tolerate me. Now I am in the same position after the Treaty. Everybody again is tending to tolerance and favour. But when the pamphlet comes out—how I shall be baited in the House and the Press!"

---

[1] The life-work of Henry Richard in the cause of peace is not forgotten, but a reference to that high-minded man is due in this place. Richard was born in 1812 at Tregaron, in Wales, and was closely identified with the Peace movement for forty-three years. Together with Elihu Burritt, the American worker in the same cause, he organized the first International Peace Congress, which was held in Brussels in 1848 and was a great success. Other early congresses were held in Paris and London (1849), Frankfort and Birmingham (1850), London again (1851), and Manchester and Edinburgh (1853). In 1848 he became secretary and organizer of the Peace Society, which dated from 1816, and besides editing its organ, the *Herald of Peace*, he was co-editor of the *Morning Star* and *Evening Star*, daily newspapers adventurously published for a time in support of Peace principles. He represented Merthyr in the House of Commons from 1868 to 1888, the year of his death. In 1873 he carried a resolution in favour of international arbitration, and in 1880 a motion in favour of gradual disarmament, which the Government accepted subject to modifications. His correpondence with Cobden covered the years 1849 to 1865.

But it had to be. Cobden was fated to be an antagonist of wrong laws and wrong causes of every kind. He was born not for peace, but for strife, and sooner or later the way of all such men, if faithfully followed, leads to the summit or the foot of Golgotha. The end came early in 1865. His last speech was made at Rochdale on November 23 preceding. It was on foreign policy, and with the Elbe Duchies dispute as a text he made another powerful attack upon the Government's interventionist policy. It was a long and an exhausting effort, and when it was over the orator confessed that he had doubted his power to finish it, for he had been in bad health for some time. Instead of recuperating for twenty-four hours in bed, as he said later he should have done, he attended another busy political function next day in the same town, and " spent the whole evening in shaking hands and talking to relays of friends." The consequence was that when he returned to the South it was to go direct home, for he feared that illness would have overtaken him had he stayed in London.

From that time he was in medical hands until the end, which came on April 2, when he was within two months of completing his sixty-first year. In February Mr. Gladstone, then Chancellor of the Exchequer, writing on Lord Palmerston's behalf, had offered him the Chairmanship of the Board of Audit, an office carrying a salary of £2,000 a year, but he had declined it at once, though with due recognition of the graciousness which had prompted the offer, on the ground of health and incompatibility. Up to within a few days of his death his active mind still found exercise in long argumentative letters to familiar correspondents.

The loss to the House of Commons and the country of Cobden's strong personality and sage counsels was handsomely acknowledged (April 3) by the Prime Minister, his old antagonist.

" Those who differed from him the most," said Lord Palmerston, ' could never doubt the sincerity of his convictions. . . . Great as were Mr. Cobden's talents, great as was his industry, and eminent as was his success, the disinterestedness of his mind more than equalled all of these. He was a man of great ambition, but his ambition was to be useful to his country and that ambition was amply gratified."

It fell, however, to Disraeli, the leader of the Opposition, then steadily soaring upward in the wide-winged flight which within three years was to bring him to the Premiership, to pay a tribute to the dead tribune which more adequately voiced the feelings of the assembly and of the nation.

" There is this consolation remaining to us," he said, " when we remember our unequalled and irreparable losses, that these great men are not altogether lost to us, that their words will often be quoted in this House, that their examples will often be referred to and appealed to, and that even their expressions may form a part of our discussions. There are some members of Parliament who, though not present in the body, are still members of this House, independent of dissolutions, of the caprice of constituencies, even of the course of time. I think that Mr. Cobden was one of these men. I believe that when the verdict of posterity shall be recorded on his life and conduct it will be said of him that he was without doubt the greatest political character the pure middle class of this country has yet produced—an ornament to the House of Commons, and an honour to England."

Bright was present, and struck a note still more personal, though excusing his few words by the fact that so short a time had elapsed since " the manliest and gentlest spirit that ever quitted or tenanted a human form " had taken flight from earth in his presence. " After twenty years of the most intimate and almost brotherly friendship with him," he added, " I little knew how much I loved him until I found that I had lost him."

CHAPTER II

THE TIMES

" English eyes are always bent upon Parliament, English history always tends to shrink into mere parliamentary history ; and there is scarcely a great English historian who does not sink somewhat below himself in the treatment of foreign relations."—PROFESSOR SEELEY, in *Lectures and Essays*.

" Our (popular) ignorance of the last sixty years is colossal."—BISHOP CREIGHTON in 1887.

SOMETHING must be said of the spiritual environment in which Cobden lived and worked—of the stage upon which his part in the many-scened drama of his day was played. First as to Europe as he saw it when in 1835 the first of the pamphlets appeared. The end of the Napoleonic era was then two decades behind, and only fourteen years had passed since Napoleon himself ended his days in solitary exile. But people still spoke of " The War," or " The Great War," meaning the series of coalitions and campaigns which ultimately brought the Man of Destiny to his knees, wound up the first Empire, and reduced France to the boundaries which existed before the Government of the Revolution began to plot against the peace and security of neighbouring territories.

The political chaos of Europe had been reduced to some semblance of order by the Congress of Vienna, which met in 1814 and 1815, and at which Lord Castlereagh, for a time Foreign Secretary in the Liverpool Cabinet, was the principal British representative. Half a century ago it was far more common than later to disparage the work of the diplomatists who met first in the French and then in the Austrian capital, —following the proposal of Metternich, that purely French concerns should be settled in Paris, and those of European import in Vienna—to determine the conditions of peace and realign the map of the Continent. Yet their handiwork, imperfect though it proved, was at least, in its main features, dictated by a genuine spirit of moderation and equity, though some Sovereigns and Governments gained less than they wished and others more than they deserved.

The leading principle followed was the restoration, as far as might be prudent and practicable, of the *status quo ante bellum*—the antithesis of the policy followed at Versailles in 1919, which was that of a wholesale revision of pre-existent frontiers. An illustration of the temper of the statesmanship of that time is afforded by the fact that France was given an equal voice in most of the deliberations in Vienna, and was even allowed to play a foremost part in the reassignment of the territories which she was required to relinquish.

Recognizing that she had so long been the mischief-maker of Europe, the Congress had to apply to her certain measures of restraint, yet, with unappreciated magnanimity, it allowed her to retain the whole of the territory subject to her rule prior to the Revolutionary Wars. There was a thought of restoring to Germany Alsace and Lorraine, forcibly annexed by Louis XIV over a century and a half before, with a view to giving to that country greater security against its restless western neighbour, and England for a time favoured the idea ; but even these alien lands were allowed to remain in French hands. The same respect for the *status quo ante* was shown in the treatment of Napoleon's fantastic system of satellite States, for these were summarily abolished. The Bourbon dynasty was also restored in the person of Louis XVIII.

Most of the territory recovered was returned to its former owners, but in the disposal of the remainder regard was paid to the need for strong barriers against future French aggression. The Kingdom of the Netherlands was created out of Holland, Belgium, and Luxemburg, as a buffer State between France and Germany in the north. Prussia was strengthened by an increase of territory on the Rhine and the cession to her of a small part of Saxony ; the Swiss Confederation was revived ; and the Kingdom of Sardinia was restored and enlarged. When the future of Saxony, which had fought on Napoleon's side, came up for decision the stoutest opposition to any cession of territory to Prussia came from Talleyrand, who, calling oblivion upon the history of the preceding twenty years, claimed for France the proud *rôle* of the disinterested friend of the small States of Europe. The economic difficulties of Danzig as a free city were relieved by its incorporation in Prussia, while Frankfort received back its earlier status as an independent republic.

The Allied Powers returned to France most of the colonial possessions which had been taken from her during the war. The reason given by Lord Castlereagh for his assent to this act was that it was not a British interest that the French should become a military instead of a commercial nation. Nevertheless, England claimed and retained several French possessions which she had seized ; she kept some of the Dutch Colonies which had been similarly occupied (Ceylon, Cape Colony, Demerara), with the Danish island of Heligoland, seized in 1801, and certain Danish territories in the West Indies ; also Trinidad, taken from Spain, and Malta, which had belonged to the Knights of St. John.

With all its merits the work of the Congress was marred by serious defects. Thus it left the Austrian grip on Italy unrelaxed, for the House of Habsburg received back Lombardy and Venetia, now constituted a kingdom ; while the rest of the peninsula was divided between two kingdoms (Sardinia and the Sicilies) and a host of petty duchies. Further, had Poland been revived at that time, so near to the date of the first partition, an act of justice and wisdom would have been done, with no intolerable injustice to the States which had divided the spoil. France, looking for allies in Eastern Europe then as in the present day, did, indeed, propose the creation of an independent Poland, but espousal of Poland's cause in that quarter was alone sufficient to discredit it, and the three monarchies in possession were allowed to divide the Sarmatian territories once more according to their wishes—Cracow being made a free city under their reciprocal guarantee.

The German question, which was already throwing its shadow over Europe, was also shelved. The Powers went so far as to devise a federal constitution for the German territories, which were to be left to find their level in a hotchpotch political system ; but the primary dispute between Austria and Prussia, the only States in the union of serious consequence, was ignored as a German domestic affair, a view which British statesmen at a later date were for a time disposed to question. It was a graver mistake that the question of Turkish rule in Eastern Europe was similarly disregarded. Greece had begged for liberation, but, as again and again in later times, the petition fell on deaf ears ; nothing was done for the Christian races suffering from oppression ; and no attempt was made to keep Turkey to her treaty engagements.

While the work of the diplomatists of Vienna was far from being based on final principles, its very defects were the result of a desire not to disturb unnecessarily an already disorganized Continent, and on the whole it must be allowed that a rough equilibrium was achieved which for a long time afforded to strong States all legitimate liberty of movement and to weak States a sense of security, since no Power was predominant. Not only so, but it left none of the Great Powers cherishing intolerable resentments, and it gave Europe peace for over a generation.

For the security of the settlement Castlereagh, Talleyrand, and others appear to have looked to the creation of a permanent system of reciprocal guarantees, in which all the European Governments were to have participated ; but, as was the case with the Versailles Conference of 1919, the final stages of the Vienna deliberations were precipitately rushed through, with the result that this scheme was not developed. The consequence was that the execution of the measures adopted by the Congress was left to the four Allies which had borne the brunt of the struggle with Napoleon, viz. Great Britain, Russia, Austria, and Prussia ; the last two, as the major States in the new German Confederation, ranking as Great Powers after 1818, though for a long time expected to sit below the salt. The arrangement suggests in our day the analogy of the Council of Four Allied States which for several years endeavoured to enforce the Peace Treaties of 1919 and 1920. The rulers of Russia, Austria, and Prussia formed separately the Holy Alliance, nominally for the preservation of the hardly won peace, though its influence was used chiefly in suppressing movements and ideas deemed to be hostile to the autocratic conception of government. Great Britain, like the United States, declined to join this coalition, suspecting from the first that the objects professed were not those intended.

In effect the settlement of 1815 based the stability of Europe on a system of checks and counter-checks, by reaffirming two principles or doctrines which had long had tacit acceptance. There were (1) the balance of power and, as its corollary, (2) the right of intervention which States sufficiently strong claimed to exercise, in the form of either diplomatic or armed interference, where and when action was taken or conditions arose that were held to be prejudicial to the established status. No Power attached greater importance to these principles or applied them more frequently during the next two generations than Great Britain, which for a large part of that time held the leading place in what came to be known as the European Concert, described by Lord Salisbury at a later date as an " inchoate federation."

The long years of war and the need for the vigilant guarding of the restored status more than ever habituated British statesmen, and in a large degree the nation, to the outward look, and the doctrine of the balance of power continued to be regarded as the sheet-anchor of foreign policy ; though so long as they continued out of office the Whigs favoured foreign intervention less, at least in principle, than the Tories. The two parties had united for the successful prosecution of the war with Revolutionary and Bonapartist France ; but when peace had been won the Whigs wished to relieve the nation's financial exhaustion by retrenchments, to be effected by the reduction of military expenditure and abstention from foreign enter-prises. Such was the policy advocated in the Upper House by men like Earl Grey, Lord Lansdowne, and for a time Lord Grenville ; in the Lower by George Tierney, Brougham, Sir James Mackintosh, and others. Since the beginning of the century, however, the Whigs had been in opposition, and it was only after twenty years of retirement that, on the Duke of Wellington's fall on the question of Parliamentary Reform in 1830, they returned to power under Earl Grey. Castlereagh had foreseen that sooner or later there would be an open breach between England and the despots of the Holy Alliance, whose antagonism to popular liberties knew no bounds, and the resolutions adopted at the conferences of Troppau and Laibach (1820 and 1821) brought matters to a head. Castlereagh died in 1822, however, and it fell to George Canning, his successor as Foreign Secretary, to dissociate this country formally from the political system which the Alliance personified.

During his tenure of the Foreign Office and, for some months of 1827, of the Premiership, Canning showed a strong disinclination to engage in foreign adventures, and it is customary to identify the principle of non-intervention with his name. Thus while England protested against the French invasion of Spain in 1823 she did no more, and though in 1826 British troops were dispatched to Portugal it was in order to counteract Spanish intrigues and maintain the independence of a threatened country, and justification could be fairly claimed by appeal to the long-standing Anglo-Portuguese treaty of alliance.

With Canning's death in 1827, whatever advance the policy of abstention and neutrality had made was checked directly Lord Palmerston's long reign at the Foreign Office began. In office for the greater part of his parliamentary career of fifty-six years (1809 to 1865), Palmerston was for over a generation England's strong man, and his foreign policy was as masterful as his character. From 1830 forward he held Ministerial office for over twenty-five years—for fourteen as Foreign Secretary and for nine as Prime Minister—and during that time the country saw itself systematically committed to diplomatic action and warlike enterprises in all parts of the world, at times over matters in which it had but a shadowy interest. He was ready to intervene anywhere and everywhere on the slightest pretext. He conceived it to be the right and duty of his country to keep Europe in order—to admonish its rulers, Governments, and Parliaments, to advise on, and if necessary uphold, its constitutions, and even to have a hand in the marriage arrangements of its dynasties. His attitude was faithfully described by a later Continental Sovereign, who might have taken Palmerston for his example, for it was his fixed determination that "nothing in the world should be settled" without the consent of England and her Foreign Secretary. He had also at times the same Sovereign's awkward and irritating way of giving effect to his country's influence. If a Continental Chancery, bent on intervention, was believed to be following certain lines of policy, Palmerston was almost sure to find pretexts for pursuing a different course. Some of his decisions and interventions in foreign affairs were as

impetuous as their consequences were disturbing. It was
after one of his sudden interferences that a famous French
financier said, " Palmerston has this drawback : he makes
the funds fall all over Europe without giving us notice."
More than any statesman of his generation he was the embodi-
ment in English political life of the restless energy which made
the British Empire and has continued to increase it down
to the present day. Unquestionably he was entirely honest
in all he did, and his motives were invariably of the best. He
had also a genuine sympathy with the politically oppressed of
other nations, so long as they were not too troublesome and
did not break treaties, and he hated despots, though himself
so despotic. He even believed that he was in the direct line
of Canning.

It was a lean, unfruitful year that gave the country none
of the sensations in which it came to take almost a morbid
pleasure. Two years particularly prolific in foreign entanglements were 1839 and 1840, when Palmerston was Foreign
Secretary in the second Melbourne Cabinet : they saw the
country at war with China in the interest of the opium
traffic ; the occupation of Cabul by British troops, leading to
the first Afghan war ; Turkey egged by Palmerston into
war with Mehemet Ali ; and a narrow escape from an armed
rupture with France over the same Minister's Eastern policy
generally.

During the succeeding Government of Sir Robert Peel the
calmer counsels of Lord Aberdeen ruled at the Foreign Office,
but with Palmerston's return in 1846 there was an immediate
revival of foreign meddling. In that year he intervened in
the Spanish marriage question, and sent a fleet to the Tagus
in order to dictate constitutional government to Portugal ;
and in 1847 he dispatched Lord Minto to Italy, there to
proclaim England's sympathy with the reform movements,
and quarrelled with the United States.

The Crimean War of the following decade was far more his
affair than that of his chief, Lord Aberdeen, though for safety's
sake he had been assigned to the Home Office ; and, forming
his own first Cabinet early in 1855, he took over full responsibility and insisted on a fight to a finish. So, with brief intermissions, his foreign exploits continued until his death, which

followed that of Cobden by only six months. If the career of Lord Palmerston conveyed no other warning, it taught the danger of allowing the Foreign Office to fall too long or too often into the same hands.

It was a source of perpetual disappointment and chagrin to Cobden that the Whigs had so little understanding of pacific Liberal principles that they persisted in idolizing the bellicose statesmen who kept the country in a fever of excitement, and by the middle of the century he had lost faith in them as " an effete and worn-out set." Henceforth he regarded them as the allies of the aristocracy rather than of the people, since they fought the Tories with gloves, not meaning to hurt them : they were " buffers placed between the people and the privileged classes to deaden the shock when they are brought into collision." What specially made Palmerston's position so powerful and practically unassailable was the fact that in foreign affairs he was almost as popular with the Tories as with his own party, and that the populace itself followed him with canine fidelity ; for severely as Cobden judged Palmerston's foreign policy, he never doubted that it was entirely to the mind of his countrymen.

With all his faults, and perhaps because of them, " Old Pam," as the bluff, impetuous, big-hearted statesman came to be affectionately called even down to our own days, was unquestionably for over a generation the darling not merely of the interventionist party, but of the whole nation. He was popular because he was ready at all times to uphold the voice and influence of England in international affairs, and because he spoke in the language of force in the name of a people which had been taught to believe in force.

Throughout his public life Cobden stood forth as the uncompromising, and apparently implacable, antagonist of that great statesman and the entire spirit of his policy, as combining mischievous meddling abroad with neglect of domestic affairs. It was also Palmerston's misfortune in his eyes that he was an aristocrat, so that he personified a class to which his critic attributed the backwardness of English political life and the unfavourable social conditions in which at that time the masses of the people lived ; but his crowning offence was that, though a representative of " the ideas of the Dark Ages," he was able to lead, as on a string, a nation which claimed and believed itself to be the most popularly governed in Europe.

As early as 1839 Cobden had convinced himself that Palmerston was politically " incurable." To a correspondent he wrote, " He is under the delusion that he is living in 1808, and as long as he lives you will not rescue him from that delusion." He never relaxed his own efforts for the great man's improvement, though some of these efforts were far too drastic to be effectual. It must even be admitted that his strong prejudices tended at times to deteriorate into personal animus. The full flavour of his antipathy and bitterness is revealed most clearly by many of the sobriquets which punctuated his criticisms of the offending Minister in indiscreetly outspoken letters. Phrases like " the old joker," " the incorrigible old dodger," " the pantaloon," " this too successful charlatan," " that venerable political impostor," " the rogue," " the evil genius of our generation," and " the old sinner " faithfully indicate the *crescendo* of hostility and wrath which there finds expression.

Even in his platform criticisms of his adversary he never minced words, though here the limits of strict decorum were rarely transgressed. Nor did he hesitate to repeat in the House of Commons the censures which he passed outside, and even to tell Palmerston to his face that he was a costly luxury which the country could not afford. Speaking in the House on August 1, 1862, he said :

" I have sometimes sat down and tried to settle in my own mind what amount of money the noble Lord has cost this country. From 1840, dating from that Syrian business which first occasioned a permanent rise in our Estimates—by the way in which, in conjunction with the late Admiral Napier, he constantly stimulated and worried Sir Robert Peel to increased expenditure—taking into account his Chinese wars, his Afghan, his Russian war ; his expeditions here, there, and everywhere ; his fortification scheme, which I suppose we must now accept with all its consequences of increased military expenditure —the least I can put down the noble Lord to have cost us is £100,000,000 sterling. Now, with all his merits, I think he is very dear at the price."

This novel way of appraising the worth of statesmen was in keeping with Cobden's habit of submitting practical questions to a practical test, though on this occasion he came out of the debate without lustre, for the House refused to have its hero valued in so mercenary a manner.

The great danger of personal resentment, as of most other ill-humours, is that it distorts judgment and destroys the sense of proportion. The more Cobden attacked Palmerston, as the enemy of his country's peace he honestly believed him to be, the more his wrath rose, until the time came when the wilful statesman's shortcomings, as he saw them, became an unhealthy obsession, which so filled the line of his mental vision as to blot out the better and finer traits of his adversary, who was much more than the querulous and fire-eating mischief-maker he was represented to be. On occasion Palmerston struck back hard blows in turn, but oftener than not he allowed Cobden to pummel away to his pleasure, knowing that in an emergency his magnetic hold on public opinion was sufficient to pull him through. The remarkable thing is that on the whole each of the combatants took his flagellations in good part, and that in the end malice remained on neither side. We have seen how Palmerston chivalrously tried to induce Cobden to enter his second Cabinet, and Cobden, for his part, had unquestionably more than a sneaking regard for his adversary.

It was in the course of the speech just mentioned that he went out of his way to pay a handsome tribute to the honesty of the Minister whose policy he had so often and so bitterly assailed. "And when I speak of the noble Lord's policy," he said, "I believe he is perfectly sincere, for the longer I live the more I believe in men's sincerity. I believe they often deceive themselves and often go wrong from culpable ignorance." That is the sort of thing that the House of Commons likes, and that lifts the level of political life, and if on that occasion Cobden weakened his case by generosity he strengthened his own reputation as a fair controversialist and an honest gentleman. To the last, however, Palmerston remained at the head of his black list of dangers to the Commonwealth. As late as December 1862 he wrote to a correspondent, " Be sure that if I can help to shelve this old dodger I shall do it as an act of piety to heaven and of charity to man."

Cobden was continually deploring the popular ignorance

of affairs as the principal reason why the nation allowed itself
to be drawn into so many needless and dangerous foreign
adventures. For this ignorance a narrow political franchise
was not the only cause. It was a misfortune that, in the
absence of the newspaper Press as it developed in the second
half of the century, public opinion was seldom able to speak
on great political issues decisively, promptly, or with collective
force. By the Press of the early-Victorian era must be understood, not the wonderful mechanism of printed propagandism
which at the present day covers the land, carrying its influences
into the remotest villages and hamlets of the three kingdoms,
but a comparatively small number of metropolitan and provin-
cial newspapers, published at a price beyond the means of the
humbler classes, and for the most part counting their readers
only by tens of thousands. The cheap Press, with its blessing
and its curse, had still to come. As late as 1836 there was a
duty of fourpence on every newspaper published ; in that year
it was reduced to a penny with another halfpenny for a sup-
plement (for the normal newspaper then had but a single
" broadsheet "), and though from 1855 the stamp became a
postal frank, it was 1870 before it was formally abolished and
newspapers were carried in the post for a halfpenny. An
indication of the limited influence of the Press at the time of
Cobden's entrance into public life is afforded by the fact that
in 1830 the total number of dutiable newspapers issued
numbered only thirty millions, which is fewer than are now
circulated in a week ; and that there are to-day London
newspapers of which more copies are printed in a single
month than were issued in a whole year by all the daily
and weekly journals of the United Kingdom in the middle of
last century.

Again, in Cobden's day the metropolitan Press stood for
public opinion to a degree incomprehensible in later times,
and the influence of influential Tory editors was always at the
service of Governments and Foreign Secretaries given to the
pursuit of prestige by foreign interventions and entanglements.
Even Lord Palmerston was not slow to benefit by support
from these quarters. Cobden quotes a London journal of
1834 as fulminating against the Ministry then in power because
a dozen Continental disputes and problems were left unsettled

owing to its lack of vigour in asserting England's influence abroad.

" The Dutch question is undecided," said the truculent writer :
" The French are still at Ancona ; Don Carlos is fighting in Spain ;
Don Miquel and his adherents are preparing for a new conflict in
Portugal ; Turkey and Egypt are at daggers drawn ; Switzerland is
quarrelling with her neighbouring States about Italian refugees ;
Frankfort is occupied by Prussian troops in violation of the Treaty
of Vienna ; Algiers is being made a large French colony in violation of
the promises made in 1829 and 1830 ; ten thousand Polish nobles are
still proscribed and wandering all over Europe ; French gaols are full
of political offenders.   In a word, nothing is terminated."

And all these things were happening because England did
not sufficiently recognize it to be her duty to keep the world
in order. The quotation reflects as in a mirror the confused
mentality of the interventionist school of politicians against
which Cobden warred for a generation.

Another and not the least notable political fact which
differentiated his time from our own was England's relationship
to France. Down to the middle of the century the memories
left by the French wars, far from having been effaced, still
chafed on both sides and had created what seemed to be a
hopeless estrangement between them. France had not forgotten the humiliation of defeat, or forgiven the Powers
which in 1815 compelled her to withdraw behind her former
frontiers, so that from a twenty years' struggle she emerged
in the end with the sacrifice at once of honour and glory, of
territory and wealth.

On the other hand, the mass of English people retained
the traditional view of France as the implacable enemy of their
country and a permanent menace to its security. " Formerly,"
Cobden said in the House of Commons in a speech on armaments on June 17, 1851, " no man could be heard in our
smaller towns and villages speaking a foreign language, let it
be what language it might, but the ruder and vulgar passer-by
would call him a Frenchman, and very likely insult him."
Indeed, there is hardly an accusation or a reproach among the
multitude made during recent years against the nation—and
not merely its Government and governing class—which bore
the brunt of the late war with the Entente Powers that was

not made during the greater part of last century, with equal
vigour, and in part with greater reason, against the French,
who represented to the majority of Englishmen of every class
a people whom it was unpatriotic to try to conciliate. Even
among responsible statesmen there were few who believed
that a neighbour who had proved himself so often either an
open or a secret enemy could ever become a reliable friend.
Down to the middle of the century, without as yet any
intermission, France had continued to be morally outlawed as
still a potential disturber of the peace ; and on two occasions
the irrational fear of a French invasion threw the nation into
panic.

Cobden was wont to regard it as one of the most serious
limitations of the national character that Englishmen were
unable to do two things at the same time. They could not
even hate two foreign nations at once. Suddenly in the early
fifties there came to a head an antagonism against Russia
which had been slowly gaining ground for some years, and the
hostility to France was suspended. Russia's crime consisted
less in any direct acts of unfriendliness committed against this
country than in her aggressive attitude to Turkey, the maintenance of whose integrity and independence was still deemed
to be a vital European interest. Great Britain and France
came together in the high interest of the balance of power, and
the alliance led them into the Crimean War on Turkey's side.
No sooner was that futile struggle over, however, than the old
distrust was revived, and a third invasion panic followed, this
time on both sides of the Channel.

Palmerston's attitude towards France was always one of
suspicion, and he never allowed himself to be off his guard.
As early as 1834 he wrote, " Paris is the pivot of my foreign
policy," and so it continued to be to the end. His quarrels
with France were habitual, and more than once, with abettors
in the opposite political camp, he nearly brought the two
countries to blows. He came to distrust Louis Philippe so
much that when the Revolution of 1848 came he helped to give
the Second Republic a fair start. But the French democracy,
still under the Bonapartist spell, promptly hailed Louis
Napoleon as the heaven-sent restorer of the great days of old.
Although Palmerston honestly tried to work amicably with the

Prince President, he soon had to abandon the attempt. That faint shadow of a colossal historical figure may not have been quite as unprincipled as he was painted by those who best knew him, but he was bad enough. On the testimony of his own Ministers, as well as of his own acts, he was a born conspirator and a master of crooked stratagem, inspired no doubt by large ambitions, yet betraying an essential weakness of character by faithlessness and falsity. He began his revolutionary exploits when a young man little over twenty, and his entire career forward to the Emperorship in 1852 was an orgy of illegality. With singular frankness the historian Guizot, one of his Ministers, wrote of him to Lord Aberdeen, " Il joue toujours ses deux rôles, le rôle d'empereur et le rôle de conspirateur ; il flotte entre ses rêves et son épicurisme, ses passions d'autrefois et ses intérêts d'aujourd'hui."— (January 24, 1850.)

Like the strong, outspoken, forthright man he was, Palmerston could not excuse deceit, and as soon as he began to know Louis Napoleon from the inside his confidence in him disappeared, never to be revived. For the last ten years of his life he followed with anxious vigilance every move of France on the political chessboard of Western Europe, knowing how the restless Emperor hankered after the readjustment of her eastern frontiers.

It is odd to recall in these days the fact that in the middle of last century this country was arming against France because she was bent on attacking Germany. Louis Napoleon divided that country, as Cæsar divided Gaul, into three parts—Austria, Prussia, and the Rhineland. He wanted nothing from Austria, but he was determined to carry the eastern frontier of France to or beyond the Rhine, and he intrigued for years before he abandoned the design as hopeless. It was from no love of Prussia or of Germany that Palmerston wanted to see both strong. His concern was for the balance of power, and that only for his own country's sake, and in his view a right balance required that Germany should be strong enough to act as a bulwark against Russia in the east and France in the west, both aggressive Powers to be watched with jealousy and, if necessary, checkmated with decision.

Cobden regarded prejudice against other nations as ungener-

ous and puerile, and just as in 1836 he wrote his second pamphlet
for the purpose of stemming a rising tide of anti-Russian feeling
at that time, so in 1853 he took up his pen in order to defend
France against the same dislike and distrust. " Our modern
history must be rewritten," he wrote in one of his early letters,
impatient with the distorted versions of political events which
were current, and kept the unlettered public in ignorance of
the truth. In the pamphlet entitled 1792 *and* 1853, *in Three
Letters*, he retold the story of one episode in his country's
modern annals—the origin of the French Revolutionary Wars
and England's participation in them. His revised version of
history cannot be accepted without qualification, yet he filled
in many important gaps, and there is at least as much truth
in his statement of the motives which led the Government of
Pitt to join hands with the Eastern Powers in 1792 as in some
of the justifications advanced by Pitt's apologists. On the
other hand, his powerful indictment of national jealousies,
competition in armaments, war, and the war spirit, as often
inflamed both in sacred and secular places, has lost none of
its force and urgency. Later he devoted another pamphlet
to the advocacy of more rational relations between the two
countries.

Cobden's public career synchronized also with a great
awakening of the spirit of nationality on the Continent, and
with that spirit he was altogether in sympathy. Everywhere
the ferment was working. In 1831 Belgium had won emancipation from the union with Holland ; in Italy the unity movement
was already on the direct way to victory ; Hungarian and Pole
alike hungered after their ancient independence. Even within
the Turkish Empire there were ominous stirrings. In 1829
Moldavia and Wallachia had been placed under the protection
of Russia by the Treaty of Adrianople ; and Greece, after four
centuries of Ottoman misrule, had thrown off the hated yoke ;
while in 1830, and again in 1842, Servia gained substantial
instalments of nationhood. Then came 1848 with its tidal
wave of political commotion, overspreading the whole of
Western Europe. In France it swept away the Orleans
branch of the Bourbon dynasty, which had been installed in
the Revolution of 1830, and replaced the monarchy by the
Second Republic. In Germany it similarly shook thrones,

though without overturning them ; it also carried the national
unity movement further, only to leave it, when the waters
receded, stranded high and dry, until a new and deeper current
of national feeling should float it again two decades later.
Austria, too, received the shock of that convulsive time ; and
there were insurrections both in Vienna and Hungary. The
despotic Metternich, who had dragooned liberal movements
for forty years, was forced to flee the country and take refuge
in England, tranquil because free. In both Germany and
Austria, however, revolution was soon suppressed, and order
having been restored the old work of repression was resumed
more drastically than before. The great tragedy of 1848 for
these countries was that both Princes and peoples forgot its
humiliations while failing to profit by them.

All such national aspirations, in so far as they were spontaneous and pursued without external interference, appealed
strongly to Cobden's love of liberty and his admiration for
independence in either individual or nation. They also
strengthened his conviction that the best service which a
powerful State like England could render to its neighbours
was to leave them alone to work out their own salvation. He
was not blind to the operation of forces making for large
political agglomerations, but then and to the last his heart
was with the little nations. " It may seem Utopian," he
wrote at a later date, " but I don't feel sympathy for a great
nation, or for those who desire the greatness of a people by the
vast extension of empire. What I like to see is the growth,
development, and elevation of the individual man."

If it be asked, what part was left to the nation to play in
the determination of foreign policy at that time, when Governments and even individual Ministers could take upon themselves
so much responsibility, the answer must be that England as
yet was only in name a self-governed country. Nevertheless,
just before the appearance of Cobden's first pamphlet a Reform
Act had been passed which greatly widened the effective
audience to which public men were able to appeal. After a
great war peoples seldom at once settle down quietly ; popular
impulses are stimulated, expectations aroused, and the ultimate
result almost invariably is that the masses move forward a
step or two—sometimes many—on the way towards the ulti-

mate goal of all government, equality of opportunity and of citizenship. The history of wars is the history of force and, on one side or, as more often happens, on both sides, of injustice and wrong ; but it contains also epilogues on the advance of political liberty and social emancipation, and often it is these alone that redeem the record from sordidness and horror.

After they had done so much for the liberties of Continental nations, the people of England thought it was meet that something more should be done for themselves in the same direction. Reform movements began as soon as the Napoleonic Wars were over, notably in the North, where so many hard blows have been given and taken in the cause of popular liberty. They were resisted by the Tory Governments which were in power until 1830, when the Whigs returned. Earl Grey took office with the promise that the policy of his party should be concentrated upon the maintenance of peace, abstention from foreign interventions, and rigorous retrenchment ; but Lord Palmerston's long reign at the Foreign Office which now began made such a policy impracticable. The new administration, however, produced a long-delayed measure of reform. Although very modest, in comparison with later measures of the same kind, some of its opponents condemned it as presaging the downfall of the monarchy. It abolished a host of " pocket " and decayed boroughs with an insignificant population, but its £10 householder qualification for borough voters and its new leaseholder and copyholder franchise for the counties meant nothing at all to the industrial and agricultural labourers, who had to wait another generation for even partial enfranchisement. The House of Lords rejected the Bill of 1831, and would have rejected that of the following year but for the knowledge that the result would be the cheapening of the peerage by a large infusion of plebeian blood. Yet the Government of the country largely remained as before in the hands of great titular and territorial lords, their wives, and their Egerias, who kept brilliant salons or coached their heroes by correspondence. To the nation at large, therefore, it mattered little which of the two parties was in power, since the ruling statesmen, whether Whigs or Tories, represented practically the same class, with all its traditions, ideas, prejudices, and interests, so that the aristocracy continued to retain besides the first choice of the plums of office, both at home and in the Colonies, the more valuable privilege of taxing the staple food of the people.

It was no wonder that the men who passed the Reform Act of 1832 grudgingly, and with the idea of finality, proved unable to guide, or even to understand, the forces which had compelled that measure of emancipation, or the new forces which were now released. Writing before his strong individualistic predilections had been modified by practical experience of the business of government, Cobden's biographer claimed that many of the social aspirations which were awakened and stimulated by parliamentary reform three generations ago " lay wholly outside the sphere of any Government." [1] But, on analysis, that plea only means that the ruling statesmen and parties of the day failed to recognize, as their successors so often did, that the scope and functions of government can never be rigidly fixed once for all, but must be indefinitely variable and adaptable, in accordance with changing social and economic conditions, the higher conceptions of manhood and citizenship encouraged by education and culture, and the moral standards which happen to be current in any given age.

In truth an old era had passed away, like a creed outworn, and a new era had opened, discovering tasks and duties ·of statesmanship of a kind undiscernible by either Whigs or Tories of the conventional schools. These men had learned nothing and forgotten nothing since the Luddite riots of 1812-18 and the massacre of Peterloo in 1819, when the Government of Lord Liverpool, with a truly aristocratic conception of the needs of society, thought of meeting the social aspirations and strivings of a restless and distempered age by providing a million pounds for the building of churches. To them the political vote was an end in itself, and having magnanimously given it they supposed that their duty had been done. The newly enfranchised classes, and still more those still left outside the pale of a full citizenship, saw in the franchise only a means to certain ends, and towards these ends they now pressed with impatient footsteps. A great awakening, bringing with it a dawning recognition of responsibilities hitherto unperceived, was to come to both of the traditional parties,

[1] *Life*, i. 89.

but the time was not yet ; and meanwhile their omission to face resolutely the oncoming new problems made these problems more complicated and the solution of them more difficult and eventually more drastic. The "hungry forties" came, bringing more persistent and now successful agitation against the taxation of the poor man's loaf, renewed endeavours to enlarge the bounds of labour combination, and the later and more violent phases of the Chartist movement.

It was in that decade, too, that Socialism and Communism passed from the stage of mere bookish theory into that of serious public controversy. At home the working class in general was still contented with its old political status as the impecunious step-brother of Liberalism, but abroad a strong movement to the left had begun, and cryptic phrases like "class consciousness" and "solidarity of labour" were to be heard from popular platforms.

It was a misfortune that at such a time of social ferment the rising estate of manufacturers and merchants, who, with greater intelligence and foresight, might have done so much to set the industrial revolution, now in full tide, in wise and safe channels, were in general ill-educated, and maintained a stolid and supercilious attitude to the intellectual and social manifestations of the time-spirit, with results injurious to their order and to society at large at a later date. They, however, were too busy in amassing wealth, more easily gotten in the middle of last century than ever before or since, and in building towns in which to make and store it, to think of the England they were creating ; though it happened not seldom that the fortunes gained with lightning speed by the fathers were squandered or lost by the sons, insomuch that in Lancashire the proverb, not altogether without point to-day, became current : "From clogs to clogs takes two generations." This hot pursuit of wealth was part of a rough, *sauve-qui-peut* endeavour to escape from the moneyless ruck of humanity, and it was specially characteristic of the North. Such a scramble can never be orderly or barely decorous, much less pay regard to altruistic considerations ; in it the stronger are certain to come to the front, the weaker to be left behind, the weakest to be trodden underfoot. For the callous neglect of social obligations shown by successive Governments in that time of transition later generations have had to pay a heavy penalty, and even yet the debt is far from liquidated.

The accident of fortune, as we have seen, cast Cobden, though by descent a landman, into the manufacturing class, but he was never in sympathy with its engrossing material aspirations. He did not grudge the nation's new conquerors their wealth, but he lamented their disregard of culture, their lack of dignity and self-respect, their proneness to hurl down the ladder upon which they had ascended from obscurity into recognition, and their readiness to play lackey to an aristocracy into which they knew they could never hope to be admitted on terms of equality.[1] The time came when his faith in the commercial middle class, which in the hey-day of his Free Food agitation had been almost unbounded, became weakened, as he saw how its ambitions were concentrated on money as a means of attaining social elevation and prominence. As this faith suffered eclipse, his hope was transferred increasingly to the toiling multitudes of the industrial towns and of the country-side, until he came to look to these for the great national impetus which was finally to overthrow the feudal incubus which had lain so long and so heavily upon the spirit and life of England.

A man of the people in the truest and best sense of the term, though one who never flattered the populace, or shrank from withholding from it truths which he believed to be for its good, he was in full accord with the democratic tendencies of the times. He sympathized keenly with the political aspirations of the working classes, herein showing a foresight far ahead of that which in general characterized the educated circles of his day, and in advocating the further broadening of the franchise he recognized that participation by wider sections of the

---

[1] Cobden's travels in Germany appear to have brought him into contact with manufacturers and merchants of a type which, to his regret, he missed at home. " It humiliates me," he wrote to his brother Frederick while on his first visit in that country in 1838, " to think of the class of people at home who belong to the order of intelligent and educated men that I see on the Continent following the business of manufacturing, spinning," etc. Not a few Germans of the class lauded by Cobden settled in this country from the second quarter of last century forward and made excellent citizens ; but it is an odd social irony that so many of their descendants should have turned from the traditional pursuits of trade and commerce to the professions, and even aspired to staff our Civil Service, which now, for good or ill, is multiracial in a higher degree than any other in the world.

population in the government of the country was not merely their just right but was in the true interest of the nation at large. In later life it was his constant wonder that the workers, who might be so powerful in union if they only knew it, had suffered indignity so patiently and so long. " Have they no Spartacus among them," he wrote to a correspondent on one occasion, " to lead a revolt of the slave class against their political tormentors ? "

Nevertheless, a warm friend of the working classes though he was, and eager as was his interest in popular education, he cannot be said to have grasped in its full proportions the condition of the people question which was already clamorously knocking at the national door, though the minds of men like Ruskin, Carlyle, and Kingsley, with many other forward-looking teachers of their generation, were proclaiming its urgency. It may also be doubted whether he saw much more clearly than the middle class in general whither the popular movements of the day were tending. Above all, there is no evidence that Socialistic doctrines ever gave him a moment of perplexed thought, though Socialism and Communism were favourite catchwords amongst advanced social reformers before the middle of the century, and though two of his contemporaries were Robert Owen, a cotton manufacturer like himself, who had both written much on Socialism and experimented a little on Socialistic lines, and Louis Blanc, of whose *ateliers nationaux* he cannot but have heard when in Paris.

What he did see, and that with growing clearness, was that labour was destined to be identified with international conceptions of the entire business of politics. It was the recognition of this fact that led him to regard labour as a necessary and natural auxiliary in every endeavour to give to foreign policy a new, wider, and humaner spirit and direction.

E

CHAPTER III

COBDEN AS CONTROVERSIALIST

" The true patriot is he who seeks the highest welfare of his country and who holds that the real welfare of his country is inseparable from right dealing. He will be jealous for the outward glory, dignity, and interest of the nation, but only so far as they are consistent with justice and honour."— E. A. FREEMAN.

" I have not, and never have had, any other criterion to guide me, nor any other standard by which to form my opinion, but the interests, the honest interests, of my country, which, with God's blessing, are the interests of mankind."—COBDEN, speech of October 25, 1862.

BEFORE Cobden's principles of foreign policy can be usefully surveyed particular reference to him as a politician seems due to those readers who do not already know him from his published memoirs—his writings, speeches, and correspondence—or from the authentic *Life* and the various studies of his work which have been published from time to time.

Perhaps, by all the rules of literary *technique*, the characterization of him as a controversialist and a parliamentary and platform figure which is here proposed should follow rather than precede the exposition of his teaching. Were this a formal biography the rule might fairly have applied, but in view of its more limited scope, and of the fact that there is in the writings and speeches so much that is alien to the dominant thought even of the present day, it seems inappropriate to allow such readers to go straight to the robust doctrine of this sturdy combatant of tradition and convention, whose maxims of foreign policy, if rigidly applied, would turn the world upside-down, without knowing more about his intimate character and the governing motives of his public life. For if an innovator, he was no mere purposeless disturber of intellectual peace ; if he endeavoured to upset

many popular faiths and cherished prejudices, it was in order
to replace them by reasoned convictions based on what to
him were clearer and sounder principles. Frankly, too, I
want the readers of this book to go to Cobden sympathetically,
since only then will they be quite sure to do him full justice.

Morley passes a carefully considered verdict on Cobden's
first parliamentary speech of August 25, 1841—a verdict based
in part, one may surmise, on the testimony of men who
heard it—and all the weightier since it comes from one who
himself was in political life at the time he wrote the biography.
He says . . .

" It sounded a new key, and startled men by an accent that was
strange in the House of Commons. The thoughtful among them recognized the rare tone of reality, and the note of a man dealing with things
and not words. He produced that singular and profound effect which
is perceived in English deliberative assemblies when a speaker leaves
party recrimination, abstract argument, and commonplaces of sentiment,
in order to inform his hearers of telling facts in the condition of the
nation."

This passage faithfully indicates both the substance and
the form of the only kind of controversy which had for
Cobden either attraction or meaning. He dealt solely with
questions and problems of life, and in so doing appealed to
actual facts and spared no pains in informing himself upon
these. Teaching of that kind involves infinite and unceasing
labour and thought. Few reformers of society have been so
self-dependent and self-contained as Cobden, and none
deduced his principles of action, so far as they went, more
completely from his own independent observation, experience,
and reflexion.

Most of us travellers through this interesting world carry
about with us well-stocked wallets of preconceptions and
prejudices, of which in the course of the journey we discard
many or few, according to circumstances, usually replacing
them by few or many others in return. From such embarrassing baggage Cobden was singularly free. He judged mankind and society, political institutions and dogmas, civilization as a whole, as he himself saw them, not as he had been
told to see them ; accepting no ready-made judgments, no

specious *dicta*, however hoary and epigrammatic, but submitting the visible facts to the play of a keen, disciplined mind, and bringing to the interpretation of them a wonderful store of sound, workaday common sense, and withal a warm and generous human sympathy. An individualist of an uncompromising type, he never judged men by groups, never confused a whole people with its Government, particularly when that Government was imposed upon it without its choice, and never awarded praise or censure upon the characteristics and institutions of other nations merely according as they happened to conform to the traditions and standards of his own country. Such a man may at times be dogmatic, as Cobden assuredly was, but he is not likely to be either intolerant or a doctrinaire.

No public man more conscientiously equipped himself for his work. He never addressed a public assembly—whether the House of Commons, an international congress, or an audience of Lancashire or Yorkshire operatives—on any question which he did not understand as well as, or better than, most other men, because he kept strictly to his own controversial province. Herein he was the antithesis of the typical party hack, who indulges in random chatter on subjects of which he is either only half informed or totally ignorant, and leaves his hearers to clarify his banalities afterwards, if able. Cobden spoke of himself as early as 1836 as "fond of digging deep into the foundations of causes." That was one of his most marked characteristics—his impatience with merely superficial facts, and his eagerness to know the origins and groundings of things, the *causae causantes*.

Reference has been made to the value which he attached to foreign travel as a means of exact and authoritative information. Morley speaks of the diaries of his wanderings as showing "a man who is acquiring knowledge not with the elaborate conscientiousness of a set purpose, but with the ease of natural and spontaneous interest." The qualification here made does not seem either necessary or just. A singular *flair* for pertinent facts was natural to Cobden, for he was a born investigator, gifted with unusually acute powers of observation ; but he has himself left it on record that he travelled and studied abroad as a duty both to himself and

to the public which he wished to instruct and influence.   It is
a characteristic which will always win for him the respect of
those who, taught by similar discipline, have most reason to
know how much thought and effort conscientious inquiry of
that sort implies.   Yet he devoted just the same painstaking
labour to the study of domestic questions.   While his writings
and speeches contain convincing evidence of this, his correspondence everywhere attests the indefatigable digger and
delver amongst histories, biographies, blue-books, and official
publications of all kinds.

His parliamentary speeches on foreign subjects bristled
with categorical statements and challenges, and justifiably
so, for he was invariably sure of his ground, and he knew that
the weakness of his opponents lay in the fact that they were
never equally sure of theirs.   After laying down the law in
his pontifical way he would admonish his hearers, remembering the average member's reliance on tittle-tattle, or at best
his favourite newspaper : "Let no one answer me with a
statement of what he has *heard* somewhere."   But the House
took the warning patiently, and could not do otherwise, for
it knew by experience that this Manchester man was too well-
informed and too wary to blunder.   It is true that the scrupulous pains which he took to ascertain facts made him seem
something of an oddity to his colleagues, but because of it
they heard him all the more readily and took him at a higher
price.   He, for his part, was unable to understand how
responsible Ministers, who were supposed to be statesmen,
could be so unwilling either to face or investigate facts, but
persisted in hugging their illusions and misconceptions in spite
of his convincing disproofs.

All testimonies agree that he had a singular power of
persuasion, the result and the reward of his sincerity, intensity
of conviction, translucent clearness of thought, and, above
all, his complete disinterestedness.   No one knew him better
than Bright, who speaks of " the absolute truth that shone in
his eye and in his countenance."   Yet he was not an orator,
like his great colleague, and his impatience with the loose
thinking which he saw went so often with empty verbosity
led him to place a low estimate on rhetoric.   Experience
even of parliamentary life convinced him that " a man may

have great oratorical gifts and be quite destitute of common sense or ordinary judgment." So great was his dislike of the artificial and the theatrical in public speaking that he never made perorations, but, as he said, "simply sat down" when he had told his tale, sometimes doing it so abruptly that the effect upon the hearer must have been that felt by the railway traveller who is dumped down upon a windy platform in the middle of the night. For appeal to emotion he had the same distaste, and his distrust of sentimentalists was so profound that he declined their co-operation, regarding them as a danger rather than a help. "These sentimentalists," he wrote on one occasion, "are very unreliable politicians. Look at the greatest of the class, Lamartine : after all his magnificent mouthings about national integrity, justice, and liberty, see how he was prepared to imitate Frederick or Napoleon in his treatment of Italy. There is nothing, after all, in a politician like the stern logic of a Jefferson or a Calhoun. They may sometimes start from false premises, but when once started you always know where they are going."

His admiration of Bright's eloquence is said to have been unbounded, but his own power lay not in any rhythmic flow of language, but rather in his sound and almost unerring practical sense and his direct and confident appeal to reason. Always he was begging his countrymen to bring questions, not merely of trade and labour, finance and education, but of war and peace, and foreign policy generally, to "the test of our own homely common sense." Employed on the platform such a ground of appeal may seem prosaic and commonplace ; but it has this advantage over the appeal to sentiment and emotion, that whereas with reflexion the influence produced by frothy rhetoric tends to evaporate, that conveyed by the plain statement of facts tends to be confirmed and strengthened. The hearer goes home, in the one case to recover sobriety, in the other to think.

Nevertheless, his command of strong, apt, and telling English was remarkable for a man in every respect self-educated who had plunged direct from business into politics. His writings and speeches abound in passages sonorous, dignified, and even stately in measure and diction, which are worthy of companionship with the accepted classic examples of English political oratory. To read almost any of his parliamentary speeches to-day is to understand how, when delivered more than half a century ago, in a still but partially democratized House of Commons, they must have fallen like a rush of fresh mountain air upon an atmosphere often heavy with convention, pedantry, and unreality.

He would not have accomplished a tithe of the work he did, or achieved a tithe of the influence which fell to him, but for the system which he applied to his public advocacy. One of the earliest of his recorded letters, written in 1836, contains the remark : " There are many well-meaning people in the world who are not so useful as they might be, from not knowing how to go to work." From that fault he did not suffer. One of the great secrets of his success in public life was his habit of concentration. In a letter written to Sir Robert Peel on June 23, 1846, he said : " The only way in which the soul of a great nation can be stirred is by appealing to its sympathies with a true principle in its unalloyed simplicity. Nay, further, it is necessary for the concentration of a people's mind that *an individual should become the incarnation of a principle.*" He had formed that conviction as a result of the struggle for untaxed food, then just won, and all his later public work was marked by the same absolute identification with and devotion to the causes which he had in hand.

He was accustomed to speak disparagingly of his country-men as a one-idea'd race, in that they were constitutionally incapable of thinking of or doing two things at once. But people who aim after great results and achieve them are almost invariably so, and Cobden himself was an example. In an early letter to his friend Mr. George Combe, he avowed that he, too, could " only do one thing at a time," and he added, " I can't help it, though I believe I am shortening my days by following strictly the rule, ' Whatsoever thou doest, do with all thy heart.' " The prospect of premature exhaustion can hardly have troubled him, if one may judge by a letter written to his elder brother—futile Frederick—in 1838, when he was still on the threshold of his public career. " Let us remember, " he said, " that to live usefully is far better than living long. And do not let us deprive ourselves of the gratification at last, a gratification which the selfish never have, that we have not embittered our whole lives with heaping up money, but that we have given a part of our time to more rational and worthy exertions." His own life fell within the narrow span of sixty-one years, and at least one-half of these years were given almost exclusively to public work. Not only during the shock attack upon vested interests which won for the people of this country cheap food, but later, in his crusade on behalf of sounder principles of foreign policy and of peace, he was a tremendous worker. He records at one time " an average mental labour of at least twelve hours a day " as his customary ration, and this effort was often increased.

In everything he was intensely practical ; he was in the best sense a realist, in that he ever kept before him the possibilities of the immediate future, reckoning with the actual as distinguished from ideal motives of human conduct and action, and never allowing his heart to run too far away with his head. An enthusiast though he was, he did not believe in tilting at windmills. Little as he liked them, there were certain facts in the political and social system of his country which he knew that it would be, for the present, hopeless to combat, and these he was prepared to accept, under protest, as logical postulates. He wrote once to Bright, so different from himself in temperament :

" You must make up your mind to accept certain conditions of things as a part of our English political existence during your time. For instance, the Church and aristocracy are great realities, which will last for your life and your sons'. To ignore them or despise them is equally incompatible with the part which I think you have the ambition to play, and which I am sure you are competent to perform."

He was proof against illusions, and though he might truly be described as one of the much-abused optimists, his was a reasoned optimism. He had no patience with chimerical schemes and Utopias which dreamers talked much about but never succeeded in putting into practical shape, or even seriously tried to do. He was one of those who, as Matthew Arnold said of Goethe, made neither man too much a god nor God too much a man. To the habit of looking the world straight in the face from the common level, instead of from an eminence, was due the fact that he came so near to the average mind, the mind that dominates public and political life, and exercised so wide and deep an influence upon his day and generation.

Catchwords and shibboleths made no impression on him— had no meaning for him. When the American Civil War was ending in the triumph of the North he warned his friend Charles Sumner [1] that the " glory " of which his compatriots were already boasting would impress no one in Europe. " It is in your superiority in other things that you can alone by your example elevate the Old World. . . . Your only title to existence as a Republic is that you are supposed to be superior to what we were sixty years ago." A hard saying, but a true one, worthy to be remembered at the present time, when old monarchies which, with all their follies and futilities, at least kept the peace and were a buttress of order, civilization, and usually of justice, have been replaced by brand-new republics, some of whose rulers and peoples have as yet to prove that they possess even a glimmering of the sense of liberty and toleration.

An individualist of the first water, in everything he went his own way ; never was he found in the crowd unless the crowd was following reason. Like a tower he stood four-square against the winds of disparagement, opposition, and contumely, let them rage as they would. Even in parliamentary life he was a difficult man to docket, for party ties held him but loosely. He both wrote and spoke only the doctrine of a sane Liberalism, yet he was the despair of the party Whips, who, though they always expected his vote, were yet never quite sure of it. Upon not a few questions he failed to see eye to eye with the mass of Liberals of the strait, synagogic type, and some issues vital and paramount to them took a back place in his mind. Thus, though he favoured a broader political franchise than the majority of his generation, he was never a zealot on the subject ; for to

[1] From 1848 forward one of Cobden's many correspondents. Sumner was a Senator for his State (Massachusetts) and one of the most powerful American exponents of Liberalism of his day. The Cobden-Sumner correspondence covers the period March 9, 1848, to March 3, 1865, though most of Cobden's letters relate to the Civil War. It is published in part in Morley's *Life of Richard Cobden*, and more fully in J. A. Hobson's *Richard Cobden, the International Man*.

him suffrages were only machinery, means to ends; what mattered was not the vote, but the use to which it was put. Before political reform also he put financial, since it stood in vital relation to the question of national expenditure, just as that in turn was determined by public policy, both in home and foreign affairs. He even went so far as to suspect that much of the popular attachment to self-government was a habit or an instinct, like the fondness of the cat for the comfortable mat, rather than the result of reasoned acceptance. This he held it could only be when the education and intelligence of the people were increased far beyond the level of his day.

He was just as little enamoured of classes as of parties. In one of his early speeches in the course of the free food campaign he said :

" I have preached from the first that we would have the co-operation of the best and most intelligent of all ranks in life—working, middle, and upper classes. No, no, we will have no war of classes in this country. It is bad enough that in free and constitutional States you must have your parties; we cannot, in our state of enlightenment, manage our institutions without them; but it shall never be our fault if this question of the Corn Laws becomes a class question, between the middle and working classes on the one side and the hereditary legislators on the other."

The division which he deprecated did, in fact, occur, yet he never ceased to regret it. In his own walk of life he never spoke or thought of the employers and labourers of industry as members of different social worlds, though it is just to remember that at the time to which his public work fell it was the literal fact that most of the rising maunfacturers of Lancashire and Yorkshire were men who had emerged from the operative status, or were related to the operative classes by a single remove, and often in education were still not divorced from it. " What interest have you of the middle class," he once asked, " that the people of the working class have not also got ? You cannot separate the interest of the one from the other." His ideal would have been an undivided nation in which there were neither bond nor free and no crass extremes of social fortune and condition. He even came to modify his early harsh judgment of the aristocracy as having been the source and origin of all past wars, to the extent of allowing that if its foreign policy had been wrong-headed and disastrous the nation at large had supported it all through and should bear an equal share of blame.

To-day as of old the vain demagogue, if unable to move the high gods, woos the favour of the lower powers. But Cobden never angled for the applause of either classes or masses. He confessed that, as a matter of controversial strategy, he found himself at times compelled to humour his popular audiences, all for the sake of the cause, and was ashamed of himself after he had done it; but he never bribed them with the small coin of flattery, though then as later there were always plenty of political leaders ready to give, and plenty of followers ready to receive, unctuous *oboli* of that kind. He had the courage to tell a popular audience in 1853 : " The mass of the English people are the least instructed of any Protestant country in the world." At that time it was still necessary for eight out of thirteen members of a Rochdale coroner's jury to sign their names by mark. He said in the House of Commons on one occasion : " You never heard me quote the superior judgment of the working classes in my deliberations in this assembly ; you never heard me cant about the superior claims of the working classes to arbitrate on this great question." And in the last of his public speeches, made to his Rochdale constituents (November 23, 1864), he said : " Now, you know if I would only flatter you, instead of talking these home truths . . . if I would get up and say you are the greatest, the wisest, the best, the happiest people in the world, and keep on repeating that, I don't doubt but that I might be Prime Minister. I have seen Prime Ministers made in my experience precisely by that process. But it has always been my custom to talk irrespective of momentary popularity." Just because of his own pride of personality and sense of dignity he credited others with the same qualities and respected them accordingly.

Flattery of himself was equally nauseous to him. Writing once to the editor of the *Star*, the organ of the Peace Society, objecting to the prominence given to his name in the columns of that journal, he offered to " make a bargain with you in the interest of your paper not to let my name appear in your leaders (unless to find fault with me) for two years." [1] To abuse and misrepresentation he was equally indifferent. Disraeli once said that when he was attacked, as he thought, unjustly he "sometimes tried to forget." Cobden did the same, with less emphasis on the trying than the forgetting. Falsehood and calumny, however, he silently consigned to the outlawry to which they belonged, and left them there, for it was his belief that the man who lied once would lie always.

He was emphatically what is called a "forward-looking" man. His eyes were set ever on the future ; the present was for him merely a resting-place for bed and board as he journeyed onward to the better time that is ever "coming." Statesmanship meant for him vision, knowledge, foresight. In his foresight more than in anything else he was untrue to the national strain. It was almost a source of despair to him that British statesmen, like his countrymen in general, refused to look ahead, and were content to let difficulties come as they would, to meet them only when they must, and to "bungle through" as best they could. "It is deplorable," he wrote late in life, "that we are never roused to the consideration of grave errors in legislation until we are suffering under the evils which they entail." What he said of legislation, however, applied to all public policy. Here he singled out a fault of which the Prince Consort, with his German love of method and thoroughness, was constantly complaining, and one to which, at a later date, Lord Salisbury was wont to attribute most of the failures of British foreign policy. Pointing the moral of the American Civil War in a speech to his Rochdale constituents on October 29, 1862, he said :

" It is not by stroking our beards, and turning up our eyes like the Pharisee, and thanking Heaven that we are not as other men are, that

---

[1] As an illustration of how manners change with the times compare the following advertisement which appeared in *The Times* not long ago : " To M.P.'s and Others.—Experienced journalist, who has had many thousands of articles published here and U.S.A., offers part-time services for publicity or secretarial work ; wide circle of acquaintances among editors and other newspaper men. Advertiser has interesting ideas, is not unemployed, holds an important journalistic post, and wishes to augment income. Time only for ' worth-while ' business. Proposition worth consideration by anyone who wishes name kept before public.—Write in strict confidence," etc. Could the desecration of the high business of politics go farther ?

we learn ; but it is by studying such a calamity as this, by asking ourselves, is there anything in our dealings with Ireland, is there anything in India, is there anything in the rights and franchises of the great mass of our own population that requires dealing with ? If so, let what has taken place in America be a warning to us, and let us deal with an evil while it is time, and not allow it to find us out in the hour of distress and adversity."

Yet with all his eagerness and zeal he had that rare quality of true statesmanship, the patient perseverance in well-doing which is more concerned that the task in hand shall be done thoroughly than quickly. He had none of the frantic hustling of the social regenerator who builds with shoddy materials and scamps his job. No man was more intolerant of injustice and wrong-doing, but he insisted that careful diagnosis of the disease must precede the application of remedies, and he condemned hasty and ill-considered action of any kind in the domain of social reform. So it was that he viewed with " suspicion and disfavour " the efforts which were made in the " hungry forties " to promote emigration even in so extreme a case as that of Ireland, fearing lest expatriation might be made a pretext for ignoring the deep-seated evils in national life which created unemployment and impoverishment.

Always his sound common sense kept him in the middle way of moderation. He hated violence of every kind—the violence of controversy and exciting rhetoric not less than civil strife at the barracades. He knew that the only safe line of progress was that of order and legality, and that to try to win political battles by overriding constitutional prin-ciples was a poor sort of campaigning, which promised at the most uncertain and Pyrrhic victories. In everything he " wanted public opinion to be ranged on the side of law." Elsewhere revolutions might still be necessary, but not in this country, for our ancestors had done that sort of thing for us once for all. Success achieved by appeal to reason was for him the true and only legitimate form of " direct action." " Let us talk over this matter as men of common sense," was the constant burden of his speeches.

Because he fought for high principles, he was sparing in his criticisms of men. His severe and often bitter references to Lord Palmerston were an exception to his superiority to personalities, but Palmerston had inspired in him deadly distrust, and he regarded him as literally an enemy of his country and of peace.[1]   His rule of political controversy was " Measures, not men."   When during the Crimean War Bright persisted in launching furious attacks against the Government in the House, as though it had been more instead of less desirous of war than the people in the mass, he wrote to a correspondent :

> " I have often tried in private to persuade our friend to rely less upon attacks on the *personnel* of the Government, and more on the enforcement of sound principles upon the public, but his pugnacity delights in a knock-down blow at something as visible and tangible as a Minister of State."—(December 9, 1854.)

He could strike hard and cut deeply, and often did, but his weapons were clean.   It was his fixed principle " never to attribute motives to any man, for there is nothing so unprofitable."   " Men of all classes," he once said, " have their good and bad individuals ;   fortunately for the world, the good predominate everywhere."   So in all his speeches he appealed to the best instincts of his hearers, and set his face sternly against anything that could degrade debate.   When one of his audiences emitted a chorus of groans at the mention of an unpopular politician, he promptly reproved it with a vigorous " No, no, no—we will deal with him with reason, and not with clamour."   " Who is Palmerston ? " he asked on another occasion ;   and when an impertinent voice cried out, " A traitor ! " the rebuke came equally short and swift : " No, I will say nothing worse of him than I have said to his face in Parliament."   Demos might like such rebukes or not :   but that was his affair, not Cobden's.   More than most known leaders of men he appropriated and lived up to the cardinal principles of a decorous public life.   Herein Peel and he had much in common, and spiritual affinity drew them more and more closely together.   A characterization which appears in

[1] The one flagrant departure from a wholesome rule was an attack made in 1846 on Peel, which he himself later described as " violent," and only excused because it was made under the influence of unaccustomed excitement and emotion.   Prompt explanations left no ill-will on Peel's side, and the two men were warm friends to the last.

a letter of 1846 from Sir Robert to Cobden may stand for both : " The world, the great and small vulgar, do not and cannot comprehend the motives which influence the best actions of public men."

Again, he sought to bring honesty and candour into play throughout the entire range of politics, whether in home or foreign affairs. He could not tolerate equivocation or any tampering with high principles. A man, even if a politician, must be true altogether or he could not be true at all. Principles were for him rules of honour and life, to be accepted and acted upon wholly and not by halves ; he would have no truck with trimmers and opportunists. There was an early stage in Mr. Gladstone's development when for this reason that rising hope of Liberalism did not satisfy him. He wrote to Mr. Richard on January 27, 1857 : " I have the highest opinion of Gladstone's powers. . . . His sway is owing mainly to the stamp of earnest conscientiousness which is impressed on the man at the moment he addresses you. But his conscience has not yet taken him in our direction, or if so he has failed to follow its dictates. And indeed I fear he sometimes entangles his conscience in his intellect." So he begged the editor of the *Star* in future references to Gladstone to be more sparing in the use of the complimentary paint brush.

He was one of the rare spirits who, in Pascal's words, " seek the truth with tears." Evidence of intense feeling, and even of mental agony, gives pathos and elevation to many passages in his writings, and still more in his letters, wherein he avows the convictions to which conscientious study and reflexion had led him. But there he stood, and he could do no other. He may be said to have exemplified in his own person the character which he saw in Lincoln, in that he proved that " great moral qualities . . . in the long run tell more on the fortunes of the world than mere intellect." One may say that in the wholesome, hard-wearing, fast-coloured virtues which he brought into public life—honesty, candour, courage, truth—he was a model of the good, solid *bourgeois* he ever prided himself on being ; while in the delicacies and chivalries of personal conduct, whether he knew it or not, he waa s true aristocrat of the spirit.

Public life was for him an alternation of ups and downs,

of successes and failures, for he was fighting for the most part for causes unpopular and little understood. Yet never did his courage fail, even in face of the severest rebuffs. When after the election of 1857, which sent Palmerston back with an overwhelming majority, his political fortunes seemed at the lowest ebb and good people were sending him sympathetic letters in the belief that " I must be very dispirited and want consolation," he wrote :

" There is perhaps no one on earth who depends so little on external circumstances as I do for cheerfulness or contentment. My object in public life being to advance objects which I believe to be true, and therefore certain to be triumphant, I never feel that kind of discouragement in temporary defeat which men must who have only personal ends in view."

No man, however sanguine, who lived so strenuous a life as his, could maintain his spirits at that high altitude. There came to him, as to all fighters in the cause of progress, moments of grief, as he saw how slow was the advance, how little had been accomplished, how much remained to be done, how the enthusiasm of associates evaporated and ardour gave place to coldness and indifference, how parties tended to forget the old clear-cut principles. It was while in such a mood that he reflected, in a speech made at Rochdale in 1861 :

" Oh ! I look back with regret sometimes, and feel ashamed of the House of Commons, when I think of the years when I first entered that assembly, when there was a great line of demarcation between two great parties, and when there was something at stake and worthy of the intellect, and worth growing older and grey to accomplish ! What is there now to satisfy the ambition of any public man ?   I have given an outline of the subject, and it will be for younger men in the country, if the country is to prosper, to carry out the details."—(June 26, 1861.)

Yet the depression was only momentary, for he fought with the old ardour for four years longer, until he fell literally with his armour upon him.

Something should be said, too, of the broader lines of his public work. He was a politician in the large sense of the word, and whether admitting it or not his attitude was in general that of Bentham's school. He never professed or

aspired to formulate a political philosophy of his own, however, since for philosophies and abstractions of all kinds he
had no liking ; yet it is none the less true that from the
disjecta membra of his teaching, his principles of practical
action, and his *dicta* of common sense, a coherent system of
political thought might be constructed, and that it might be
definable as an altruistic utilitarianism. " The greatest good
of the greatest number " would accurately describe his view
of the purpose of all political action. His business, however,
was with certain large basic principles and concrete facts of
life. Assuming peace to be better than war, friendship better
than enmity between nations, prosperity better than poverty,
stable social order better than ever-menacing chaos, he asked,
how were these better things to be achieved, the worse to be
avoided ? His answer to this question was—transform the
entire relation between nations, give to foreign policy a higher
and humaner purpose. To this end his educative work as a
public man and his efforts as a parliamentarian were directed,
and he tried to find allies in every social sphere ; for he rejected
the idea, favoured by the governing class, that politics, and
especially foreign policy, was a recondite business, the rightful
affair only of the lettered and the bookishly wise. On the
contrary, it was a simple, everyday matter, within the capacity of the meanest minds to understand—it was pre-eminently
the concern of the common people. For him the master
principles of foreign policy were that the moral law is one and
indivisible, hence that what is morally wrong cannot be
politically right ; that actions which are right or wrong for
individuals are equally right or wrong for nations ; and that
the duty of these in their intercourse one with another is simply
to act justly and honourably, in accordance with the rules
which govern ordinary civil relationships.

Such a conception of foreign relations bears the stamp of
the " international mind," and no man of his day had more
of that mind, with its freedom from prejudice, bigotry, and
narrowness. Foreign travel and contact with people of many
nations and races may have strengthened this admirable trait
of his character ; but large minds are born and not made,
and a fine breadth and generosity of outlook was native to
him. Looking to the future, he conceived of mankind as a

great co-operative commonwealth, knit together by free and untrammelled intercourse, material and intellectual, each part contributing to the weal and happiness of the whole. He criticized other nations freely, but with great restraint, seeking ever to understand their habits of mind and to judge their problems and difficulties from their points of view ; yet while he did so disclaiming any virtue of " toleration "— itself the most intolerant of words, since toleration assumes superiority, and is the brand of arrogance and conceit.

In his controversies he applied the Socratic method, insisting on clear definitions, laying bare sophistry, emphasizing the importance of knowledge as distinguished from mere information and hearsay opinions, contending against ignorance as the real enemy of truth, and holding wisdom to be the surest foundation of justice and virtue. The folly of fools is raw material for much of the wisdom of the wise. Cobden did not suffer fools gladly. He turned their minds, so to speak, inside out, exposed their shallowness and emptiness, tore to pieces their specious platitudes, refuted the fictions which they airily advanced as facts, and by contrast made the more obvious and impressive his own sane and well-grounded convictions.

And how he understood his countrymen—their failings as well as their virtues ! He was willing enough to praise, when praise seemed likely to do good, but he felt that he could best serve his generation and help it forward by pointing out the weak places in the national character. They made an appalling indictment when taken in the aggregate : chief among them he singled out the " ever-ready-primed pugnacity " of his countrymen, their readiness to lecture other nations and, if not too strong, to keep them in order, their general arrogance towards " foreigners," their illusions and gullibility, their impatience of general principles, their imperviousness to new ideas, the lack of culture characteristic of so large a part of his own class, and the illiteracy of the masses both in town and country, which kept them down, prevented them from realizing the best in themselves, and made them the sport of the governing classes. Of such defects he never ceased to speak in season, regardless of the danger to public reputations of telling unpleasant truths.

The extent of the prevalent popular ignorance was at times his despair. He saw it at the very outset of his public work, which began, as we have seen, with a village effort in the cause of popular education. " Do not let your zeal for democracy," he wrote to a literary correspondent in 1838, " deceive you as to the fact of the opaque ignorance in which the great bulk of the people of England are wrapt. If you write for the masses politically, and write soundly and honestly, they will not be able at present to appreciate you and consequently will not support you. . . . The great body of the English peasants are not a jot advanced in intellect since the days of their Saxon ancestors." By way of holding the balance he said a few years later, when he had had experience of parliamentary life, that he had never seen amongst an equal number of North of England workmen ignorance equal to that shown by the Tory members of the House of Commons. Nevertheless, in one of the latest of his public speeches, he came back to the old lament : " I do not know, perhaps, any country in the world where the masses of the people are so illiterate as in England."

One of his countrymen's illusions which he strove in vain to dispel, in the hope of spurring them to reflexion, was the belief that they were the only democratic nation in the world. His examination of the claim fits as exactly to-day as ninety years ago when it was penned, so slowly do national characteristics change.

" Democracy," he wrote in 1835, " forms no element in the materials of English character. An Englishman is, from his mother's womb, an aristocrat. Whatever rank or birth, whatever fortune, trade or profession may be his fate, he is, or wishes, or hopes to be an aristocrat. The insatiable love of caste that in England, as in Hindustan, devours all hearts is confined to no walks of society, but pervades every degree from the highest to the lowest."

The Englishman who does not recognize the truth of these words does not know himself. It was with something like moral nausea that he saw, in the middle of the century, the growing snobbishness of the manufacturing middle class, to which he had been proud to belong, now grown to be a new and powerful estate, and observed how with the expansion of their wealth their independence and manliness had contracted.

It has been said that reverence cannot be imparted to others by one who himself lacks the reverential spirit; and so likewise only the man of truly moral character can hope to exercise moral influence and achieve moral ends. Cobden was such a man. He emphasized conscience, its demands and prohibitions in public life, and more particularly in foreign policy, in a way they had never been emphasized before and have seldom been emphasized since. He never unduly paraded his moral principles, however, and few intimations of his thought upon the deeper things of life will be found outside his correspondence. Yet he was old-fashioned enough to believe that controlling human destiny and the world's affairs there is a Power—he calls it variously Moral Law, Providence, and God—which is ever working out a beneficent purpose, and that though human folly, blundering, and crime might impede this purpose, right must ultimately triumph over wrong and good prove the final goal of ill.

He wrote in one of his letters, " There is an obstinate tendency for the right to get its own, even in spite of the powers and authorities of the world."   It was this faith that reconciled him to the American Civil War, deeply though he deplored it. " There is something more than accident," he wrote midway in the struggle, " which seems in the long run to favour the right in this wicked world, and I have a strong persuasion that we may live to see a compensating triumph for humanity as the result of this most gigantic of civil wars." He even believed that, taught by experience, all States would in the end " turn moralists in self-defence."

It was the ethical aspects of the question of war that weighed with him so much more strongly than the material. When, after carrying the anti-Corn Law agitation to a successful issue he entered upon his crusade against armaments, he wrote to George Combe, the Scottish phrenologist (January 5, 1849) :

" You know that of old I have felt a strong sentiment upon the subject of warlike armaments and war. It is this moral sentiment more than the £ s. d. view of the matter which impels me to undertake the advocacy of a reduction of our forces. It would enable me to die happy if I could feel the satisfaction of having in some degree contributed to the partial disarmament of the world."

Great as was his faith in humanity, he was painfully conscious of its moral backwardness and proneness to revert to grim rule of tooth and claw, and knew that it would be long before society accepted the moral law as the standard of public policy.   In another of his letters to Combe, he said :

" You ask me whether the public mind is prepared for acting upon the moral law in our national affairs.   I am afraid the animal is yet too predominant in the nature of Englishmen, and of men generally, to allow us to hope that the higher sentiments will gain their desired ascendancy in your lifetime or mine.   Our international relations are an armed truce, each nation relying on its power to defend itself by physical force.   We may teach Christianity and morality in our families ; but as a people we are, I fear, still animals in our predominant propensities."

All that has been said so far may seem to have been in praise of Cobden.   It is fair to consider what is sometimes said on the other side.   For example, was he lacking in patriotism, as critics have sometimes contended ?   Here, as he would have told us, definition is necessary.   Those who confuse patriotism with an exclusive concern for what are obscurely called " national interests " may be assured that he was not a patriot of their sort.   What he contended for was equality in justice and right, moral law and sanction, for all nations alike.   He urged without ceasing the interdependence of mankind, taught that its true and enduring interests were the interests which men held in common, and that no society, large or small, could live to itself without loss and hurt to the entire human family.   Hence everything that alienated men and nations was to him unnatural and wrong, an obstacle to mutual understanding to be set aside ; while everything that brought them together was to be fostered and sought after.   That attitude may be regarded as connoting a " larger patriotism " of a kind that in the present stage of human progress may leave the mass of people cold and apathetic, but it is the one to which we must all come if the errors of the past are to be avoided and mankind is to advance not by fits and starts, here and there, but steadily and all along the line.

In modern phrase Cobden was " a good European," and

one of the best, though that did not prevent him from being also one of the best of Englishmen. M. Drouyn de Lhuys called him the typical "international man," and few men have carried catholicity of spirit to so high a degree of understanding of and sympathy with other peoples and races. He was acutely conscious that national characteristics differ fundamentally, and whatever was good in any of these anywhere he was prepared to admire. He recognized, for example, that the great difference between the Englishman and the Frenchman was that the latter hugged his idol of equality, while the former specially loved liberty; yet here he entirely shared the preference of his countrymen, asserting that he "would rather live in a country where the feeling in favour of individual freedom is jealously cherished than be without it in the enjoyment of all the principles of the French Constituent Assembly."

Cosmopolitan in his desire to promote, and see promoted, the happiness of every nation, he was an ardent lover of his own land, so much so that he objected to English Governments troubling so much about the affairs of other countries until they had put their own house in order, or indeed interfering abroad in any way except for overpowering reasons. Again and again, in speech and writing, he stops short in his argument for a wider conception of human fellowship, a broader outlook, a larger charity, in order to prove by the ardour of his own national sympathies that the "international mind" is not antagonistic but complementary to sound patriotism. He writes in one place: "We are proof against despair when the energies of our countrymen are the grounds of hope," and again he boldly declares: "Let but Englishmen know of a danger to face and of a difficulty to surmount, and there is nothing within the compass of human capacity which they will not accomplish."

M. Émile de Girardin, one of his many French friends and admirers, wrote truly: "Richard Cobden was English, proud and happy so to be, admirer of his country and its institutions, though not blindly and without reserve. For while remaining English in his habits and affections, he firmly believed that here below a man has two fatherlands, the community in which he first saw the light of day, and the world—the common patrimony of the human race." It was from visits to M. Girardin's country that this widely travelled man returned with the conviction that " The race of men and women in the British Islands is the finest in the world in a physical sense, and although they have many moral defects and some repulsive qualities, yet on the whole I think the English are the most outspoken, truthful men in the world, and this virtue lies at the bottom of their political and commercial greatness." It would be absurd to accuse the man who could thus speak and write of lacking a proper national pride and patriotism. Cobden was all-English except in his comprehensive sympathies and his freedom from irrational prejudices, and no truer, prouder, or manlier patriot ever gave himself to the service of his country.

Again, he has been reproached for having entertained a too materialistic estimate of civilization. At one stage of his career there may have been some justification for this disparagement. In a large degree he was the creature of his age, the age of steam, machinery, and the factory, of the first railways, of steamships, and telegraphs ; he was, in short, a product of the time-spirit which expressed itself in the endeavour to annihilate both time and space. Accordingly it was natural that the aspect of modern life which specially appealed to him, at least at the beginning of his public career, when he was still combining business with politics, should have been the materialistic aspect. In his first glorifications of all-conquering trade there was unquestionably more than a trace of commercial class consciousness, the pride of the self-made man, and even of that national vanity which he was wont to censure. In one of his early writings he lauded commerce with far more ardour than in later years. He wrote :

" In the present day commerce is the grand panacea which, like a beneficent medical discovery, will serve to inoculate with the healthy and saving taste for civilization all the nations of the world. Not a bale of merchandise leaves our shores but it bears the seeds of intelligence and fruitful thought to the members of some less enlightened community ; not a merchant visits our seats of manufacturing industry but he returns to his own country the missionary of freedom, peace, and good government ; whilst our steamboats, that now visit every port of Europe, and our miraculous railways, that are the talk of all nations, are the advertisement and vouchers for the value of our enlightened institutions."

One can only imagine how such an outpouring of mercantile enthusiasm would have called forth the cutting satire of Matthew Arnold had it fallen into his hands—how it would have found its way to the philosophic Armenius, and served him as an apt illustration of the ideal of " the beatification of a whole people through clap-trap," which satisfied the Bottles tribe of that day, in contrast to his own ideal of " the elevation of a whole people through culture." Arnold himself would have concentrated upon the unhappy ebullition a whole flood of devastating scorn in the scathing comment " Machinery ! " It was certainly a paradox that not long after this panegyric on trade appeared its author was agitating against laws which, on his own showing, were grinding the poor and compelling the labouring classes of town and country to live the lives of helots.

It is also to be remembered that Cobden's special mission, from the anti-Corn Law campaign forward, brought him into contact predominantly with commercial audiences—merchants and manufacturers, shopkeepers and working-men. These he perhaps knew best, and if in addressing them he was apt to emphasize the material aspects of the causes he advocated, it was because he knew that by so doing he could best drive home his arguments and teaching. Yet when it has been granted that his early estimate of concepts like " progress " and " civilization " was inadequate, and that the materialistic appeal was overdone in the first rush of his public agitation, it remains to be said that he came to see, as time passed and his knowledge of men increased, that while the creation of material values was in measure a legitimate object of national policy it could never alone be a sufficient or a safe basis of national life.

In order to show how far he travelled from his first exaltation of material prosperity it is only necessary to recall later words like these : " Nations have not yet learnt to bear prosperity, liberty, and peace. They will learn it in a higher state of civilization. We think we are the models for posterity, when we are little better than beacons to help it to avoid the rocks and quicksands." In his own country prosperity, while it fattened the bodies, was starving the souls of men. When he observed the generation of thriving manufacturers and merchants which was growing up in the North under the influence of Free Trade, and saw how easily and rapidly they were amassing wealth, while remaining unrefined by education and dignity, or any sense of responsibility—how, as their social ambitions increased, they tried to disown their order, throwing down the ladder by which they had climbed from obscurity to recognition, he was moved by a sorrow not unmixed with contempt.

It was not for " progress " of that kind that he had toiled to break down the barriers which fettered trade ! The time came when he ceased to extol " the mighty influence which now slumbers in the possession of the commercial and manufacturing portions of the community," and recanted his description of this class as forming a " great and independent order of society."

He was the more disappointed that his own class was failing him since for the present he saw no substitute. The aristocracy, still in possession of social and political power, had manners ; but, as Arnold was beginning to tell them, enlightenment was lacking to the barbarians. The mass of the manual workers, much as he sympathized with them, were still as sheep without a shepherd, devoid of aspirations or ambitions, apparently resigned to a status of servility, the ready prey of the selfish exploiter or the scheming demagogue. Nevertheless, in the end he came to the conclusion that in the best of the toilers lay the hope of the future, and it may be that history will yet confirm his forecast, though the genius of history is ever chary of saying his last word. Meanwhile, Cobden's greatest wonder was that the workers, who might be so powerful in union if they only knew it, were willing to tolerate so patiently the disparagement and contumely from which they suffered.

One other count in the case against Cobden as a teacher must be mentioned. He has been accused of under-culture— the usual argument of superior persons who have nothing better to say. It is a somewhat unchivalrous reproach to make against a man who, during all his public life, was so strong an advocate of popular education. But once more definition is called for. It is true that he entered life unequipped by a university or any other so-called " higher " education, and of the deficiency he never ceased to be conscious. With perhaps an unnecessary emphasis he once publicly spoke of himself as owing " nothing to birth, parentage, patronage, connexion, or education "—words that recall Plato's rebuke of the pride of Diogenes on a certain occasion. It is true also that in classical allusions, when he was betrayed into making them, he was apt to lose his way ; and the most indulgent of his admirers may not be able to forgive him for a certain disregard of contemporary literature.[1] But if the classicists, with their lore of Greece and Rome, beat him on some dead subjects, he beat them on many living ones ; while his remarkable command of robust, vivid, direct, and telling English enabled him, on whatever subject he spoke, at once to get near to the minds and sympathies of his audiences in a way that scholarly orators seldom do, and to maintain a profound and unique influence upon public opinion and affairs for a full generation. His mind was singularly well and wisely stored, if not with the peptonized and capsuled lore of the examination schools, with that compendious knowledge which makes the well-informed citizen. If he could not be called a scholar in the conventional sense, he was a diligent student of history, practical economics, and life, and he had a rare mastery of his own subjects, at least in their large aspects.

It is true that, stung by the criticisms of the intellectuals, he once sneered at Oxford and its scholarship in return, yet after a visit to that seat of learning he recanted handsomely, knowing better. " After seeing some of the examinations," he wrote somewhat naïvely, " I am inclined to think there is a greater effort required to face the ordeal than we generally suppose." There was dignity as well as a gracious humility in the tribute which he paid to scholarship in the last speech which he made (November 23, 1864). He had spoken of the prevailing English ignorance of America, even on the part of men who were brimful of the history, geography, and literature of ancient Greece and Egypt, yet had made it clear that he

---

[1] Thus he wrote to a correspondent on December 30, 1863, fifteen months before his death : " Can you get me Carlyle's address ? I don't find it in the *Court Guide*. His name is Thomas, is it not ? " Carlyle had then been writing for thirty years, his *French Revolution* appeared twenty-six years before, his *Oliver Cromwell* eighteen years before, and he was nearing the completion of his monumental work, *Frederick the Great*.

did not disparage classical learning in itself. Then he continued :

> " I am a great advocate of culture of every kind, and I say, where you can find men who, in addition to profound classical learning, like Professor Goldwin Smith or Professor [Thorold] Rogers, of Oxford, have a vast knowledge of modern affairs, and who, as well as scholars, are at the same time thinkers—these are men I acknowledge to have a vast superiority over me, and I bow to these men with reverence for their superior advantages."

Those who still disparage Cobden's culture are advised to consider the fine instinct which led him to protest against the barbarism of removing memorials of Egyptian history to the crowded streets of Northern capitals.

> " Mark the folly and injustice," he wrote from Egypt in 1836, after visiting the site of Cleopatra's Needles, " of carrying these remains from a site where they were originally placed, and from amidst the associations which gave them all their interest, to London or Paris, where they become merely objects of vulgar wonderment. It is to be hoped that good taste, or at least the feelings of economy which now pervade our rulers' minds, will prevent this vestige of the days of the Pharaohs from being removed."

One of the obelisks still stood *in situ* at the time Cobden wrote : another, which had long lain prone, embedded in the sand, was conveyed to London in 1878. How far reverence, piety, and good taste in this matter have advanced in later times is, perhaps, best attested by the spectacular disinterment of Tutankhamen.

Such was Richard Cobden. To whom and to what can he be compared whose personality was so rich and many-sided ? He was an Ishmael amongst politicians, a strong man who went his own way, and, smooth or rough, held to it to the end ; a rebel against convention and tradition, not harsh of tongue, yet very hard of stroke ; a high priest of reason of the order of Socrates, who pierced to the marrow sophistry and falsity, and probed the inner meaning of things ; a gallant Crusader who bore upon his shoulder the white cross of an unblemished repute ; a torch-bearer whose welcome ray gave guidance to confused and floundering wayfarers ; a messenger of peace, who yet was the doughty and tireless combatant of all injustice and wrong. For he was not one man but many men merged in one ; yet out of the diversity of his characteristics was shaped a splendid unity in that powerful individuality of his which he had " a horror of losing," since it was to him " as existence itself."

It might seem that our world of to-day no longer produces such men. Is the reason only that the mould has been broken, or has the material itself for the present given out ? And if the latter, whence and when shall come the sorely needed supplies ?

CHAPTER IV

THE LIMITS OF INTERVENTION

" Is England so uplifted in strength above every other nation that she can with prudence advertise herself as ready to undertake the general redress of wrongs ?   Would not the consequences of such professions and promises be either the premature exhaustion of her means, or a collapse in the day of performance ? "—Mr. GLADSTONE in 1869.

" Is the present a struggle for a just and secure peace, or only for a new balance of power ?   If it be only a struggle for a new balance of power, who will guarantee, who can guarantee, the stable equilibrium of the new arrangement ?   Only a tranquil Europe can be a stable Europe.   There must be, not a balance of power, but a community of power ; not organized rivalries, but an organized common peace."—PRESIDENT WILSON, speech in the United States Senate, January 22, 1917.

COBDEN placed in the forefront of his indictment of the foreign policy of his day the doctrines of the balance of power and intervention.   These were, on his reasoning, the major and minor premises of a syllogism of which war was the inevitable conclusion.   First as to the balance of power.   The familiar phrase may have been less often on the lips of statesmen when he entered public life than earlier in the century, but the doctrine itself continued to be regarded as the mainstay of European stability, and only some violent challenge of the existing territorial status was needed to ensure its active and prompt assertion.

It is customary to date the first formal recognition of the doctrine in the political relations of Europe from the Treaty of Westphalia (1648), which ended the Thirty Years War. It has, however, a longer lineage, for there never was a time, from classical antiquity forward, when military rulers possessed of sufficient power did not attempt to enforce the rough principle of equilibrium.   In application to modern Europe, misleading and unreal as have often been the pretences advanced in its defence, the policy of the balance of power has meant, on the best justification, the creation and maintenance of such an apparent equipoise between the stronger States as might prevent the menace of domination by any one of them. One unchanging peculiarity of that policy, however, has been that while the Great Powers have usually been ready to see it applied to their neighbours, no Power, however ambitious and aggressive, has ever recognized as legitimate attempts to enforce it against itself.

We have seen that it was Cobden's rule, a rule which made him one of the most awkward of controversialists to contend with, never to accept political theories or opinions on faith or authority, but to require them to explain and justify themselves. He first came to close quarters with this doctrine in his second pamphlet, that on *Russia* (though it deals with much else), written in 1836.

" Our history during the last century," he there wrote, " may be called the tragedy of British intervention in the politics of Europe, in which Princes, diplomatists, peers, and generals have been the authors and actors—the people the victims ; and the moral will be exhibited to the latest posterity in eight hundred millions of debt." [1]

This tragedy, this debt, and the resulting impoverishment he attributed solely to the constant wars and foreign interventions into which the larger Powers were led by their pursuit of the illusory idea of equilibrium. What was the origin of this doctrine ; what authority was behind it ; from what date did it begin to operate ? When our conscientious student, eager to obtain answers to such questions, consulted accepted authorities on the subject, like Vattel and Gentz, he found that the only point of agreement between them was that some sort of " union " had existed for a certain indefinite time in virtue of which Europe was supposed to have enjoyed peace and prosperity.

Gentz, for example, defined the balance of power as " that constitution subsisting among neighbouring States, more or less connected with one another, by virtue of which no one among them can injure the independence or essential rights of another without meeting with effectual resistance on some side and consequently exposing itself to danger." Cobden

[1] In 1914 the national debt still stood at 650 millions ; the Great War increased it to some 8,000 millions gross.

wished to know when this constitution was entered into and signed, for no one seemed to have heard anything about it. Was it prior to the Peace of Utrecht, or to the Austrian War of Succession, or to the Seven Years War, or to the American War ? Did it exist during the French Revolutionary Wars ? Did it function when Great Britain was appropriating Dutch colonies in South Africa and the East, seizing French territory in Canada, and wresting Gibraltar from Spain ? Did Russia, Prussia, and Austria belong to it when they partitioned Poland, or France when she took a slice of Switzerland, or Austria when she seized Lombardy, or Russia when she dismembered Sweden, Turkey, and Persia, or Prussia when she annexed Silesia ?

Merely to state searching questions like these was sufficient to prove that equilibrium meant in theory what it had never meant in practice ; in fine, that it was a figment of the imagination, signifying anything or nothing according to circumstances, since every State had claimed the right to define, assert, or repudiate it arbitrarily according to its temporary power and interest. Far from the doctrine being the result of either a union or a concordat between the Great Powers, it had been invented for the very reason that these Powers had never agreed to recognize any durable state of equilibrium in Europe. Talk as rulers and statesmen might about the balance of power, it had meant always just such a status as the strongest State or group of States had been able to create in any given time and circumstances. Even Napoleon put forward the plea that he, too, was asserting the balance of power when on one occasion he refused to allow Russia to occupy the Dardanelles after he himself had invaded Turkey. Since his day, the " balance of Europe " had been in England's hands, as honest Dutch William designed.

Nevertheless, this doctrine, so unsubstantial and illusory, had for generations proved a source of infinite mischief. Invoking its sanction, England had at different times fought either for or against every European State, seas of blood had been shed, old dominions had fallen and new ones had arisen, political changes of many kinds had taken place all over the Continent, yet all to no good ; for a real balance of power had never existed and was still as far off as ever.

Some of the earlier defenders of the doctrine contended that it had nothing in common with alliances, and was indeed intended to be a substitute for them. It was an easy task for Cobden to show that it had been fruitful at all times in such combinations, sometimes of the most incongruous character, as in the case of the alliance of Louis XIV with Turkey in the seventeenth century. At the very time he was writing his early pamphlets the doctrine was being revived by the British and French Governments owing to suspicion that Russia was meditating aggressive designs against the same Mahomedan Power. The prospect of England fighting to uphold Turkish misrule incensed him, and both then and later he condemned the idea of an alliance with the Turks as a stain upon the national reputation.

The war for Turkey's sake which seemed to be impending in 1836 was staved off, but within twenty years Cobden was to see his own country and France allied with Mahomedanism against a third Christian Power in defence of a vicious system of government which in the interval had become worse instead of better. Had he lived still another twenty years he would have seen how this country narrowly escaped, almost against its will, an identical struggle. He would, however, have regarded as a crowning refutation of the doctrine of the balance of power the spectacle presented during the Great War of the reconciliation of the Christian Powers which fought against each other in the Crimean War, their repudiation of the settlements of 1856 and 1878, and Turkey bound in an alliance to Germany and Austria, who in 1854 had refused to side with her against Russia.

The importance of a doctrine lies in its practical application. The doctrine of the balance of power would have been harmless had the acceptance of it gone no farther than passive assent. Necessarily, however, it led the Powers which attached importance to it to intervene, either by diplomatic or military action, whenever they believed the existing equilibrium to be endangered. Here Cobden had to arraign his own country as the chief offender. At the time he began to write Lord Palmerston ruled at the Foreign Office, and the meddling spirit was in consequence particularly active there, with the result that the nation lived in constant anticipation of surprises, alarms, and scares, and armaments were maintained at a ruinous level.

He treated the historical aspect of the interventionist policy in some detail in his pamphlets, but most of his speeches on foreign policy dealt at greater or less length with the same theme ; and it took a foremost place in all his platform work on behalf of peace. He gave also a stricter meaning to a well-known phrase, for in opposing foreign intervention he wished to apply the ban to every kind of interference in the affairs of other countries. With the recent victory of the anti-Corn Law movement in mind, he wrote to Bright in October 1846 :

" I began my political life by writing against this system of foreign interference, and every year's experience confirms me in my early impression that it lies at the bottom of much of our misgovernment at home. . . . I have always had an instinctive monomania against this system of foreign interference, protocolling, diplomatizing, etc., and I should be glad if you and our other Free Trade friends, who have beaten the daily broadsheets into common sense upon another question, would oppose yourselves to the Palmerston system, and try to prevent the Foreign Office from undoing the good which the Board of Trade has done to the people."

His advocacy of non-intervention, the most fundamental article in his political creed, was based upon the contention that every nation has a right to manage its own affairs ; that only in extreme cases, involving issues of immediate and urgent concern to other peoples, could outside interference be justified ; and, further, that such interference was inevitably injurious to the State which devoted to other countries energy and money which ought to be employed at home. He wished to apply to England Washington's maxim, as contained in his Farewell Address to the American Nation : " The great rule of conduct for us in regard to foreign nations is, in extending our commercial relations, to have with them as little political connexion as possible." He also dreaded the effect of continually consorting with the great military Powers of the Continent, for he saw that if England once began to enter into competition with such companions she would inevitably be committed to a policy of alliances, which would compel her, while still maintaining her invincible and costly navy, to emulate them in land power.

G

His experiences abroad confirmed his conviction that the policy of meddling only led to irritation and mischief. He wrote to Bright : " In all my travels three reflexions constantly occur to me : How much unnecessary solicitude and alarm England devotes to the affairs of foreign countries ; with how little knowledge we enter upon the task of regulating the concerns of other people ; and how much better we might employ our energies in improving matters at home." British Governments were for ever endeavouring to reform other nations, not only against their will, but in disregard of their traditions, forcing upon them constitutions which they had not asked for and did not want, presuming to tell them what they might and might not do, not merely in relation to other countries but in their own households. Wherever there was an upstart Sovereign to instal or a discarded one to convey to a place of refuge, a British vessel-of-war was sure to be in readiness for convoy service. " We are general carriers for erratic royalty all over the world," he wrote from Greece in 1837 ; " when will this folly have an end ? "

At that time our Government had assumed responsibility for the personal safety of King Otho of Greece and his consort, of the Donna Maria Miquel of Portugal, and of Ferdinand II of Naples (King Bomba). To the end of his life he never ceased to urge fussy Foreign Secretaries to cease interference, to be patient, and trust more to the " natural course of events," instead of impetuously rushing into difficult places where even angels would have hesitated to tread. When the Marquis of Lorne, before his departure for Canada as Governor-General, was troubling himself over difficulties which had not arisen, Disraeli comforted him with the assurance, " My dear Lord, as you grow older you will find that affairs of State develop themselves." Cobden was willing to go a long way in applying the policy of *laissez faire, laissez passer* to policies of State in general, but he would have applied it altogether to foreign affairs, except in the rare case in which overwhelmingly urgent reasons made intervention a national duty and interest.

He was also one of the very few English public men of that or of any time who refused to believe that their country could not do wrong, and he did not hesitate to castigate with impartial hand acts of injustice committed by Governments of either party in the nation's name. There was much in the foreign policy of his day which justified his stern protests, but what most offended his sense of right and honour was the fact that most interventions took the form of punitive or coercive action against small and weak countries. A case in point was the blockade of Greece in 1850 owing to the refusal of its Government to pay extortionate bills of compensation to British subjects, notably one Don Pacifico, a Portuguese Jew domiciled at Gibraltar, who claimed five or six times more than was ultimately found to be due—" an atrocious attempt at swindling," as Cobden truthfully called it.[1] It was in reference to this episode that he said, in the course of a speech at Manchester on the policy of the Whig Government (January 1, 1851) :

" I have set myself the task of accomplishing certain things, and amongst them that which is most dear to my heart is the advocacy of a more peaceful and conciliatory policy in the intercourse of nations, or, as I would especially say, in the intercourse between this country and weaker nations. If you want to wound my principles most acutely, it will be to show me England violating the principle of a conciliatory and humane policy when it has to deal with a weak Power which is like a child in its grasp. I look upon inhumanity, rudeness, or violence on the part of England towards a powerless State, like Greece, with additional resentment, just as I should regard that man as a coward as well as a despot who molested and ill-used a child."

Immersed in mercantile interests as he was until public life monopolized his time, he abhorred the manner in which commercial treaties had been forced on the Chinese by powder and shot, and he protested that arguments of that kind were only applied to China because she was unable to resist. The Chinese war of 1858, in which Great Britain and France acted together, excited his deep indignation. The Chinese were soon beaten, as was inevitable when disciplined troops equipped with modern rifles confronted untrained irregulars armed with primitive weapons only fit for pig-sticking, and by the Treaty of Tientsin China was required to open more of her ports and rivers to foreign trade. But the chorus of jubiliation which at home greeted the victory and the treaty left unshaken his horror of " our criminal policy in the East,"

[1] See pp. 139–40.

and his disbelief that trade could be successfully promoted by killing our customers.

Little more than a year later another war with China was provoked by the rash and unauthorized action of a British admiral, in attempting to force a passage up the Peiho on the way to Pekin, whither he was conveying the British envoy charged with the ratification of the new treaty. The Chinese authorities had refused to remove the barriers which obstructed the river, so the admiral began to clear the way for his gunboats, on which the adjacent forts opened a destructive fire. No right to navigate the river existed, and the action of the British officer was not defended at home, but as the Chinese declined to make amends they were again engaged in hostilities by the allied Powers, who only halted at the gates of Pekin. On the way there the French force plundered the Emperor's magnificent summer palace, then, on the directions of Lord Elgin, the ambassador, the British destroyed it.

While all such episodes filled him with disgust, he regarded as equally reprehensible the diplomatic interferences which created the false impression that there was behind them a force which would be used if words failed of effect, and, by thus encouraging friendly Governments to entertain baseless expectations of active support, lured them into disastrous decisions. Criticizing the speeches of Lord John Russell on the Italian question in 1856, so full of grandiloquent generalities, he wrote :

" What does Lord John, and what do our aristocratic politicians, who have our foreign policy in their hands, propose to do ? Do they intend to set up the peoples of the Italian States to force their Governments to give them constitutional freedom ? If so, are they prepared to help them ? No, a thousand times no, must be the answer of all who know what our Government is. . . . The truth is, it must be again and again told the English public and the world that our aristocratic politicians make political capital out of the Italians, Poles, Circassians, etc., for purposes of their own, and not with any intention of promoting liberty anywhere. And this game will go on so long as the English public allow them to parade their sympathies for the grievances of foreigners instead of doing the work of liberty at home."

The policy of admonishing, browbeating, and threatening usually succeeded when its objects were little States, but danger arose when they were powerful. Where in such cases imprudent action had been taken without effect, safety lay in timely withdrawal, even with loss of dignity and prestige. Criticizing in the House of Commons in 1850 Lord Palmerston's meddling propensities, Sir Robert Peel bade him " beware that the time does not arrive when, frightened by your own interference, you withdraw your countenance from those whom you have excited and leave upon their mind the bitter recollection that you have betrayed them."

The words received unhappy confirmation fourteen years later, when Palmerston's Government deserted Denmark in the Elbe Duchies dispute with Prussia, after allowing her to believe that if the worst came the strong arm of Great Britain would be at her service. On the eve of the failure of the London Conference, Lord John Russell said in the House of Lords (June 17, 1864), " Her Majesty's fleet is ready for any service which it may be called on to render." It was required to render none at all, for the end of all Russell's threats and bombast was that the British Government left Denmark to her fate, just as it abandoned Turkey in similar circumstances thirty-three years later.

A vote of censure, moved by Disraeli, charging the Government with having " failed to maintain their avowed policy of upholding the independence and integrity of Denmark, lowered the just influence of this country in the councils of Europe, and thereby diminished the securities for peace," was only lost by eighteen votes. Cobden's verdict at the time was justified : " There is no doubt in the world that England and her Government encouraged that small country of Denmark to hopeless resistance by the false expectation excited from the first that we should go to its help." [1]

To do Palmerston justice, there was one notable occasion

---

[1] Referring to this episode, Spencer Walpole writes of Palmerston in his *History of Twenty-five Years* (i. 528) : " He liked to play a game of brag on the card-table of Europe, and habitual success had convinced him that he was a master of the game. He was fated, before his life closed, to meet a player far stronger than himself, whom it was his misfortune to misunderstand and despise. He met Herr von Bismarck with the same confidence with which he had met other antagonists, and he retired from the contest a broken and a beaten man." But in fairness to Palmerston it should be said that it was Russell, then Foreign Secretary, who on this occasion prematurely took the bit within his teeth. To the eleventh hour he blustered with more than Palmerstonian energy.

when he did not intervene, though he might have been expected to do, and Cobden praised him for his restraint. In 1859 he kept his country out of the Italian war between France and Austria, and instead of losing prestige, as had been predicted, England gained it by neutrality, insomuch that the belligerent Powers were both eager for her participation in the peace negotiations. Nevertheless, it may be doubted whether Cobden was justified in concluding that it was the nation's known objection to further armed interventions that led Palmerston to keep the sword in the sheath on that occasion.

And yet, while unsparing in his censures on the Foreign Secretaries and Governments which meddled in other nations' affairs, he was just enough to apportion equal blame to the nation which approved these interventions. Thus, during the Crimean War, the folly and wrongness of which he condemned from beginning to end, he disagreed entirely from the peace advocates who wrote and spoke as though the Government alone were responsible. In one of the fine-toned speeches which he made before his constituents at that time he told them : " You cannot separate yourselves from the honour or dishonour of your Government, or from the acts of those Cabinets and legislators whom you allow to act on your behalf and in your name." If Palmerston mesmerized England at that time it was with the nation's willing assent. Individual statesmen carried out the policy of intervention and waged the wars which sprang from it, but the nation at large applauded them and by so doing took the responsibility upon its own shoulders.

" You must not disguise from yourself," he once wrote to Bright, ' that the evil has its roots in the pugnacious, energetic, self-sufficient, foreigner-despising and pitying character of that noble insular creature John Bull. Read Washington Irving's [1] description of him, fumbling for his cudgel always the moment he hears of any row taking place anywhere on the face of the earth, and bristling up with anger at the very idea of any other people daring to have a quarrel without first asking his consent or inviting him to take a part in it."

It was a source of distress to him that, because of their own aggressive policies and acts, British Governments were

[1] In his *Sketch Book*, published in 1819, after a visit to England.

disqualified from protesting against similar wrongful proceedings by other powerful States. So it was that when Russia invaded Hungary in 1849, in order to assist the Austrians to suppress the Kossuth rebellion, he recognized how difficult it must be for the Foreign Secretary to protest, and could almost find an excuse for his passive attitude. Many years later, when the same Power was ruthlessly suppressing a Polish revolution within its own borders, he said (November 1863) : " When I see Russia is burning Polish villages I am restrained from even reproaching them, because I am afraid they will point Japanwards and scream in our ears the word Kagosima." [1]

There was, however, a more egoistic objection to foreign interventions and the resulting wars, since they were the cause of extravagant budgets, heavy national debts, oppressive taxation, and excessive armaments in time of peace, as a result of which industry, trade, and agriculture were handicapped, and the material life of the nation was kept at a needlessly low level. His strong sense of justice also revolted at the thought that, though his country had borne so large a share in the Continental wars, the nations for which it had lavishly sacrificed both life and treasure had repaid their debt with ingratitude.

One of the worst national effects of the interventionist policy was that it prevented concentration upon the humdrum tasks of government at home, so that progress in civil and political liberty was held back. Holding that no nation which was continually meddling in the affairs of other peoples could be sufficiently careful about its own, he deplored the fervent popular acclamations which greeted Garibaldi on his visit to England in 1864, for creditable as he allowed this manifestation of hero worship to be he saw in it new possibilities of meddling in matters which did not concern this country. He wrote to a friend at the time :

" When will the masses of this country begin to think of home politics ? Our friend Bright observed, as he gazed from a window in Parliament Street on the tens of thousands that cheered the Italian, ' If the people would only make a few such demonstrations for them-

---

[1] Bombarded and destroyed by British vessels-of-war in 1863.

selves, we could do something for them.' But nothing except foreign politics seems to occupy the attention of the people, Press, or Parliament."

On this occasion Cobden's apprehensions were soon allayed. " The Italian's " visit had a speedy and an abrupt ending. So long as the lion of Caprera could be led about on silken strings from London salon to salon all went well. But Garibaldi was a man of the people, and when he showed eagerness to visit the democratic towns of the provinces the Government saw in him a source of public danger and whisked him off to his island home with unseemly expedition.

Had, then, nations, had the British nation in particular, to be indifferent to the welfare and happiness of the less advanced communities ? Cobden answered that his objection to intervention implied no such thing. Of course, he wanted to see " Poland happy, Turkey civilized, and Russia conscientious and free." The only question was how these transformations were to be effected, whether by moral or material influences, whether by internal regeneration and independent effort or by interference from outside. In his view it was the duty of every nation to work out its own destiny, and all it had a right to expect from its neighbours was a fair field for its efforts and abstention from interference.

" I think," he once said, " as a corporate body, as a political community, if we can manage to do what is right and true and just to each other—if we can manage to carry out that at home, it will be about as much as we can do. I do not think I am responsible for seeing right and truth and justice carried out all over the world."

Thus while he denied to his country the right to impose the yoke of dependence upon other peoples, so also he repudiated all obligation to fight their battles for freedom. He told the House of Commons on one occasion :

" I yield to no one in sympathy for those who are struggling for freedom in any part of the world ; but I will never sanction an interference which shall go to establish this or that nationality by force of arms, because that invades a principle which I wish to carry out in the other direction—the prevention of all foreign interference with the nationalities for the sake of putting them down."

Pointing to the history of his own country, he claimed that it was by such self-dependence that its liberties had been won. It may be said that for so ardent a humanitarian he seemed at times to show a singular toleration of evil political and social conditions in other countries. The answer is that he did not tolerate such conditions any more than the citizen of a monarchical country can be said to " tolerate " the constitution of a neighbouring republic ; all he did was to deny the right or duty of outsiders to interfere, holding that arbitrary meddling, even in a good cause, was likely in the long run to be worse for a country than any temporary evils resulting from faulty government. For always he looked beyond the present, and the study of history had taught him that to do another nation's work for it was to paralyse its powers and stunt its growth. He also believed that the life and affairs of nations were everywhere subject to a " natural " course of development which—in some countries more slowly than in others—inevitably made for amelioration, provided only that events were not precipitated by artificial influences, such as the intrusions of outside meddlers concerned to recommend their short cuts to the millennium.

In some statesmen such an attitude might have argued cynicism, or at least a selfish indifference to the well-being of others. In Cobden it was rather the expression of his profound respect for the independence of nations, of the importance which he attributed to human individuality, of an invincible faith in mankind, and a conviction that patient plodding was the safest and surest way of progress. Assuming that the level of civilization must always be relative, according to people, place, and time, he was convinced that a nation's elevation must come in the main by the force of its own moral and intellectual resources, and that the best service which the advanced peoples could render to their less fortunate neighbours was to exercise patience and leave them to find salvation in their own way.

He went further, for he was old-fashioned enough to believe that the world was not altogether without the guidance and care of a wisdom higher than that of statesmanship, which, indeed, he never rated highly. Avowing this deeper faith in one of his latest speeches, made at Rochdale in November 1863, he said :

" Some people will say, Do you intend to leave these evils without a remedy ? Well, I have faith in God, and I think there is a Divine Providence which will obviate this difficulty, and I don't think that Providence has given it into our hands to execute His behests in this world. I think, when injustice is done, whether in Poland or elsewhere, the very process of injustice is calculated, if left to itself, to promote its own cure ; because injustice produces weakness—injustice produces injury to the parties who commit it. But do you suppose that the Almighty has given to this country the power and responsibility of regulating the affairs and remedying the evils of other countries ? No ! We have not set a sufficiently pure example to be entitled to claim that power."

In dealing with this subject of intervention he incidentally laid down a high standard of propriety for the acceptance of public men and the Press in all allusions to foreign nations, their Governments, and their affairs. Here he called for the utmost restraint and reticence, even going so far as to discourage unfavourable criticism as impertinent. For he held that a nation's constitution and the persons of its rulers and Government were its own business, and that other people should either keep a civil tongue when speaking of them or be silent. He told his countrymen that instead of being so ready to criticize and censure foreign nations they should study them, with a view to revising their stock prejudices, correcting their wrong impressions, and even improving their national customs and institutions, where something better was offered abroad.

Disregard of so wholesome a rule of restraint was commoner in his day than in ours, but he at least practised as he preached. He was even better than his word, for however much he might differ from the policies of other Governments he invariably tried to view questions from their standpoints, and the test which he was accustomed to apply in so doing was this : What should we have done ourselves in the same circumstances ? It was the test of the international mind, and in adopting it he was far ahead of any of his contemporaries. Obviously such an attitude of detachment cannot affect the justice or morality of any given act of policy. His point was rather that it creates a judicial frame of mind, which gives value to opinions formed, and by forcing men to self-examination and scrutiny leads to a broader outlook and to charity, which are long steps on the way to mutual understanding.

How, then, was the principle of non-intervention to be made effectual? Cobden saw no hope in the Governments of the day, whether in his own or any other country, independently of the creation of a strong driving force in the form of public opinion. He wrote to Bright, " It is opinion and opinion only that is wanting to establish the principle of non-intervention as a law of nations as absolutely as the political refugee in a third and neutral country is protected now by the law of nations." Public opinion might operate in three ways. One was by a common accord of the Great Powers binding them not to interfere in their neighbours' affairs. Another was by the application of force to States which arbitrarily resorted to such interference—a method obviously contrary to his principles. The third way, and the one which he favoured, was that of example. Recognizing that a formal international agreement was for the time impracticable, and that the employment of force was undesirable at any time, he was willing to stake his faith on the influence of a bold British lead.

" We all wish," he wrote of the non-intervention party on December 5, 1856, " to see the principle universally adopted. But there are some who think that the first step is to act up to our own professions, and thus try, at least in the first instance, what moral means can be adopted to carry out our views. Mr. Roebuck [1] is all for force, for cannon and squadrons, and regiments and fleets. Let us try, in the first place, the force of a good example and of an honestly expressed opinion. *England will never speak in vain when she has moral power to back her.*"

Meeting the objection that this would be a one-sided arrangement, he answered that if the policy proposed were wise it could need no further justification. He was even convinced that, however other Powers might continue to carry on the old meddling policy, England's prestige would be increased rather than diminished by the acceptance of a self-denying ordinance imposing on her abstention and

[1] John Arthur Roebuck (1801–1879), the honest, impeccable, but also incalculable Radical reformer who represented Bath and Sheffield in Parliament at various times.

neutrality in European affairs. Freed thus from complications and prior commitments, she would be free to exert her influence as she would in any given situation, as indeed happened at the close of the Italian war of 1859.

Further, on this question he was uncompromising. His opposition to intervention was hedged round by no reservations, no exceptions, no craven-hearted options such as to-day stand in the way of the acceptance of any genuine system of international arbitration. When he had been preaching the doctrine for over twenty years, and may be supposed to have grasped its full significance and implications, he wrote (1858) :

" I am opposed to any armed intervention in the affairs of other countries. I am against any interference by the Government of one country in the affairs of another nation, even if it be confined to moral suasion. Nay, I go further, and disapprove of the formation of a society or organization of any kind in England for the purpose of interfering in the internal affairs of other countries."

Such an attitude may seem to the modern mind just as hopelessly doctrinaire and unpractical as the non-resistance attitude of the orthodox Quakers. But, like the early Quakers, Cobden saw that to attempt to set limits and qualifications to his principle would be to weaken it, make it less of a reality, and rob it of attractive force. No doubt thorough-going advocacy of that sort ruled him out of court with conventional politicians of both parties, but its very straightforwardness and definiteness enormously simplified his popular crusade, and it was the masses of the people that he wished first to capture, knowing that without them on his side he would never be able to move the House of Commons and the ruling classes.

Did he really believe that the principle of non-intervention would ultimately triumph ? There can be little doubt that he did, though he never expected speedy success. At times, indeed, he professed a confidence which it is difficult to regard as quite genuine, and which was certainly not well founded ; for in his eager look-out for allies in his peace campaigns, he was apt to mistake platoons and companies for battalions. He greeted with enthusiasm all signs—or what to his optimistic mind seemed to be signs—which now and then, and here and there, appeared to show that his policy was steadily gaining ground. Thus, midway in the American Civil War, he wrote to his friend Charles Sumner (January 23, 1862) : " If our Government were not pressed forward by this question of material interest (i.e. the blockade), there never was a time when the doctrine of non-intervention was so strongly in the ascendant in our maxims of foreign policy as at present." Alternating with such moments of confidence, however, there were depressing times when he almost despaired of his country, as he saw how ready it still was to allow itself to be stampeded into foreign adventures at the beck and whim of a masterful statesman.

The year before his death was for Cobden and his work a year of great fear but also of great hopes, since owing to the assertion of a sane and strong public opinion the country had been saved, so as by fire, from the catastrophe of participation in two wars—the American Civil War and the war between Prussia and Denmark. It was natural, therefore, that he should make the most of this happy immunity, and regard it as a good omen and the earnest of a new era in diplomatic life. In a mood of unaccustomed confidence he wrote on November 3, 1864 : " I defy us to go to war for any of the old European issues, the balance of power, the Eastern Question, or any dynastic or territorial question whatever, and I shall say so at Rochdale." He did not precisely say that when, three weeks later, he made in that town his last public speech —the most impressive which he ever devoted to this subject— yet he indulged in justifiable satisfaction that for once in a while England had not gone to war when she might have done. Yet that he regarded the struggle for non-intervention as still far from finished may be concluded from his confession :

" We shall have to do with this foreign policy, and this non-intervention, just what we did with the Corn Law question—reiterate and reiterate, and repeat and repeat, until that comes to pass which O'Connell used to say to me, ' I always go on repeating until I find what I have been saying coming back to me in echoes from other people.' "

At heart he knew that a great transformation of national thought must come before foreign policy would be moralized as he wished to see it. With such a change, however, the practice of intervention would cease automatically, in the " natural course of events."

It is plain to see that on both of the twin questions of the balance of power and intervention Cobden was altogether in advance of his own century and so far of ours. In later times the Great Powers may occasionally have given to these doctrines greater refinements, and justified them with greater subtleties, than in his day, yet they have continued to be the foundation of European diplomacy, with recent results only too tragically apparent. Not only so, but owing to the aggressive forms taken by imperialism and colonial expansion the leading States have since applied them in directions never dreamt of half a century ago. Cobden was wont to say that the doctrine of equilibrium had ceased to have any meaning for Great Britain since the national life had become so deeply involved in that of countries outside the Continent. Had he lived into the present century he would have seen, to his despair, how the insatiable craving for territory led to the application of the doctrine in Asia and Africa.

It was his hope that " when the affairs of the British Empire are conducted with as much wisdom as goes to the successful management of a private business," the nation's immediate, and pre-eminently its domestic, interests would be made the exclusive study of its Governments, and non-intervention would in consequence become the guiding principle of foreign policy. It is true that after his day arbitrary and one-sided meddling of the Palmerstonian kind became increasingly uncommon, giving place to collective action by the Concert of the Powers, as in the winding up of the Russo-Turkish war by the Congress of Berlin in 1878, and more recently in the Balkan settlement of 1913. That the older tradition was only dormant, however, became apparent when in the summer of 1914 the Serajevo murders brought Austria-Hungary and Servia into collision. Over the controversy which arose out of that crime, all the Great Powers, forgetting its enormity, promptly took sides in accordance with the grouping formed some years before in pursuance of the elusive *fata Morgana* of equilibrium, and within a few days plunged into the fiercest and longest war of European history.

However indecisive and disappointing the results of that struggle were in most other directions, it left the doctrine of the balance of power discredited beyond possibility of recovery. Never since the doctrine was first formulated did there exist so unique an opportunity of proving its utility as was afforded by the formation of the Triple Entente of 1904-7, ostensibly as a pacific counterpoise to the Triple Alliance, or more accurately the *Zweibund* or Dual Alliance between Germany and Austria-Hungary. Yet the way in which the new combination, from the first, stimulated on both sides jealousy, arrogance, and defiance, lessened increasingly the disposition to smooth away recurrent misunderstandings, and made war inevitable directly a serious dispute should acutely divide the opposing groups, nicely balanced though they were, has once for all demonstrated the doctrine to be what Cobden called it nearly a century ago, a phantom, a chimera, and an illusion.

As he and many later writers have abundantly shown, it has never been possible to define the doctrine except in the most general terms, and the question whether it would or would not be applied in any given set of circumstances which *ex hypothesi* made its application appropriate has always been a matter of chance. The end desired has seldom been long and never permanently achieved, for no sooner has some sort of equilibrium been arrived at, as a rule at great cost of life and treasure, than it has been upset. At times its effect may have been to defer wars ; but it has never set a limit to the aggression of ambitious Governments and rulers, whether those of the Great Powers or of petty States infected by their evil example, directly they have found it contrary to their interests, and have believed themselves strong enough to challenge opposition. To that extent the future will hardly be different from the past. So long as nations continue to harbour aggressive designs against each other, active opposition from other nations, which hold their interests to be menaced, will be certain to follow. If, for example, owing to the temporary eclipse of Germany and Russia, France were to use her present dominating military strength in such a way as to weaken independent States and to become again, as a century ago, " the mischief-maker of Europe," forcible intervention would follow from one quarter or another, whether on the plea of equilibrium or not.

Not the least deplorable effect of the doctrine in the past has been that the superstitious belief in its efficacy has diverted the thought of Governments and peoples from wiser and surer methods of reconciling opposing interests, discouraging the spirit of aggression, and so of preserving international peace. It may be recalled that it was on the plea that there existed no supreme authority able to enforce the decisions of the majority that Russell refused to take part in the congress of the Powers which Louis Napoleon wished to convene in 1863 for the purpose of revising the European status, i.e. the balance of power, in the interest of France ; for he feared that in the absence of such sanction the members would separate with less amicable feelings towards each other than when they met.

The formation of the League of Nations, with the object, amongst others, of holding a sort of watching brief for the welfare of the civilized world at large, puts the entire question in a new perspective. The League will fulfil its highest purpose when it comes to embody in its own person a rational conception of a balance of power. Then it may be found that amicable conference and negotiation at the council board will succeed in achieving that position of stability and that reconciliation of interests which the interventions and wars of the past have failed to give to the world.

The question of future methods of international conciliation, however, leaves untouched the wider question whether interference in the affairs of sovereign States is justifiable at all. Cobden's contention that it is unpermissible in any circumstances, even where the clear interests of justice and humanity are at stake, will be likely to command even less assent to-day than when he lived. Perhaps few of those who are most in sympathy with his general principles of foreign policy will be prepared to go further with him on this point than to concede that intervention of any kind is defensible only over issues of supreme importance affecting the common interests of nations, and when the absence of intervention may lead to still greater evils.

The truth is that the principle of intervention, like some other political principles, is neither all right nor all wrong.

It was often wrong in the way Palmerston applied it, if for
no other reason than that he usually made the power of this
country felt when he was dealing with weaker States ; it was
wrong in particular in almost all our early dealings with
China, and the proof of this is found in the fact that they
have imposed on us an accumulating penalty of unpopularity
and dislike ever since.   It is just as true, however, that Palmerston was right in what he did—little though it was—to prevent
Russia, after her troops had trodden out the last embers of
revolution in Hungary, from wreaking vengeance upon the
leaders of that desperate gamble for independence.   In his
severe indictment of the long tale of British interventions
which fell to his day Cobden failed to give sufficient weight to
the fact that some of these interferences were undertaken,
more or less benevolently and disinterestedly, for the purpose
of preventing aggressive action by other Powers.

Perhaps it was in his wholesale repudiation of intervention
that Cobden came as near to being doctrinaire as he ever was,
though it is probable that if his sympathies had been put to a
severe practical test his heart would have proved more
generous, if less logical, than his head.   He did, indeed,
contradict himself rather flagrantly on one notable occasion.
It was when in 1860, turning a blind eye upon his former
professions, he tried to persuade Prince Metternich, the
Austrian Ambassador, that unless Austria were to evacuate
Venetia at once England would be almost certain to join
hands with the Italians.   How easily he fell into an order of
ideas which he was never weary of condemning in others is
shown by the account of this conversation which is contained
in his journal :

" I began," he writes, " by explaining very frankly . . . that the
popular sympathies were everywhere strongly in favour of the Italians ;
and that if another struggle should arise for the independence of Venetia,
and especially if it were attended with slaughter of civilians, or such of
an unarmed community, it would be very difficult for any Government
in England to prevent the feeling of honour and resentment from
assuming the form of material aid to the Italians."

That so sturdy an advocate of unconditional neutrality
should have used the threat of armed action as an argument,

H

in language which would have been altogether to the mind of "the old political juggler" and Lord John, only shows how difficult it was for even a straight-thinking man of his acutely logical mind and strong convictions to resist the promptings of a generous enthusiasm.

At the same time there is force in his contention that even intervention from motives of genuine altruism may in certain circumstances do more harm than good. History furnishes illustrations of forcible interferences in the affairs of mis-governed countries which, by weakening the authority and capacity of the responsible executive powers, have accentuated the very evils which they were designed to remove. It may be arguable, for example, whether on the whole there was any great balance of advantage to the Christian races under Moslem rule in the policy of spasmodic interference and pres-sure exercised by the Great Powers in Turkey during the past century, seeing that it was never accompanied by effective control and often lacked energy sufficient to convince the Sultan and his Government that his many masters were in earnest. Granting that much good was accomplished, yet it was at a heavy cost, not only to the victims of misgovernment, even those who were eventually emancipated, but to the inter-vening Powers themselves. How far humaner government would have come without this intervention must be a matter of speculation, but it is certain that coercion, even of the diplomatic and moral sort, often stiffened the obstinacy of the Porte, while armed interference threw back progress altogether.

All that Cobden says about the propriety of greater res-traint and decorum in public references to the statesmen and affairs of other countries has still point for the present day. No doubt most of the politicians and journalists who so often offend in this respect do so in complete ignorance of the fact that the code of good manners accepted in social intercourse applies equally to international relations. Even in the House of Commons there are always members ready to ask questions of a character insulting to foreign States; and though on such occasions the Foreign Office adopts the correct attitude of refusing to reply, its silence does not wholly prevent, though it may minimize, the mischievous effects of such impropriety. It would be a wholesome rule if no question relating to a foreign

State or statesman were allowed to be asked in either House, or even to appear on the notice-paper, until it had passed a severer scrutiny than parliamentary order and practice now require. It is not enough that impertinent and offensive questions are not answered and at times are even rebuked. Harm is done by the publicity given to them. The praiseworthy action taken by the Speaker prior to the debate on Russia on July 24, 1926, was highly commendable, but some of the succeeding speeches showed once more the great need for a more drastic revision of parliamentary procedure in this matter.

CHAPTER V

THE CASE AGAINST WAR

" We think our civilization near its meridian, but we are yet only at the cock-crowing and the morning star."—EMERSON, Essay on " Politics."

" You cannot redeem under any circumstances the naked and horrid aspect of war, the offspring of brutality, and civilization's adopted child. War in itself is a mighty evil, an incongruity in a scheme of social harmony, a canker at the heart of improvement, a living lie in a Christian land, a curse at all times. We confess that we regard with infinite satisfaction every endeavour, come whence it may, to destroy the supremacy of a cruel deity acknowledged on every ground."—Quoted from *The Times* by Mr. MILNER GIBSON in the House of Commons, June 12, 1849.

WRITING at a time when, in this country at least, the " pride, pomp, and circumstance of glorious war " have temporarily ceased to captivate even the popular imagination, it might seem purposeless to recall Cobden's argument on this subject. Nothing, however, can be super-fluous that can in any degree whatever help to focus public attention upon war as a gigantic evil, and to lay bare any of the fallacies and deceptions which are still current regarding it.

In time of tranquillity it is the first duty of the soldier to study how war may be waged with success, but it is then the urgent duty of the statesmen to study how war may be avoided. Cobden complained that in the discharge of the latter duty the statesmanship of his country and day conspicuously failed. Parliament after Parliament and session after session Speeches from the Throne reiterated the old platitude, " My relations with foreign Powers are friendly and promise so to continue," but always there followed a reservation to the effect that " the necessity of maintaining the strength of the country's defensive forces requires some increase," etc. The specious doctrine that to be prepared for war was the best way of preserving peace still claimed general assent, though here and there wise men were abandoning it. Such a man was the Earl of Aberdeen, who in a speech of 1849 said that " Men, when they adopted such a maxim, and made large preparations in time of peace that would be sufficient in the time of war, were apt to be influenced by the desire to put their efficiency to the test, that all their great preparations and the result of their toil and expense might not be thrown away," and added that he " could not be at ease as regarded the stability of peace until he saw a great reduction in the great military establishments of Europe."

Yet the piling up of armaments went on, until at last Europe became a fortified camp. At the time these words were spoken it was computed that one-half of the able manhood of the Continent was under arms. Five years later, when Aberdeen was Prime Minister, England joined France in a war with Russia—the culmination of a long and subtle conspiracy against peace, engineered with unwearying persistence. In his pamphlet 1793 *and* 1853, *in Three Letters*, published in 1853, Cobden wrote that " never even in England was the military spirit so much in the ascendant in the higher circles as at the present time." Patriotic gatherings were then accustomed to drink to the toast of " Ships, Colonies, and Commerce," the chain of reasoning being that as colonies were necessary to the maintenance of powerful trade monopolies, so naval armaments were needed to the maintenance of colonies. Further, the minds of the masses of the nation had been unbalanced by the flashy policy of foreign interventions long pursued by Lord Palmerston, and the bitter experiences of the early years of the century were almost forgotten.

Perhaps also the persistence of the martial spirit of which Cobden complained was in part due to the fact that under the system of fighting by proxy which allowed stay-at-home patriots to buy their soldiers for a shilling a day the realities of war—and few of them—were seen only when the maimed and broken victims of the battlefield returned, and to the comparative cheapness of warfare and its machinery in general at a time when the price of half a dozen modern men-of-war would have paid for a considerable campaign.

British soldiers never talked of the immoral doctrine of " preventive war," that is, the permissibility of anticipating an attack which is expected to come sooner or later, so taking the hypothetical enemy unprepared ; but Cobden perpetuates a bellicose Member for Birmingham of his day who from his seat in the House of Commons dared to assert that this was his country's traditional way. In an outburst of anger against Russia in 1833 this pugilistic patriot lamented that

" We, the people of England, who have never known what fear is, who have been accustomed for seven hundred years to give a blow first and to receive an apology afterwards, we, who have borne the British lion triumphant through every quarter of the world, are now forced to submit to insults from this base and brutal and in reality weak Power."

A wholesome change has come over the public attitude to war since nonsense of this sort was tolerated in parliamentary debate ; though even to-day we are so habituated as a nation to the idea of war as a normal pursuit that we still cling to phrases like the " War " Office, the " Fighting Services," and the rest. Merely to recall this unremembered flash of oratory, however, is sufficient to show that peace advocacy was then a far bolder and more difficult occupation than it is to-day. Cobden entered the lists against war and its mechanism in his first pamphlet, *England, Ireland, and Russia* (1835), a writing which in some ways may be regarded as a synopsis of his later more systematized political thought. His method of attack was to prove the futility of war and its inability to achieve any result except harm, and he pressed the attack from different directions.

Being then still engaged in cotton manufacturing, the commercial argument against war naturally appealed to him with special force. The old idea that war was good for trade was still popular, and in illustration of it he pointed to the inscription on the monument which had been erected to Lord Chatham in the London Guildhall in recognition of the benefits which the City had received by its share in the public prosperity created " . . . by conquests made by arms and generosity in every part of the globe, and by commerce for the first time united with and made to flourish by war." He combated this view as both fallacious and vicious. War was not creative, but only destructive. While it was the purpose of agriculture, industry, and commerce to multiply and diffuse wealth and build up prosperity, war squandered the national resources in costly, disastrous, and usually purposeless foreign adventures, battening leech-like upon the body politic, sucking the life-blood which should give to it energy and vigour.

He admitted that both agriculture and trade might enjoy a temporary fillip owing to war ; but later came the inevitable reaction, when the apparent advantages gained disappeared, leaving the latter state of things worse than the first. From the economic standpoint war was at best " a kind of inter- mittent fever, and the cure or death of the patient must at some time follow." What was it but stupendous folly to close beneficent avenues of trade and commerce, to cut off from their natural markets vast food-yielding territories, and to inflict poverty, privation, and suffering upon whole populations ? Yet such were the results of war.

While thus war could ruin trade, it was powerless to promote it. Here he endorsed Sir Matthew Decker's dictum, " Trade will not be forced." Nearly all the wars in which Great Britain had been engaged during the preceding century and a half had been undertaken for the preservation of our com- merce, yet he denied that in a single instance a favourable tariff or a beneficial commercial treaty had been extorted from an unwilling enemy at the point of the sword. In a forcible passage in the pamphlet *Russia*, 1836, he contrasted the commercial argument for war with the reality, the promise with the fulfilment. Trade, instead of being furthered, was crippled ; nations, instead of being enriched, were impoverished and ruined ; and the glory which fell to the favoured few was purchased by the misery of the many.

Some of his references to the intimate relation between war and unemployment have peculiar relevance to the present day. Thus, in addressing a Manchester audience just after the close of the Crimean War (March 18, 1857), he said :

" Now, what do we see in London ? Twenty or thirty thousand unemployed workmen. Why are they unemployed ? You don't find that the newspapers connect cause and effect. They are unemployed because capital is scarce. Who will lay out his money in building houses, to pay him at the rate of 6, or 7, or 8 per cent., if he can get that percentage for the money he puts into the banks ? Consequently there is no money being invested in buildings, because you have now such a high rate of interest. And why is there such a high rate of interest? Because the floating capital of this country has, during the last two or three years, been wasted in sudden and extraordinary expenses.

" But you don't see your newspapers, that were bawling for the war, honestly tell the people in London that the reason they are suffering want of employment is that this floating capital, which is always a limited quantity in the country—the floating capital which sets all your fixed capital in motion—has been exhausted, wasted by the course that has been pursued. They tell these poor people in London they may emigrate; but I say it is downright quackery to talk of relieving the country of 20,000 or 30,000 people by means of emigration."

Long before people began to recognize as a " great illusion " the idea that nations could permanently benefit by wars of conquest, or that wars could even, in Bismarck's memorable phrase, " pay their expenses," he had exposed the fallacy, for it never imposed upon him at all. He once wrote to a correspondent : " I often wish I had the leisure to do justice to the argument which is always uppermost in my mind, that the modern application of the principles of political economy has destroyed the motive of self-interest which formerly tempted us to wars of conquest. I could turn the batteries against the £ s. d. argument most successfully."

On this question, as on so many others, he saw eye to eye with Peel, who told the House of Commons in 1841 :

" You can't conduct war as Bonaparte did. No Power in Europe can do it. You can't make the country you conquer bear the price of the conquest. The thing is impossible. With States as with individuals that most unpleasant day, the day of reckoning, comes round, and when in their sober moments men calculate the relative advantages of immense armaments, and the illusions of military glory, with the cost of the taxes to pay for such exploits, they come to take a calmer and more discreet view of the comparative advantages than they could be expected to do in the moment of excitement."—(August 27.)

In pressing the case against war from the political stand-point he ridiculed the claim that great campaigns were necessary from time to time in order to preserve the equilibrium of Europe or the integrity of Turkey, and begged the statesmen who indulged in argument of that sort to condescend to give a thought as to the effects of war upon the " equilibrium of our cotton manufactures." Seldom, if ever, did war settle

the issues over which it was professedly waged.   For the effect
of aggression and defeat was always to stimulate the spirit
of the injured people and to provoke the craving for revenge.
Speaking at Manchester in January 1849, when nationalist
aspirations were ominously stirring in Europe, he said :

> " I defy you to show me how any Government or people on the
> Continent can strengthen themselves, even if they chose to carry on a
> war of conquest.   Let France invade Germany ; it only makes Germany
> unite like one man—the whole Teutonic race are united as one man to
> repel the French.   What is their predominant sentiment ?   The union
> of Germany, not for aggressive force, but for defensive succour.   What
> is the cry of Italy ?   Italian nationality.   What is the contest between
> Lombardy and Austria ?   The House of Austria may call Lombardy
> part of its territory, but there . . . the Latin race say, ' We will not be
> governed by a Teutonic race ' ; and, though the Austrians may keep
> down the Italians by Radetzky and his 100,000 troops, Lombardy will
> be a source of weakness, not of strength, to them.   I defy you to show
> me any partition where an accession of territory has not been rather
> a source of weakness than of strength."

Still more emphatically he combated the opinion that
popular liberties could be established by war.   Criticizing in
the pamphlet *1793 and 1853, in Three Letters* (1853) the common
plea that the coalition with Revolutionary France was in
defence of the liberties of Europe, he wrote :

> " Where are they ?   *Circumspice* !   I can only say that I have
> sought for them from Cadiz to Moscow without having been so fortunate
> as to find them.   But in truth the originators of the war never pretended
> that they were fighting for the liberties of the people anywhere.   Their
> avowed object was to sustain the old Governments of Europe.   The
> advocates of the war were not the friends of popular freedom even at
> home.   The Liberal Party were ranged on the side of peace—Lans-
> downe, Bedford, and Lauderdale in the Lords, and Fox, Sheridan, and
> Grey in the Commons were the strenuous opponents of the war.
> Not only are we constrained, by the evidence of facts, to confess that
> we were engaged in an aggressive war, but the multiplied avowals and
> confessions of its authors and partisans themselves leave no room to
> doubt that they entered upon it to put down opinions by physical
> force."

Far from war having ever been the parent of healthy
national development, far from it fitting people for the better

exercise of the rights of citizenship and the enjoyment of ordered freedom, it threw back all progress of the kind and tended to destroy the spirit of order and legality.

He also rebutted the idea that the question of war and the preparations for waging it was primarily one for soldiers ; it was the business of civilians, since they provided the armies and bore the cost of the campaigns in life and treasure. He therefore warned his countrymen that if they wished to make the world better their duty was to begin reform at home, and first to recognize, by the study of their country's history, that no nation had meddled more in foreign affairs, waged more wars, and showed itself generally more militant than their own.

" We shall do no good," he wrote in a letter, " until we can bring home to the conviction and consciences of men the fact that, as in the slave-trade we had surpassed in guilt the whole world, so in foreign wars we have been the most aggressive, quarrelsome, warlike, and bloody nation under the sun." And in another letter, " We have been the most combative and aggressive community that has existed since the days of the Roman dominion. Since the Revolution of 1688 we have expended more than 1,500 millions of money upon wars, not one of which has been upon our own shores or in defence of our hearths and homes."

He allowed that some of the wars waged by this country had been disinterested, but looking back upon national history as a whole he was more impressed by the sordidness of motive behind the martial record. Moreover, in his indictment of his own nation he included all classes and conditions of men. When he began his crusade against war he was disposed to lay the entire blame for the nation's unenviable record of violence on the aristocratic ruling class. " Wars," he once wrote, " have ever been but another aristocratic mode of plundering and oppressing commerce." Time and experience moderated that attitude, and he ceased to blame any one class for the guilt which belonged to the whole nation. In 1852 he wrote to Mr. Thomasson, of Bolton, a strong peace advocate of his day :

" Before you and I (men of peace as we are) find fault with the Whig chiefs, let us ask ourselves candidly whether the country at large is in favour of any other policy than that which has been pursued by the aristocracy, Whig and Tory, for the last century and a half. The man who impersonated that policy more than any other was the Duke of Wellington ; and I had the daily opportunity of witnessing at the Great Exhibition last year that all other objects of interest sank to insignificance even in that collection of a world's wonders when he made his entry in the Crystal Palace. The frenzy of admiration and enthusiasm which took possession of a hundred thousand people of all classes at the very announcement of his name was one of the most impressive lessons I ever had of the real tendencies of the English character."

Not much will be found in either writings or speeches on the ethical and religious aspects of this question, partly, no doubt, because of a characteristic reticence on such matters, but also because he believed that he had a better chance of influencing public opinion when he dealt with the subject, as he said, " as a politician strictly on the principles of policy and expediency." Nevertheless, his views on the ethical issues involved in war-making are stated freely and at times vehemently in his correspondence. Holding war to be essentially wrong, he was more than dubious as to any results of moral value to be expected from it. He rejected with scorn the plea common amongst religionists of a certain type in his day, and not uncommon in ours, that the doors which were forced open by sanguinary wars of conquest were designed by a wise Providence for the admission of the messengers of peace.[1] Though a passionate friend of liberty, as much for other nations and races as for his own, he yet wrote to his friend Charles Sumner during the American Civil War : " You know I would never have fired a shot for the freedom of the negro, because I believe that God in His own good time would have found a way of emancipating the slave at a less cruel cost to his master." So profoundly was he convinced of the evil and hatefulness of war that to the end of the struggle he never wholly abandoned that position.

As in relation to the doctrines of the balance of power and intervention, so in regard to war, Cobden looked for amendment to the spread of knowledge and education, the elevation of the tone of national opinion, the cultivation of a more

---

[1] In a letter he records a remark made by Bright, as a parliamentary colleague of this type passed him in the House of Commons lobby, " There's a little fellow that will vote for any amount of slaughter on Evangelical principles."

generous faith in mankind, and, on the part of statesmen, a greater patience and willingness to wait on the "natural course of events." He told the House of Commons after it had voted the country into the Crimean War : " It is because you do not sufficiently trust to the influence of the course of events in smoothing down difficulties, but will rush headlong to arms, which never can solve them, that you involve yourselves in long and ruinous wars."—(December 22, 1854.)

Much of his argument clearly presumed a standard of international relationships which had never yet been reached, yet at times, with an exaggerated optimism which one must suppose to have been in part assumed as a stimulus to his fellow-workers for peace, he professed the belief that the age of wars of conquest and ambition was closed, never to be reopened. At heart, however, he knew that the berserker instinct was too deeply rooted in human nature to be overcome by shock-attacks, or even appeals to material interest. Upon this, as upon other questions, his true convictions find most candid statement in his letters, and in one of them he wrote : " You may reason ever so logically, and never so convincingly as through the pocket, but it will take time to play off even John Bull's acquisitiveness against his combativeness. He will not be easily persuaded that all his reliance upon brute force and courage has been a losing speculation."

How far, then, was Cobden prepared to go in proscribing war in the conditions of the world as he saw them ? He has been unreasonably and ignorantly described as a weak, milk-and-water pacifist, too timid to say " Boo " to a goose. He was, of course, nothing of the kind, and if the truth were known, he was probably more combative than one-half of his detractors. He hated all war in general, as every moral man must do, but he did not condemn war waged in a right cause, provided the circumstances were so urgent as to require it and that no other solution was possible. In truth he was an advocate neither of peace at any price nor of war at no price, but a level-headed patriot who never wanted to fight, but was prepared, if the clear necessity for so doing existed, to throw into the breach the whole of his nation's resources. His position on this question was perfectly sane and practical. He said in the House of Commons on one occasion : " I am prepared to assume that wars may be inevitable and necessary, although I do not admit that all wars are so." No attitude could be more reasonable, and if challenged not one of his opponents could honestly have spoken differently.

Wars against injustice he held to be theoretically permissible, every such case being judged on its merits, and he would not have ceded one tittle of his country's just rights except by force —and much of that would have been needed. By nature he was himself somewhat of a militarist, though he could capitulate gracefully when policy dictated that course. One of his most striking characteristics was his large fund of human nature and healthy, vivid animal spirits. In 1837 he met Grote the historian, and was disappointed ; for he says of him, " He is a mild and philosophical man, pursuing the highest order of moral and intellectual endowments, but wanting something which for need of a better phrase *I shall call devil*." Answering the foolish accusation of a weak pacifism in a speech made at Manchester in 1853, just before the Crimean War, he said :

" I have never avowed—I should be hypocritical if I avowed—that I entertained the opinion that, if attacked, if molested in an unprovoked manner, I would not defend myself from such an act of aggression. Nobody, I presume, who wishes to do me justice, ever dreamed that I would do so. But it was not necessary because I found everyone bullying and crying, ' We will remind them of Waterloo ; we will sing " Rule Britannia," we will remind them of Trafalgar and the Nile ' ; —it was not necessary I join in reminding them of that. But I hold opinions which are held by the great body of my countrymen, and an unprovoked attack would find, I dare say, as resolute a resistance from me as from many of those who are now crying out in a panic, and who, I suspect, would be very likely to run away from the enemy." [1]

Cobden had, in fact, two selves : the one was the ardent cosmopolitan philanthropist, to whom war was a cruel, revolting, heart-breaking affair, and who deplored every appeal

[1] How little the most pronounced of theoretical pacifists at times know themselves may be illustrated by a humorous incident which was reported to me during the late war from a certain North Country recruiting tribunal. A local pacifist had obtained exemption by reason of his conscientious objection to war. The day following he reproached a member of the tribunal who had opposed his release, and ended by thrashing him. Hearing of this, the tribunal cited him to reappear, and, informing him that he was clearly just the sort of man needed in a time of national extremity, withdrew his certificate of exemption.

to its monstrous arbitrament, let the cause be never so good and strong; the other was the impulsive, justice-loving, pugnacious Englishman—a refinement of the very type against which he was never tired of tilting—jealous of his just rights as such, and ready to defend them to the last trench. He was also perfectly conscious of this antinomy of a double nature, but the difference between the avowed militarists of his day, whether professional or lay, and himself was that while they acclaimed war as "all in the day's work" of a great nation, he regarded it as the humane surgeon regards a dangerous operation, as an act only to be performed in dire necessity.

Not the least valuable of his opinions on the subject of war are those which relate to the finance of militarism. Intimate as this connexion was in his day, few people recognized so clearly as he the sinister part which money played in the lives and policies of nations. He both wrote and spoke strongly against the practice of making loans to the Governments of impecunious countries for expenditure on armaments, and some of his warnings on this subject, uttered three-quarters of a century ago, have been emphasized by later experience. As early as 1849 he induced the Peace Society to undertake a crusade against the system of foreign loans in general, in the hope of handicapping warlike Continental Governments, by stopping their financial supplies. In informing his correspondent Sumner in America of this new crusade, he wrote with his habitual assurance: "In proportion as we succeed in this we shall drive the bankrupt rulers back upon their own subjects for the pecuniary means necessary for their own subjection. This plan will do more than anything besides to hasten the financial crisis which must precede any change." It cannot be said that the efforts of the Peace Society in this direction were attended by any very practical results, but good was unquestionably done by enlightening public opinion on the moral issues raised by some of these international money transactions.

He dealt with the subject in public speeches in the same and the following year, when the Austrian and Russian Governments were floating loans on the London market. These Governments had just suppressed the rising of the Hungarians in circumstances of great ferocity, and Cobden, in effect, charged them with sending in the bill of costs to the British nation.   In a speech made on October 8, 1849, he said :

"The Austrian Government comes now, and stretches forth its blood-stained hand to honest Dutchmen and Englishmen, and asks them to furnish the price of the devastation which has been committed. For there is little difference whether the money subscribed to this loan be furnished a little before or after. The money has been raised for the war by forced contributions and compulsory loans, for which Treasury receipts have been given, in the confident expectation that this loan would be raised to pay them off."

Challenged by London journals to say whether he opposed the loan on the ground of its immorality or of its insecurity, he replied that he opposed it on both grounds since in his opinion what was immoral was unsafe.   He reminded investors who were tempted by the promise of a high rate of interest that the borrowing Governments were insolvent, since they were only able to make ends meet by contracting new loans, and he warned them that if they parted with their money they might never see it again.   He also condemned such loans on purely economic grounds—as the frittering away of capital which ought to be employed in reproductive ways.   Opposing the Russian loan in a speech made on January 18, 1850, he said :

"It is so much capital abstracted from England and handed over to another country to be wasted ; it alienates from the labouring population of this country a part of the means by which it is employed, and by which it is to live. I say that every loan advanced to a foreign Power to be expended in armaments, or for carrying on war with other countries, is as much money wasted and destroyed for all the purposes of reproduction as if it were carried into the middle of the Atlantic, and there sunk in the sea. . . . It stops employment, impedes industry, and withdraws from us the very sources of profitable labour."

The speeches just cited were made in London, and to utter such language in the hearing of City men at that time was like talking in a foreign tongue, but the Press had much to say. Shallow-minded critics told him that in thus proposing to restrict traffic in money he was unfaithful to his favourite doctrine of Free Trade.   To this objection he made the sufficient reply that whereas food was meant to maintain life, the foreign loans which he had attacked would be used in destroying it. He did not accept the doctrine which Ruskin was propounding at that time, that interest-receiving was as sinful as war-waging, but far ahead of his age in general he laid down the doctrine that the possession of money, as of any other kind of property, was attended by responsibilities and duties as well as by privileges and rights, and that the neglect of the one might justly entail the loss of the other.

He even anticipated certain much controverted acts of fiscal policy done abroad in our own day. Recognizing that loans raised by foreign Governments, whatever the pretexts put forward by the borrowers, were so often used for purposes in direct conflict with the interests of civilization and humanity, he believed that " future generations will raise the question whether they shall be held responsible for debts incurred, often for keeping their own country in slavery, and for foreign wars in which they can have no possible interest."—(November 14, 1850.)

This, however, was only a forecast, and injustice would be done to him by the suspicion that he entertained light views regarding the inviolability of public debts. He was a foe to debt repudiation in every form as on principle indefensible and as undermining public faith. "Nothing," he warned his countrymen in his first pamphlet, " can be more certain than that the National Debt (which never ought to have been incurred, and the authors of which some future generation will, probably, deem to have been madmen) must be borne by the people of England, entire and untouched, so long as they can stand beneath the burden." He predicted, however, that if the day should come when its public debt crushed the nation there would be buried in the ruins " the monarchy, Church and aristocracy, and every vestige of our feudal institutions, and every ancestral precedent." From such a catastrophe there could be no escape but in " either honestly paying off the principal of the public debt, or in continuing to discharge the interest of it for ever," and he stigmatized all proposals of a composition with the State's creditors as the " ravings " of men who wished to precipitate political disaster, ending with the categorical dictum, which for him closed the discussion, " The national debt, then, is inviolable."

Nevertheless, Cobden's voice was one of the first to be raised against the habit of private creditors looking to the Government to act as " bumbailiff " for the forcible collection of their claims against defaulting States. At the time he was attacking foreign loans the British admiral on the South American station, acting on instructions, was interfering in Venezuela in a case of the kind, and the demand had been made that the same thing should be done in Spain. Jealous for his nation's honour, and apprehensive of all foreign interventions, he followed these proceedings closely and critically. He argued that inasmuch as Government loans floated in London were largely subscribed by foreigners, interferences of the kind made England a debt collector for other States, and he objected to such a function as undignified. There was talk of naval measures against Venezuela, and these he strongly condemned, for if we blockaded the coast of Venezuela how could we decently refuse to blockade the American coast in the interest of the creditors of repudiating States of the Union, for there would be " obvious disgrace as well as injustice in dealing differently with weak and with powerful States."

At the time these words were written and long after this was precisely the distinction made by strong European Powers in their dealings with weak ones. As late as 1902 Great Britain, together with Germany, once again assumed the debt collector's *rôle* in the case of the same State of Venezuela, and effectually blockaded its coast until satisfaction had been obtained. In the meantime a courageous stand against the rent-collector function of British Governments had come from Lord Salisbury, whose resistance as Foreign Secretary in 1879 to the attempts of France to drag him further than he liked in pressure upon Egypt in the interest of French bondholders was one of the manliest acts of his career.

" It may be quite tolerable and even agreeable to the French Government," he wrote to Lord Lyons (April 10, 1879), " to go into partnership with the bondholders, or rather to act as sheriff's officers for them. But to us it is a new and very embarrassing sensation. Egypt can never prosper so long as some 25 per cent. of her revenue goes in paying interest on her debt."

Lord Beaconsfield shared the opinion of his colleague, and doubted whether the country would approve " a mere bondholders' policy." (June 24, 1879.) It was a creditable achievement that while France wished to compel the Egyptians to pay to the last farthing the loans made by her financiers on scandalous terms to the prodigal Ismail, the British Government succeeded, after a long and difficult struggle, in having the rates of interest scaled down and the arrears in part wiped out.

In uttering his repeated warnings of the ruinous cost of wars, and of their disastrous social consequences, Cobden cannot have anticipated how small was to be their practical effect. He described the public debt of his day as due to a policy of madness, yet two succeeding generations continued the hitherto unbroken sequence of wars, interventions, and imperialistic adventures on a scale never before equalled, with the result that the nation's indebtedness has risen to catastrophic proportions. When Cobden wrote the public debt amounted to 800 millions, or £33 per head of the population ; it is now nearly 8,000 millions, or £190 for every inhabitant. The population has barely doubled in the interval, but the public debt has increased tenfold.

CHAPTER VI

PEACE AND ARBITRATION

" We have shared deeply in that widely extended calamity : the bitter draught which France prepared for herself has flowed into our cups. Let us at least derive from it the benefits of an experience so dearly purchased."— Speech of LORD GRENVILLE on the prevailing discontents, made in the House of Lords, November 30, 1819.

" The commonest error in politics is sticking to the carcasses of dead policies."—LORD SALISBURY, May 25, 1877.

IT has been said that one of Cobden's most marked characteristics as a public man was his habit of concentration. " To confess the truth," he wrote once to a friend, " I can only do one thing at a time." No sooner were the corn duties repealed, and Free Trade accepted as the basis of England's fiscal system, than he turned his mind to practical work on behalf of the peace movement. Was the abolition of the Corn Laws or this longer and harder crusade his first love ? A study of his writings, even more than of his speeches, which began at a later date, makes its fairly certain that the order in which he publicly advocated these two great causes was not that which they took in his thought. His systematic work for peace came second in time, but that it was no after-thought, no mere enlargement or by-product of the Free Trade agitation is shown by his own words. For it was while he was working for repeal that he came to recognize how Free Trade was, after all, only part of the larger peace movement and should properly be worked into it. Thus we find him writing to Mr. Henry Ashworth in 1842, when the anti-Corn Law agitation had covered half the way to victory :

" It has struck me that it would be well to try to engraft our Free Trade agitation upon the peace movement. They are one and the same cause. It has often been to me a matter of the greatest surprise that the Friends have not taken up the question of Free Trade as the means —and I believe the only human means—of effecting universal and permanent peace. The efforts of the Peace Societies, however laudable, can never be successful so long as the nations maintain their present system of isolation."

This idea of the inter-relation of the two causes grew on him, and was never afterwards lost sight of. " Free Trade ! What is it ? " he asked in a speech made in London a year later, and he answered :

" Why, breaking down the barriers that separate nations ; those barriers behind which nestle the feelings of pride, revenge, hatred, and jealousy, which every now and then burst their bounds and deluge whole countries with blood ; those feelings which nourish the poison of war and conquest, which assert that without conquest we can have no trade, which foster that lust for conquest and dominion which sends forth your warrior chiefs to scatter devastation through other lands, and then calls them back that they may be enthroned securely in your passions, but only to harass and oppress you at home. It is because I think I have a full apprehension of the moral bearing of this question that I take a pride and gratification in forming one in the present agitation."—(September 28, 1843.)

His profound belief in free commercial intercourse as the great palliative of international jealousies and frictions, and a sure panacea against militarism and war, may seem quixotic in the present day, but it is necessary always, in judging Cobden's apparent over-confidence, to allow for his intense nature and his exaltations, and to remember that when he so spoke he was under the influence of a great faith and hope. No formal co-ordination of the two movements such as he suggested took place, yet their interdependence was taken for granted, and from the time that Free Trade was safely entrenched he turned to the larger campaign.

Accordingly, from 1847 forward, side by side with his more or less critical work as the antagonist of war, and of the national mentality and temper which conduce to war, he was actively engaged in the positive work of peace propagandism in this and other countries. For some years he practically directed the work of the Peace Society, whose secretary then and for long after his own life's end was the Reverend Henry Richard.

True to his nature and methods of controversy, he refused to approach the question on sentimental lines. Peace was for him a question of morality, but he knew his countrymen too well to expect that the peace movement would succeed by appeal to that high sanction alone. It was for this practical reason that in 1850 he decided to have nothing to do with a League of Brotherhood which was being formed in the interest of international peace, feeling that the sentimental idea which it suggested would prejudice that cause. For " Brotherhood is fraternity, a word dragged through the mire by red Republicans and Socialists, and to adopt it in this country is only to burden ourselves with a needless disadvantage."

In the summer of 1849, though not formally a member of the Peace Society, he attended an International Peace Congress held in Paris. Victor Hugo presided, and the French were admirably courteous as entertainers and masters of ceremonies, but not as enthusiastic in the cause of peace as he and his colleagues had hoped to find them ; some notable men, who had been regarded as pillars of the movement, even failing to make an appearance. This lack of ardour was a matter of national temperament ; for while the Englishman invariably means all he says, and sometimes a little more, the Frenchman usually means a good deal less. Knowing this by earlier experience, Cobden refused to be discouraged. In a letter to his wife (August 19) he wrote :

" The good men who have come out here from England to make the arrangements are sadly put out in their calculations of French support by having taken too much to heart all the professions, promises, bows, and compliments which they met with on their first arrival here. They are now taking such demonstrations at their just value."

Yet in spite of the abstention of so many of the expected great and wise ones of the French political world, the Congress drew together two thousand people on each of the three days of its meeting, and he was satisfied with the result. " Everything is sure to succeed that has a good principle in it," he wrote home when the turmoil was over. " All our good Quaker friends are in capital spirits. There can be no doubt that our meetings will have done good. Everybody has been talking about them during the week, and the subject of peace has for the first time had its hearing even in France." It is worth recording that by its resolutions the Congress affirmed the duty of Governments to submit all differences arising between them to arbitration, and the necessity of a general and simultaneous measure of disarmament ; condemned all loans and taxes for wars of ambition or conquest ; urged the friends of peace in all countries to agitate for the formation of an international congress, to revise the existing law of nations, and to institute a High Tribunal for the decision of disputes between nations ; and invoked the aid of Press and pulpit in securing peace and goodwill among men. The resolutions were all in Cobden's spirit, and it is probable that his experienced hand had much to do with the drafting of them.

Abroad as at home he was already an influence to be reckoned with in public affairs, and in Paris he added to his laurels. Charles Sumner, already mentioned, was the chairman of the American delegation to the Congress, and he described Cobden at the time as " the world-renowned British statesman, the unapproachable model of an earnest, humane, and practical reformer," paying also a well-deserved compliment to the "characteristic common sense" which had marked the whole of his contributions to the proceedings. To this friend, as he now was, Cobden wrote later in the year, reporting progress :

" You will have seen that we have been trying to lead the wicked Old World into a new and hitherto unknown path. You have too much practical knowledge to require to be told by me that our Peace Congress and public meetings are but the faint glimmerings of a new light which is dawning upon the nations, and that we do not deceive ourselves with the belief that we are near to that perfect day when they shall learn war no more. And yet I think the last two years (for which I have been co-operating directly in the peace agitation) have produced visible results. In the peace controversy we have brought the sneerers into serious debate. They tell us that the vast armaments of Europe are not now maintained for purposes of external warfare, but to maintain order at home. This is a damaging admission, for it converts the army into a *gendarmerie* and robs it of its chivalry. There is henceforth no popularity for armies in Europe."

But Cobden was never satisfied with abstract theories ; always he worked for concrete results, practical measures, and if his ends could not be attained by a single rush he was ready to advance towards them by stages. Recognizing that universal and permanent peace must be regarded as a " far-off divine event," he accepted the prospect of peace by instalments as a tolerable second-best. The first instalment upon which his mind was set was a partial scheme of arbitration, and he was willing to begin with a treaty with a single nation. He was not one of the earliest pioneers of the arbitration movement, for earnest friends of peace in this country had been working for it even before the Peace Society was founded in 1816, yet his resolute efforts on its behalf earned for him, as for Richard, Bright, and many other contemporaries, the recognition and gratitude which are due to all men who do the spade-work of civilization, by steering moral causes through the stage of unpopularity and opprobrium and making them socially respectable. To this cause he brought, if not original ideas, a unique force of advocacy which, combined with his opportunities of influencing public opinion as a Member of Parliament, materially helped to gain for the arbitral method of adjusting international disputes its first serious parliamentary recognition.

In June 1849 he succeeded in obtaining a formal debate on the subject in the House on a resolution proposed by himself for a " humble Address to the Throne," praying that the Foreign Secretary might be directed " to enter into communication with foreign Powers, inviting them to concur in treaties binding the respective parties, in the event of any future misunderstanding which cannot be arranged by amicable negotiation, to refer the matter in dispute to the decision of arbitrators." In introducing the motion he claimed to do so as representing " that influential body of Christians who repudiate war in any case, whether offensive or defensive," and also " that numerous portion of the middle classes of this country, with the great bulk of the working classes, who have an abhorrence of war greater than at any former period of our history, and who desire that we should take some new precautions, and if possible obtain some guarantees, against the recurrence of war in future." His argument was commended by all his habitual " homely common sense " and by marked temperateness of statement, in so much that he was at times almost apologetic, perhaps remembering that there were lying in wait opponents bent on destroying him.

" It is not necessary," he said, " that anyone in this House, or out of it, who accedes to this motion, should be of opinion that we are not justified, under any circumstances, in resorting to war, even in self-defence. It is only necessary that you should be agreed that war is a great calamity, which it is desirable we should avoid if possible. My object is to see if we cannot devise some better method for attaining those ends (" the just interests and honour of the country "), and my plan is, simply and solely, that we should resort to that mode of settling disputes in communities which individuals resort to in private life. I only want you to go one step farther, to carry out in another instance the principle which you recognize in other cases—that the intercourse between communities is nothing more than the intercourse of individuals in the aggregate."

He even went out of his way to make it clear that he had no idea of proposing a " congress of nations with a code of laws, a supreme court of appeal, and an army to support its decisions." " I am no party to any such plan," he said. " I believe it might lead to more armed interference than takes place at present." Nor did he appeal to feeling or sentiment, talk morality, or draw lurid pictures of the horrors of war. All he did was to invite nations—and his own as an encouragement to others—to be willing to settle their disputes in the rational manner recognized in civil life. As he put it in another arbitration speech made in the following year :

I ask Governments to do in the case of a nation what we always do in the case of individuals. If a Frenchman living in London commits a crime, the law—and Englishmen may be proud of it—allows him to claim to be tried by a jury, half of whom are foreigners. Now, all I want is that the nations of England and France, and other countries, should carry the same principle into operation, and that when they have a dispute . . . let two arbitrators, one for each nation disputing, be appointed ; and if the two cannot agree, let them appoint an umpire to settle the dispute according to reason and the facts of the case."

Answering the objection, " What would be the use of a treaty of the kind between France and England ? The parties would not observe it, but in the event of a serious dispute would treat it as a piece of waste paper and go to war all the same," he said :

" It would be a sufficient answer to say, What is the use of the Foreign Office ? What is the use of your diplomacy ? You might shut up the one and cashier the other.   I maintain that a treaty binding two countries to refer their disputes to arbitration is just as likely to be observed as any other treaty.   There would be this advantage, at all events, in having a treaty binding another country to refer all disputes to arbitration.   If that country did not fulfil its engagement, it would enter into war with the brand of infamy stamped upon its banners."

With the single exception of his repudiation of an international peace tribunal almost every word of this speech of eighty years ago is applicable to present conditions—a painful reminder of the world's distrust and slow acceptance of all great, basic moral principles.

In view of the later friendly relations of the two men, it is interesting to recall the fact that on this occasion Disraeli and Cobden fell foul of each other. Just before the motion came on Disraeli, then Member for Buckinghamshire and as yet uncalled to office, had referred to a recent exchange of courtesies between America and England on the subject of the Franklin Expedition, winding up with the remark that such an international incident was better than " the phantasies which were now in circulation and the political and international crotchets which would soon occupy their attention." Cobden rebuked his flippancy, though assuming that it arose from a misconception. Many years later Disraeli was to make handsome amends.   Lord Palmerston himself moved the previous question, and with his speech the issue of the debate was no longer in doubt, the motion being rejected by 176 against 79 votes.   Mr. Gladstone, still bound to Oxford, its losing causes and its impossible loyalties, did not speak or vote.

No doubt the time was inauspicious for experiments of the kind. Everywhere on the Continent the spirit of reaction was visible. The revolutionary movement which had passed over the Continent in the previous year had now been suppressed, and despotism, recovered from temporary abasement, had once more set the axe to the pernicious tree of liberty. France had, indeed, exiled her Bourbon-Orleans sovereign, yet, in spite of much rhetorical talk about the " rights of man," she was already eager to prostrate herself before another dictator, and he was near at hand. At the very moment that Cobden was lauding the gentle principles of arbitration a Russian army was assisting Austria to stamp out Kossuth's insurrection in Hungary—a task satisfactorily accomplished within a month directly the ruthless Hainau set his hand to the bloody work. In Germany likewise reaction had triumphed, and her score of potentates were engaged in repressing popular manifestations, even to the extent of denying the right of free speech and free thought.

When practically all Europe was in a condition of unrest and dissonance a proposal to maintain the world in peace by friendly argument had little chance of success. Yet, though or the time defeated, Cobden was not discouraged. Nor would he admit that his action had been inopportune, for, as he once said, he " never knew a good motion brought forward in a bad season." A week after the debate he wrote to his friend George Combe :

" The more I have reflected upon the subject the more I am satisfied that I am right at the right time. Next session I will repeat my proposition, and I will also bring the House to a decision upon another and kindred motion, for negotiating with foreign countries for stopping any further increase of armaments, and if possible for agreeing to a gradual disarmament. These motions go naturally together. They are called for by the spirit of the age and the necessities of the finances of the European States."

He did, in fact, move a resolution on the armament question on March 8 of the following year, but with even less success, for it was rejected by 272 votes to 59. Nevertheless, to the close of his parliamentary career questions of peace, like arbitration and disarmament, were " hardy annuals " which he never wearied in pressing upon the attention of the House in one way or another ; and all the time he continued his platform work on behalf of the same causes.

The year 1851, which was that of the Great Exhibition,

gave to the Peace Society an exceptional opportunity of reaching an international audience and it was not neglected. Cobden again tried to gain a sympathetic hearing in the House of Commons for a motion in favour of a reciprocal reduction of armaments (June 17), an agreement to be made first with France. Palmerston professed to be favourable, but preferred not to have his hands tied by a resolution, and the question did not go to a division. Reconciliation with France continued, however, to be one of Cobden's cherished ideas, and in a letter written in January of the following year we find him talking about an *entente cordiale*.

In his letter to Sumner cited above Cobden had spoken of the popularity of armies as belonging to the past. The daring statement, in its innocent exaggeration so much in his way, could only be justified by the fact that he was addressing a correspondent in a country which had never had a large standing army and had no present intention of having one. The succeeding year, in fact, was to bring a serious set-back to the peace movement. The occasion was the notorious Don Pacifico episode. The part played therein by the British Government was humiliating and unchivalrous, and for a long time it provided Cobden with material for pointed censure at the expense of his old adversary at the Foreign Office. Don Pacifico was a Portuguese Jew who lived in Athens, but as a native of Gibraltar he was a British subject. In 1847 his house had been attacked and rifled by a mob ; the outrage had its origin in religious prejudice against the Hebrew, but it was indefensible and Don Pacifico had a just claim to compensation. What he did was to ask for a total sum of £32,000, a sum vastly in excess of his losses, for it was found later that the value of nearly every item in the inventory had been fraudulently increased many times over. The Greek Government refused to pay the amount, whereupon the Jew, trading upon his nationality, invoked the help of the British Foreign Office. The exorbitant bill was presented again with a demand for payment within a fixed time, and as the Greek Government still failed to comply Lord Palmerston dispatched to the Piræus a fleet which promptly, in violation of international law, seized all the Greek vessels within hail and blockaded the Greek coast.

Invited by the weaker side to interpose, both France and Russia offered their good offices as mediators, on which the Foreign Secretary curtly told them that no outside interference was desired. Russia remonstrated with undiplomatic candour, lecturing Great Britain on the duty of strong States towards weak ones, and quoting against her sententious maxims of moral conduct uttered by British statesmen in the past.

Cobden's blood ran hot at the spectacle of a Goliath of a nation bullying a little David over so trivial a matter, and at an early stage of the dispute he strove with might and main to secure its submission to arbitration.

" It is just the case for arbitration," he wrote to Bright in April. " Here is a dispute about a few thousand pounds or of personal insult, matters which might be amicably adjusted by two or three impartial individuals of average intelligence and character, for the settlement of which a fleet of line-of-battle ships has been put in requisition, and the entire commerce of a friendly nation largely engaged in trade with our own people has been for months subjected to interruption. Apart from the outrage which such proceedings are calculated to inflict upon the feelings of humanity and justice, they must tend to bring diplomacy into disrepute."

French co-operation with the minister at Athens in the adjustment of the dispute was accepted, but just when an agreement came within sight misunderstandings arose between the two Governments which nearly led to a rupture with France, whose ambassador was recalled from London. In the end the Greek Government was ordered to pay Don Pacifico a mere fraction of his original inflated claim as a just and final settlement. When the episode was ended Cobden wrote bitterly : " I suppose the affair is finished, disgracefully, I think, to ourselves." In truth, all through, little that was creditable had been on the side of the British Government, which not for the first or the last time found its reputation compromised by indiscreet association with people of mongrel nationality.

There was an important sequel to the affair in the form of a set debate in the House of Commons. On the motion of Lord Stanley (later Lord Derby) the Upper House had censured the Government by a majority of 37. In the Lower

House on June 28 the same question was debated on a motion of an ambiguous character, which allowed members to vote as their convictions bade them. Palmerston's conduct, however, was warmly impugned by influential men belonging to different parties—Peel, Disraeli, Gladstone, and Cobden himself, the last-named making a comprehensive survey of the Foreign Secretary's interventions in all parts of Europe. The arraigned Minister defended himself vigorously and impenitently in the course of one of his most powerful parliamentary efforts, turning the temper of the House so entirely in his favour that a division gave him a majority of 46 votes (310 against 264). It was the clearest and most direct rebuff which Cobden's peace doctrines had received. Intervention and force were rehabilitated for the remainder of Palmerston's career.

The following day saw the death of Peel. It was to Cobden a heavy and almost irreparable blow, since he had hailed him with joy as a comrade-in-arms in his peace crusade. He wrote several days later : " I had observed his tendencies most attentively during the last few years, and had felt convinced that on questions in which I take a great interest— such as the reduction of armaments, retrenchment of expenditure, the diffusion of peace principles, etc.—he had strong sympathies—stronger than he had yet expressed—in favour of my views."—(July 5.) In August he again attended an international congress, this time at Frankfort. Only between 500 and 600 persons appear to have attended, and they were mostly from England. Nevertheless, he was " upon the whole very well satisfied with the meeting : we are gaining ground." During the greater part of that year and of the following one he was practically directing the operations of the Peace Society at home, in intimate and cordial collaboration with its secretary, Henry Richard.

It is unnecessary to follow in detail his further association with the Peace Society and peace propagandism. There were ebbs and flows, as in the case of every great public movement ; and owing to the troubled condition of Europe, the unsympathetic influences dominant in English political life under a still semi-oligarchic constitutional system, and the prevailing ignorance and immaturity of public opinion on all questions of international policy, jubilation one day was apt to be followed by depression on the morrow.

In 1852 Mr. Sturge, a Quaker friend, proposed to visit the Continent as a peace apostle, but Cobden dissuaded him, advising him rather to stay at home and try to convert his countrymen. " At this moment we are doing more than any other people to keep up the vast peace armaments of which we complain. Can you, in face of such facts, travel to the Continent to advocate a reduction of establishments ? "

Yet all the time there was progress, though it was never of the rushing, whirlwind kind which made the anti-Corn Law agitation a triumphal march to the fanfare of trumpets and drums. For not only was the cause radically different in character, motive, and appeal, but it was necessary to create in its service a new and different army of comrades. Never was the peace party to the same extent as the Free Trade party a homogeneous force. The demand of the earlier campaigners was for the unconditional repeal of harsh and grinding taxes ; there was no question of compromise, of any distinction between much or little protection : the one aim and object was the clean sweep of a hoary and oppressive privilege. While no doubt other motives inspired isolated leaders of the anti-Corn Law movement, the attitude of the great mass of its adherents, whether working-men or manufacturers, was determined by a justifiable egoism—the hope of immediate material advantage.

Behind the peace movement, however, there was no momentum having its source in a consciousness of worldly interest ; its appeal, in the main, was moral rather than material, universal rather than individual, and for that reason it presupposed both a higher order of intelligence and a more advanced civic spirit and conscience. Cobden early saw that he could not count on the co-operation of the old Leaguers in his new crusade, and that to expect it was " about as rational as to argue that the tree which has yielded a good crop of oranges must be able to give you some apples also." It was a further source of deep disappointment to him, though hardly one of surprise, that Manchester, his political birthplace, which had so nobly championed the cause of Free Trade, responded but coolly to the call for a new departure in foreign policy.

" Manchester," he wrote at a later date (November 30, 1856), " has never been more than a ghost of its former self in the agitations that have been attempted there since the League shut up shop. . . . It is perhaps contrary to human nature to expect that the same community which has won one great triumph should be the first to re-enter the political arena for other victories. People naturally feel a wish to enjoy what they have been for seven years fighting to obtain. Besides, the truth must be told that people in Lancashire are growing conservative and aristocratic with their prosperous trade."

He suspected that the fallen mantle would best fit Birmingham, a rising centre of progressive influence which he trusted would remain immune from the virus of " aristocratic snobbery," owing to the fact that its industry and wealth were still in the hands of a large class of small manufacturers, in contrast to Manchester with its great centralized staple industry. In the event London continued to be the base of the Peace Society's operations, while for recruits Cobden came more and more to look to the " common people." " After all, our business," he wrote (January 25, 1853), " must be with the masses—keep them right and we can't go wrong."

But there were also difficulties in the temperament and preconceptions of some of his more energetic associates. His co-operation in the work of the Peace Society threw him into a heterogeneous company, not all of whose members were congenial to him. Together with a stalwart and devoted band of thoroughly level-headed men, who clearly understood what was and what was not practical politics, and sought their end only by rational and temperate methods, there was the usual sprinkling of extremists, hot-heads, and cranks, those good, futile people who have compromised and impeded so many useful movements, and always will do the like. If lacking in prudence, however, all were in deadly earnest, and Cobden was too big-minded to refuse to work with other men in a common cause simply because their ideas and ways were not in all respects like his own ; though differences on questions of tactics and policy meant loss of energy and wasted opportunities.

One of his greatest difficulties on the score of incompatibility was with the Quakers of the orthodox school, who persisted in riding hard their traditional doctrine of non-resistance.

He respected their scruples, but rejected their doctrine, and the division between them was at times acute. For the Quakers formed the backbone of the Peace Society, and they naturally strove to keep its work on lines consistent with their historical attitude towards war and all invasions of individual liberty. Cobden made the generous admission on one occasion. " The soul of the peace movement is the Quaker sentiment against war. Without the stubborn zeal of the Friends there would be no Peace Society and no Peace Conference " (September 19, 1853). Nevertheless, more than once he differed fundamentally from them, as on the Hungarian question in 1851, when we find him writing to Mr. Richard (November 9) :

" I have always endeavoured to avoid being brought into collision with the Friends' principle, and I had thought they were similarly minded towards those who were, like myself, labouring to give practical effect, as far as they could, to their doctrines. But I doubt whether it will not be necessary for the two societies [the Peace Society and the Peace Congress Committee, the latter an international organization] to make a more clear avowal than they have hitherto done of their principles. If the agitation is to be based entirely on the non-resistance principle it will cease to occupy its present position in the domain of practical politics."

It may surprise many people to-day that Cobden, though so prescient, daring, and responsive to new influences and outlooks, never accepted the idea of a permanent international tribunal of peace answering to the League of Nations. Did he not see so far, or did he see farther ? The extract already quoted from his parliamentary speech of 1849 shows that the idea was known to him, and that he had given thought to it ; indeed, he used part of the now familiar terminology. Writing to his friend Combe just before the speech, he said explicitly, " My plan does not embrace the scheme of a congress of nations or imply belief in the millennium "—perhaps a significant conjunction of ideas. In his fifth pamphlet, published in 1856, he again alluded to the subject :

" For a century and a half," he there wrote, " we have been fighting with occasional intermissions for the balance of power, but I do not remember that it has ever been made the subject of peaceful diplomacy, with a view to the organization of the whole of Europe. Now if such a pact or federation of the States of Europe as is implied by the phrases balance of power or International Law should ever be framed, it must be a work of peace and not of war."

This was as far as Cobden went in the advocacy of a political union of States, and the context plainly shows that he had in mind what would be called to-day a Pact of Security or of Mutual Assistance. He made no suggestion of a permanent Council of States nor yet of a formal international tribunal of justice, to be charged with the duty of settling disputes, but continued to advocate the simplest possible method of arbitration—a body of *ad hoc* arbitrators chosen by the disputing Governments in every individual case—and eschewed the idea of a permanent piece of international mechanism.

Remembering his strong antagonism to intervention, as the source of so many wars and so much mischief to his own country, it is easy to understand this attitude. He was clearly prepared to tolerate further the evil of occasional, and as he held illegitimate, interference by one State in the affairs of another rather than see Europe place herself under a system of legalized interference on possibly an indefinite scale—a cure for war which, on his argument, would have been like trying to cast out devils by the prince of devils. No outside tampering with the rights of sovereignty, though the heavens should fall! That was his contention to the last, and because he held it so staunchly he preferred arbitration by ordinary unornamental citizens rather than by Sovereigns or States.

The adoption of a League of Nations with a Covenant postulating, theoretically, an unlimited right of intervention was perhaps the last thing in the world which he would have thought of as a means of promoting international peace. Herein he may have been right or wrong, but at least from his own standpoint in that day he was consistent. Nevertheless, a letter written to Mr. Richard shows that he advanced later so far as to favour the informal and passive ostracism of Governments which, like those of Austria and Russia at that time, tyrannized over their subjects.

K

" Now here is a programme of foreign policy," he wrote : " will our Liberal politicians, our Radicals and democrats, as they profess themselves, join us in this policy ? If it can be carried out, depend on it we shall do more than by any intermeddling to bring the Austrian Government upon a proper footing of dependence upon its people. . . . Now we recommend a course, a principle of action, which will tend to leave their Government more at the mercy of the people they are oppressing. We would keep aloof from the blood-stained oppressors at Vienna. We would have no compliments passing, no secret diplomacy, no dependence in any way on that central authority ; we would cultivate friendly intercourse and trading relations as far as possible with the people throughout all the Austrian Empire, and we would be on a courteous footing diplomatically with the Government."

Beyond that he was unwilling to go in bringing external pressure to bear even upon Governments which had forfeited the confidence of their neighbours. His opposition to direct intervention and coercive measures of any kind in international relations never weakened.

Many as were the discouragements which had to be encountered, Cobden's confidence in the ultimate triumph of the peace movement never wavered. While still on the threshold of this second crusade he ended a public speech on the subject with a passage to the point which perhaps came as near to the proscribed peroration as any other.

" I will say once for all," he said, " that I am not dreaming of the millennium. I believe that long after my time iron will be used to make the spear as well as the pruning-hook and the ploughshare. I do not think the coming year is to produce any sudden change in the existing practice or that the millennium will be absolutely realized in my time ; but I think, if the principles of the Peace Society are true, we are engaged in a work in which conscience and, I believe, Heaven itself will find cause for approbation."

Not always had his faith the wide vision of the mountain-top, and towards the end of his life, at a time when still another French scare had led to a demand for larger armaments, he confessed to Bright :

" Perhaps we were wrong in aiming at producing too large results within a given time. I do not, as I grow older, lose my faith in humanity and its future destinies, but I do every year—perhaps it is natural with increasing years—feel less sanguine in my hope of seeing any material change in my own day and generation."

Yet in the meantime new recruits were coming forward on every hand, and therein lay assurance for the future. Peel had more and more adopted his peace standpoint, and Gladstone was following in his train. The time even came, though Cobden did not live to see it, when Earl (Lord John) Russell, who had often been a man of war in his early days, preached with a convert's fervency the duty of universal trust and good will amongst nations, and urged that Governments should pursue such peaceable and benevolent policies as would " forge a chain of love which shall unite all the races of mankind."

Since Cobden's day the arbitration movement has made slow but steady progress, more in this country and America than in most other parts of the world. It fell to Cobden's friend, Mr. Richard, to carry in the House of Commons for the first time in 1880 the resolution affirming approval of this method of settling international disputes for which he himself failed to win its acceptance. Since that time Great Britain has done much of the preliminary spade work which has brought the question to its present hopeful position. During the nineteenth and the early years of the twentieth century —that is, before the institution of the League of Nations— she was a party to fifty arbitrations of various kinds with other countries out of a total of about two hundred known to have occurred. Further important advance was made when in 1899 the Peace Conference held at the Hague, on the invitation of the Emperor of Russia, agreed to create a permanent tribunal for the optional adjustment of differences between States. A second conference, held in 1907, improved and extended the machinery of arbitration in the light of the experience gained. Largely owing to the stimulus thus given to the question, many arbitration treaties have been concluded during late years between European countries and between these countries and States of the American Continents, and in this movement Great Britain has taken a foremost part.

What this country has not yet done, and still hesitates to do, is to accept arbitration in all cases—in other words, to rule war out of court altogether, instead of reserving the right to resort to it when disposed. At the present time progress in this direction is checked by British obstruction more than by any other cause. Not only did the British delegate at the 1925 assembly of the League of Nations, acting on his instructions, hold back the many countries which were eager to make arbitration the universal rule, but our Government has since refused to submit certain classes of disputes, mostly of a judiciable character, to the competence of the International Court of Justice which the League has been instrumental in establishing, so checkmating the Governments which make no such reservation. In adopting this course we are adhering to a long-standing if little-appreciated British tradition, and are as usual taking it for granted that merely to plead precedent is sufficient justification for our attitude. So long, however, as every country claims the right to maintain its own traditions it is obvious that the arbitration movement will never achieve its great object, which is not merely to minimize the risk and reduce the frequency of war, but to supersede it altogether. Remembering its relatively creditable past record on this question, it would be lamentable if, now that the victory of the arbitral method of settling disputes is in sight, the impression were to be created abroad that this country is bent on fouling the course just at the winning-post.

While arbitration complete and unqualified would alone have satisfied Cobden to-day, there can be little doubt as to what would have been his attitude to the League of Nations. He would no longer have opposed such an institution in principle, but the only League which would have had his full sympathy would have been one in which all States, strong or weak, would meet on equal terms and with equal rights under the shadow of an impartial and wide-embracing law, and which could be counted on to mete strict and even-handed justice to all its members alike. To that end he would have contended that in constitution it should be a true union of peoples, directly chosen by the free Parliaments of the world, and not a magnified conference of ambassadors, and probably he would have kept the entire hierarchy of diplomacy out of it. Above all, he would have resolutely insisted that the elevated principles of the League's Covenant should have formed the basis of the treaties of peace, instead of being adopted as an ingenious device, at least in the veiled intention of some of the League's leading members, for guaran-

teeing the stability of the territorial settlements and so securing
to the victors the continued possession of the spoils of war.

One can picture the cold, hard disdain with which this
hater of insincerity and sophistry would have turned from
the lofty sentiments of the Covenant's preamble, with its
talk of " just and honourable relations between nations," the
acceptance of " the understandings of international law as
the actual rule of conduct among Governments," and " the
maintenance of justice and a scrupulous respect for all treaty
obligations," to the Treaties of Versailles, St. Germain, Neuilly,
and the rest. Merely to paraphrase some of his speeches
on peace and war is to suggest the verdict which would have
followed.

" Let us clearly understand each other," he would have said to the
authors of these documents.   " Let us bring to this matter our ' homely
common sense.' What you mean to say by the Covenant is really
this, that from to-day you agree to be honest, and not again to covet
your neighbours' vineyards ; but you insist on retaining all the ill-gotten
gains of countless yesterdays.

" You representatives of Great Britain propose to apply a Statute
of Limitations to your seizures of territory from Holland, Spain,
France, Denmark, and the Dutch republics of South Africa, the last
going back only twenty years.[1] But why do you refuse to apply the
same principle to the Polish territories which have been part of Russia,
Prussia, and Austria for a century and a half ? Why do you break the
treaty by which fifty years ago France swore to give back to Germany
' for ever ' the Rhenish lands which were once taken from her by force,
and which she had never renounced ? Above all, why herald your good
resolutions by annexing the territory of your late enemies in all parts
of Asia and Africa ? Must not that inconsistency throw doubt upon
your profession of a change of heart and your intention to be virtuous
henceforth ? If you are entitled to retain your own prizes of war,
by what right do you impose these wholesale renunciations upon other
nations ? Either all the annexations should be returned or none.

" You speak of your ' scrupulous respect for treaties,' but the
treaties which you have in mind are the new treaties of expropriation
and subjection. What about those past territorial treaties, not forced
on disarmed and helpless nations, as these are, but concluded by the
free action of independent Governments, and bearing your own signa-

---

[1] It should be needless to say that the suggestion that these territories, or
any part of them, could now be returned is not intended even by implication.
Without some large condonement of the past the world would never have
hope of tranquillity.   But it is good for all of us to look at facts honestly,
and as other nations see them.

tures, which you are now treating as ' scraps of paper ' ? Your Covenant, with all its moral unction, condones the wrong done by yourselves in the past, and invites the world to sanction and uphold the injustices of the same kind done again by your treaties of peace.

" ' I come now to the logical deduction from all this—that we find that not only do not your late enemies recognize your authority as a judge, but that the rest of the world does not acknowledge it.' " [1]

That, with no exaggeration of phrase, is how Cobden would have judged the League and Covenant in relation to the treaties which they are intended to maintain—as noble achievements put to ignoble purposes ; and to that view the world has come more and more since 1919.

[1] Cf. Cobden's speeches in the House of Commons on the Crimean War, December 22, 1854, and June 5, 1855, and at Manchester, March 18, 1857.

CHAPTER VII

THE BURDEN OF ARMAMENTS

" Our influence, if it is to be maintained abroad, must be secure in its sources of strength at home; and the sources of that strength are in the sympathy between the people and the Government, in the union of the public sentiment with the public counsels, in the reciprocal confidence and co-operation of the House of Commons and the Crown."—Letter of CANNING, September 16, 1823.

" I find that the protection of which States stand in need is the application of moral remedies chiefly."—BARON STOCKMAR, January 27, 1850.

JUST as Cobden advocated international arbitration as a present check upon war and, as he hoped, a future permanent substitute for it, so he worked for the limitation of armaments by international agreements as a means of correcting the war spirit and removing out of the way of pugnacious Governments and Foreign Ministers the constant temptation to weight their arguments by appeals to force. This question he began to agitate publicly in 1848, when addressing a meeting in Manchester (January 27) apropos of an appeal which had just before been made by the Duke of Wellington for a large addition to the military strength of the nation as a measure of security against France, and from that time forward it occupied a prominent place in his peace crusade.

Jeremy Bentham had written " Whatever nation should get the start of the others in making the proposal to reduce and fix the amount of its armed force would crown itself with everlasting honour." Cobden coveted for his country the still " vacant niche in the Temple of Fame " open for the ruler or minister who should be " the first to grapple with this monster evil of the day." It had been said from old times that the best way of maintaining peace was to prepare for war. In spite of its classical ancestry, he rejected as an imposture this hoary sinner of a political maxim, which has led mankind a dance of death for centuries. Here he was in good company, for Sir Robert Peel had repudiated it before him. When, on taking office in succession to Lord Melbourne in 1841, Peel explained to the House of Commons the broad lines of policy which he intended to follow, he gave prominence to the question of excessive armaments as one of the greatest urgency.

" Is not the time come," he asked, " when the powerful countries of Europe should reduce those military armaments which they have so sedulously raised ? Is not the time come when they should be prepared to declare that there is no use in such overgrown establishments ? What is the advantage of one Power greatly increasing its army or navy ? Does it not see that if it proposes such increase for self-protection and defence the other Powers would follow its example ? The consequence is that the end of this state of things must be that no increase of relative strength will accrue to any one Power, but there must be a universal consumption of the resources of every country in military preparations. They are, in fact, depriving peace of half its advantages and anticipating the energies of war whenever that may be required."

He added the warning : " The danger of aggression is infinitely less than the danger of those sufferings to which the present exorbitant expenditure must give rise." An utterance like that, coming from a man of Peel's great moral influence, gave Cobden a helpful start on his disarmament crusade, and he often recalled it in writings and speeches. Yet the question had made little or no progress when Cobden became its champion. Powerful influences, political, social, and professional, were behind the ever-swelling army and navy votes, and in the background he still saw the aristocratic class, jealous for the security of its great possessions and its vested interest in all the best public offices. Upon the concentrated hostility of this class he knew from the first that he must count, for it feared him, and fear has torment. His old antagonists still writhed under the remembrance of the defeat which they had sustained in the struggle for cheap bread. What if the Manchester manufacturer should repeat his success in the attack upon the " fighting services ? " The money power represented in so many seen and unseen ways by the military system was thus the lion in the way. " The peace party in England," he once said, " raise £3,000 a year to maintain a contest against a system which is subsidized every year by the State to the amount of 15 or 16 millions sterling. There must be great pluck in the men who dare enter the lists in such an unequal contest."

The first important speech which he devoted exclusively to this question was made before a mass meeting held at Manchester on January 10, 1849. In that year Lord Aberdeen, too, formally gave his support to the cause, declaring that the very possession of large and powerful armaments was a danger to peace, since it made nations eager to test their efficiency. Just before Cobden spoke a well-known parliamentary colleague had warned the House of Commons that the longer the country remained at peace the greater would be the likelihood of eventual war—a warning held to be justified by the law of probabilities as disclosed by the sequence of wars in the past. Lord Palmerston had challenged this view, contending that the long duration of peace made its continuance more rather than less probable, since it would tend to dispose countries to settle their differences otherwise than by appeal to arms. For once Cobden found himself in agreement with Palmerston, whose doctrine admirably suited his book. From the Foreign Secretary's proposition, however, he drew the conclusion that the gain of a prolonged period of peace would be diminished, and the prospect of its permanence be menaced, unless the opportunity which it afforded for curtailing armaments were courageously used.

Citing figures to show the inordinate growth of both army and navy during the preceding decade, in spite of the fact that the time had been for England one of peace, he complained that Governments were ready enough to demand increased armaments on the slightest pretext, but they never thought of diminishing them when the danger, real or imaginary, had passed away. He justified the demand for retrenchment by the fact that the menace from France which lately had been assiduously preached by the military party had proved to be a manufactured scare. Louis Philippe, " the Napoleon of Peace," had been dethroned, but the French nation had settled down under a republican President. In Germany thrones had been shaken, and Italy had also shared in the convulsions of the time ; yet in neither of these countries did a warlike spirit exist. " Where in all Europe," he asked, " has there been among the mass of the people one sign or symptom of a desire for aggressive war on their neighbours ? "

The conclusion he drew was that in the absence of danger from abroad it was the duty of the Government to economize on armaments :

" You must be content with a smaller manifestation of brute force in the world. You must trust something to Providence—something to your own just intentions and your good conduct to other nations ; and you must rely less upon that costly, that wasteful expenditure arising from so enormous a display of brute force."

At the same time he took care to say a word in season for the doctrine of non-intervention, warning his hearers that there could never be a serious reduction of armaments, or any real approach to international fraternity, without a radical change of public opinion in relation to foreign policy, and the abandonment by the nation of the idea that it was the business of its Governments to regulate the affairs of the whole world. Accordingly he urged his countrymen to be contented to occupy a more modest place in the scheme of the universe, and to give other nations credit for the honesty which they claimed for themselves.

A year later he succeeded in gaining for the cause of disarmament the distinction of a formal parliamentary debate (March 8, 1850), when he brought forward a motion to reduce national expenditure " with all practicable speed to an amount not exceeding the sum which within the last fifteen years has been proved to be sufficient for the maintenance of the security, honour, and dignity of the nation." At that time the national budget stood at nearly 50 millions, of which amount $15\frac{1}{2}$ millions covered the cost of the army, navy, and ordnance, while 28 millions more were for the service of the national debt, " that debt of nearly 800 million pounds having been almost every farthing contracted in former wars." He held the reduction proposed to be both possible and safe in view of the settled political outlook at home and abroad, though he anticipated some further relief owing to the intention, recently avowed by the Prime Minister (Lord John Russell), to give self-government to the larger Colonies.

At the close of his speech he avowed the conviction that England would have no need to fear menace from without so long as her attitude towards other nations was pacific and friendly.

" Is there not less danger," he asked, " in trusting to our good intentions and to Divine Providence instead of ten million pounds being expended on our armaments ?   Is it not better to trust to those elements of security, and have it in our power to relax taxation and give contentment to the people in the way which I have put before the House."

Among the supporters of the motion was Milner Gibson, while Russell opposed it on behalf of the Government. An unconventional orator who proposed economy on the defence estimates and was prepared to base England's security upon Providence had little chance as yet of a sympathetic hearing, and the motion was rejected by the large majority of 183—272 to 89. It was a gain, however, that Peel, in speaking several days later on the pressure of taxation, came out still more strongly on the side of peace and this method of promoting it.

" In time of peace," he said on March 12, " you must, if you mean to retrench in good earnest, incur some risks.   If in time of peace . . . you adopt the opinions of military men, naturally anxious to throw upon you the whole responsibility for the loss, in the event of war suddenly breaking out, of some of our valuable possessions, you would overwhelm this country with taxes in time of peace.   The Government ought to feel assured that the House of Commons would support them if they incurred some responsibility with respect to our distant colonial possessions by running a risk for the purpose of effecting a saving. *Bellum para, si pacem velis*, is a maxim regarded by many as containing an incontestable truth.   It is one, in my opinion, to be received with great caution and admitting of much qualification."

The following year was that of the Great Exhibition, and international fraternity and the solidarity of the working classes were the watchwords of the day. Three years before the historical Communist Manifesto of Karl Marx and Friedrich Engels, issued from Paris, had bidden the proletaires of all nations unite. They were uniting, and London was now at once the refuge, the workshop, and the power station of not a few Continental organizers, chiefly German, French, and Russian. There was a certainty of a large foregathering of races and nationalities in England. The Exhibition had, indeed, been trumpeted as a great gesture in favour of universal peace and amity. Ever ready to take occasion by the hand, Cobden judged the event opportune for another attempt to obtain a reduction of armaments, and he introduced in the House of Commons (June 17) a motion calling on the Government to open negotiations with France with a view to reciprocal action in that sense. " All I stipulate for," he said, in the course of a very conciliatory speech, " is that diplomacy should put itself a little more in harmony with the spirit of the times, and should do that work which the public thinks ought to be the occupation of diplomacy."

Lord Palmerston gave platonic support to the idea, but declined to institute immediate action on the lines proposed, pleading as his reason that the peace spirit did not as yet go deep enough. What he was prepared to do was, so to speak, to accept from the House a watching brief on the subject. The motion did not go to a division, though had it done it is unlikely that the vote of a year before would have been reversed. This time Palmerston and not Cobden was in the right, for at the end of the year peaceful republican France gave Europe another evidence of political instability, and threw England again into alarm, by welcoming the *coup d'état* of her ambitious President, Louis Napoleon, soon to revive the Empire of his more famous uncle.

Though rebuffed, Cobden continued to press the expediency and need of a reduction of armaments, preferably by Great Britain and France reciprocally, in virtue of a formal convention, or, if that were impossible, by this country alone. He had, nevertheless, convinced himself by this time that much uphill fighting would have to be done before the strongholds of fear, prejudice, and interest which impeded progress would be reduced. His suspicion of the aristocratic class as the main obstacle to his peace programme appears to have been for the time allayed as he saw how the nation at large continued, with insuperable stolidity, to ignore its vital interests. Writing to Mr. Sturge on March 11, 1852, in criticism of the Militia Bill which was introduced at that time, under the influence of renewed anxiety as to the intentions of France, and which, owing to an amendment carried by Lord Palmerston, had led to Russell's resignation and the formation of the Earl of Derby's first administration, he said, " I am more and more convinced that we have much to do with the public before we can with any sense or usefulness quarrel with this or that aristocratic party." Later in that year he even confessed his belief that " if the European Governments were to meet together for the purpose of promoting a reduction of armaments there is not one which would enter upon the movement with less earnestness or sincerity than our own."

For a full decade after this all hope of the success of any measure of disarmament, however partial, was dispelled by wars and rumours of wars. First came the Russo-Turkish War of 1853-6, in which Great Britain and France, burying for a time the hatchet of ancient feuds, fought together against Russia, nominally on behalf of the Christian races under Turkish rule, but actually for the maintenance of the full integrity and independence of the Ottoman Empire ; and in 1859 there followed the Italian war, in which France aided Piedmont in its successful struggle with Austria, leading to the latter's cession of Lombardy and to the annexation by France of Nice and Savoy—" two days' pay for half a day's work," as the historian Freeman put it, and a transaction which finally shattered British faith in Louis Napoleon and turned Palmerston's long waning distrust of him into active hostility. In the Far East, too, Great Britain had embarked in a series of wars against China, beginning in 1857 and lasting until 1860.

Nevertheless, Cobden, with the divine hope of the passionate enthusiast, never despaired of bringing together two neighbouring countries which had quarrelled and warred with each other for centuries, and knew by dolorous experience that no good had ever come of it. While resting in Algiers in January 1861, after the arduous work of negotiating the Commercial Treaty with France, he returned to the fray, and in a letter to Mr. Samuel Morley discussed the conclusion of a convention with that country for the mutual reduction of naval armaments. He held that such an agreement would be just as acceptable to France as it would be beneficial to England, and would tend to bring the political attitude of the French Government into greater harmony with its new commercial policy. His idea was that a memorial with this end in view should be addressed to the Queen by a body of City of London bankers, merchants, and others; the Peace Society and the spokesmen of the "Manchester school" being kept out of the affair. He had in mind, by way of analogy, an address to the French Emperor which had been signed by the City some years before.

The time for such an agreement seemed to him the more opportune since a momentous departure in shipbuilding was impending. Wooden line-of-battle ships had been doomed, and there was a general belief that no more would be built; while at the same time the great cost of their replacement by iron and steel vessels remained to be faced. Moreover, it was certain that many ships of the new type would only be built in order to be immediately discarded in favour of others better in material and design. If, therefore, shipbuilding were checked by an agreement not to replace obsolete vessels as they passed out of service, an enormous economy would be effected by automatic process.

"Now then," wrote the indomitable optimist to Mr. Richard (April 17, 1861), "is the time for common sense to interfere. Let England and France only set a limit to their iron-cased ships; the rest of our gigantic waste will disappear in time." He was confident that America, Russia, and the other maritime Powers would fall into line as a matter of course. So strongly did he feel on this question that he addressed a memorandum to the Prime Minister setting forth his views in detail. But once more he overrated the wish of his own and other Governments for peace. Even his argument that, greatly though the rival armaments had been increased, their relative strength had tended to remain the same, and that this would be the case in future, had no effect.

While he was still abroad the disarmament question was raised indirectly in the House of Commons. A fresh shipbuilding programme—the building of new iron for old wooden vessels which Cobden had wished to prevent—was brought forward, and Disraeli, taking the side of the angels, gave his support to the proposal that the British and French Governments should agree upon some limitation of their insensate naval rivalry. "What is the use of diplomacy?" he asked.

"What is the use of Governments? What is the use of cordial understandings if such things can take place?" A year later (May 8, 1862) Disraeli formally appealed to Palmerston to "put an end to these bloated armaments which only involve States in financial embarrassment." The phrase "bloated armaments" captured the nation's imagination at once, though it left its reason still unconvinced.

Recognizing that speeches were in vain, Cobden now determined to try another method of educating public opinion. Later in the same year he wrote to Mr. Richard (August 17) :

"I had an idea of writing a pamphlet giving a running history of the Anglo-French armaments, with extracts from speeches since 1844, when the game of beggar-my-neighbour began. But I don't know whether I shall have the courage to do it. I get discouraged as to the effect of reason and argument and facts in deciding the policy of the country. We are a very illogical people, with brute combativeness which is always ready for a quarrel and which can be excited at the will of a governing class that has subsisted for centuries upon this failing in John Bull's character. Is it not vain to expect any honest attempt to put a limit to our expenditure so long as Palmerston rules and Gladstone,[1] whilst protesting against the waste, lends his eloquent genius to its perpetuation ? "

The idea took shape in his mind, and on his return to England he at once buried himself in Hansard, Blue-books, and Parliamentary Papers, with the result that the last of his pamphlets, *The Three Panics : an Historical Episode*, appeared in 1862. Six editions were published, besides a French translation, edited by M. Chevalier, the economist. It contained a searching examination of the alleged justifications—which he scornfully denied—for the invasion panics of 1847–8, 1851–3, and 1859–61, which embittered English feeling against France in so high a degree, and, as a necessary part of his argument, of the relative expenditure of the two countries on armaments during the period covered by his survey. What made this naval rivalry doubly insensate was the fact that the fear of invasion fomented by politicians and half-pay officers of both services at home excited French public opinion in an equal degree. People had become so anxious and unsettled by the

[1] Chancellor of the Exchequer in Palmerston's second Administration of June 1859, as he was in Russell's second and succeeding Administration of November 1865.

perpetual warnings of impending attack that they had begun to say : " Let us fight it out at once, and have done with alarms for at least a generation ! " Apart from the immediate purpose of the pamphlet, the essay is full of *dicta* of sound common sense on international relations and foreign policy, and may be read to-day with no less advantage than when it was written.

Throughout his advocacy of this question he was careful to show how closely it bore on the question of foreign policy. " What has been my argument for the last seven years on this question ? " he asked a Manchester audience in 1857. " You cannot have a reduction of taxation unless you have a reduction of your military and naval establishments ; and you cannot have a reduction of your military and naval establishments if you allow a Minister to be constantly involving you in wars or in danger of wars." Let the people take matters more into their own hands and see that their interests were better looked after ! After all, the question of disarmament was one for civilians, and not soldiers, to decide :

> " When we are at war, then the men with red clothes and swords by their sides may step in to do their work. But we are now at peace, and we wish to reap the fruits of peace, and in order to do so we must calculate for ourselves the contingency of a possible war. That is a civilians' question—that is a question for the decision of the taxpayers who have to pay the cost of war. It is a question for the merchants ; it is a question for the manufacturers, for the shopkeepers, for the operatives, for the farmers of this country—ay, and it is a question for the calico-printer."

Incidentally he administered a rebuke to the people who called most boisterously for large armaments and were most boisterous in resenting the idea that they should pay for them. " I do not sympathize with those who advocate armaments and then grumble at the cost. For my part I would make the influential classes pay the money, and then they will be more careful in the expenditure."

While, however, strenuously contending for smaller armaments and economy on defensive expenditure in every direction, he never even hinted at entire disarmament, but, on the contrary, repudiated the idea as absurd. Speaking both for himself and for the " Manchester school " of politicians, he said on one occasion :

" Now, what is it, after all, that the so much abused ' Manchester school' wants ? Why, they say we want to abolish all our standing armies and navies, and leave you, like so many Quakers, at the mercy of the whole world. Any man who has lived in public life, as I have, must know that it is quite useless to contradict any falsehood and calumny, because it comes up again next day just as rife as ever. Here is my programme : ' Non-intervention '; here is my programme : ' Diminished expenditure on your armaments, and diminished taxation if you follow that policy.' "

Doubtful though he was whether " constitutional freedom could coexist with large standing armies," he favoured " the maintenance of a small disciplined force to serve as a nucleus around which the nation might rally to defend the country in the event of war," but in writing to this effect to a military correspondent in 1855 he took care to add : " There is hardly a case to be imagined or assumed in which I would consent to send out a body of land forces to fight the battles of the Continent." To another correspondent he wrote in 1859 : " I have no prejudice against a voluntary armed force like the riflemen of Switzerland or the militia of America."

Nor was he prepared to see the navy reduced beyond strictly safe and prudent limits. As France was at that time Great Britain's only possible menace at sea he advocated the regulation of our naval power accordingly. In a speech at Rochdale in 1861 he said :

" I am not one to advocate the reducing of our navy in any degree below that proportion to the French navy which the exigencies of our service require. . . . Besides, this country is an island ; we cannot communicate with any part of the world except by sea. France, on the other hand, has a frontier upon land, by which she can communicate with the whole world. We have, I think, unfortunately for ourselves, about a hundred times the amount of territory beyond the seas to protect, as colonies and dependencies, that France has. France has also twice or three times as large an army as England has. All these things give us a right to have a navy somewhat in the proportion of the French navy which we find to have existed if we look back over the past century. Nobody has disputed it. I would be the last person who would ever advocate any undue change in this proportion."
—(June 26, 1861.)

L

It is certain that Cobden never suspected that the time would come when France, with an army larger than nearly all the other Continental armies put together (that of Russia excluded), would also have at command an air force which practically placed the British shores of the Channel at her mercy. What he might have done in these circumstances, in the absence of a reciprocal disarmament agreement, may perhaps be surmised from the following passage, which may be commended to those of his critics who, knowing nothing about him, still persist in regarding him as more eager for economy than for his country's security. It occurs in his pamphlet *The Three Panics*. There he wrote that if the ruler of France, with her much smaller mercantile marine and colonial empire, and her access by land to the entire Continent and thereby to the rest of the world, " attempted to equal if not surpass us in naval armaments," he would regard it as " a reasonable conclusion . . . that he had some sinister purpose in view or that he was a rash and unreflecting and therefore a dangerous neighbour. If, after the offer of frank explanations on our part, with a view to avert so irrational a waste, that ruler persisted in his extraordinary preparations, there is no amount of expenditure which this country would not bear to maintain our due superiority at sea."

Cobden's attitude towards another aspect of the armament question, of minor importance in his day, though later it took dangerous forms, may surprise those who do not bear in mind the logical unity of all his political thought. This was his consistent opposition to the manufacture of armaments of war in Government factories. In the last speech which he made in the House of Commons (July 22, 1864), he recommended the immediate transfer of all such work to contractors, though he was willing to allow the Government to advance money for the equipment of private factories where that seemed needful. It was the staunch individualist and opponent of State interference in trade and industry who here spoke. Few people, however, can have foreseen in his day how powerful a factor in influencing the attitude of Governments on the issues of peace and war the armament industry was destined to become, or have anticipated the time when great armament companies would station in every important capital in the world trade ambassadors ever on the look-out for commissions and ready not only to wait for their money but to provide credit for impecunious Governments to spend in other directions.

At the same time he was able to establish an overwhelmingly strong case against State enterprise and bureaucratic incompetency at that time when he compared the cost of goods produced in Government workshops with that paid for goods bought by contract. For he contended, and proved by actual instances, that the Government was able neither to buy goods cheaply nor to produce them economically, a reproach which has not lost point even in the present day. He also exposed the ludicrous notions of business current in public Departments which, in order to persuade the nation that their enterprises were well run, systematically falsified their balance-sheets and never dreamed of charging to the debit side of a trading account such items as interest on capital, rent of land, depreciation of plant, rates, taxes, insurance, and the like.

Some of his scathing judgments on this subject are still opportune. He had served on Committees of Account and Enquiry and he knew what he was talking about when he said : " I find that you can never make the conductors of these Government establishments understand that the capital they have to deal with is really money. How should it be real money to them ? It costs them nothing, and whether they make a profit or a loss they never find their way into the *Gazette*. Therefore to them it is a myth—it is a reality only to the taxpayers." To all which a modern Government Department might be disposed to reply by asking, Where would be the individuality and the *raison d'être* of a bureaucratic hierarchy if its members were expected to act like ordinary mortals ?

It might appear that, in spite of all his efforts, Cobden left the disarmament question not little different than he found it. In season and out of season he preached the prosaic, unsentimental, but eternally needed, though eternally disregarded, truism that there could be no reduction of taxation without a reduction of expenditure, and that a reduction of expenditure must begin where expenditure was highest, and at the same time least remunerative and least necessary, and that was in the excessive accumulation of armaments in time of peace. Twice in the early months of 1870, indeed, Lord Clarendon tried his hand at the disarmament question and approached Bismarck on the subject ; but his idea was not that Great Britain should reduce her navy but that Prussia and France should reduce their armies. Bismarck courteously rejected the one-sided proposal, but he told the British Ambassador that it was " the act of a cool friend," which indeed it was.

Upon this as upon most other questions near to his sympathies, however, Cobden indulged in over-confidence. " What do other men propose—those most opposed to the Peace Society ? Do they say that the system which we are opposing will last for ever ? Why, every man admits that it will not last five years." That was said in 1850, yet the five years became seventy before the Governments of the Great Powers took seriously to heart Peel's counsel and appeal of 1841, and action then came too late to prevent the greatest catastrophe of history. By the naval disarmament conference of 1920, however, one of Cobden's earliest political predictions was fulfilled, for it fell to America to show Europe a way out of the toils in which she had entangled herself.

CHAPTER VIII

INTERNATIONAL SEA LAW

" Peace cannot be had without concession and sacrifice. The statesmen of the world must plan for peace, and nations must adjust and accommodate their policy to it as they have planned for war and made ready for pitiless contest and rivalry."—PRESIDENT WILSON, speech in the United States Senate, January 22, 1917.

" A nation . . . cannot risk to place itself outside the pale of the opinions of mankind, because a nation never dies, and the conscience of mankind never dies, and when the orgies of successful force have spent their strength the day comes when it has to live not with its own recollections, but with those which mankind have preserved of it."—SIR ROBERT MORIER, Letter of May 1875.

A QUESTION, closely bearing upon harmonious international relations and the conditions of world peace, which Cobden took up at a later stage of his public life was the reform of the international law in relation to maritime usages in time of war. It was a question upon which he felt very strongly and was able to speak in the double capacity of a man of commerce and a politician. He dealt with it in a long letter addressed to the Chairman of the Manchester Chamber of Commerce which was appended to the later editions of the *Three Letters* pamphlet of 1853, and also in parliamentary and public speeches, notably a speech made before the members of the organization named on October 25, 1862.

In all that he wrote or said on the law of the sea in war he argued from the standpoint of the interests of commerce and of non-combatants. Just as England in this matter has consistently championed the rights of belligerents, so America has always been the spokesman of the rights of neutrals, and it is but fair to say that both countries have been specially concerned about their own interests. He adopted the American standpoint, as became the " international man." An uncompromising advocate of Free Trade, he sought to apply that principle in all directions with the severest consistency, and as far as possible in war just as in peace.

His strongest criticism was reserved for the practice of blockade, which, even as limited by the Declaration of Paris of April 16, 1856, he condemned as an irrational weapon of war and an indefensible infraction of the rights of neutrals. But he was also insistent on the desirability of exempting private property at sea from capture under any pretext.

> " It is a most important principle," he wrote in 1856 to a correspondent ; (it) " tends to rob the spoiler of his prey and make war a game of blood and bruisings without the attractions of plunder and prize money. Hurrah for anything that tends to make war a mere duel between professionals, for it will make the calling less profitable and therefore less popular."

Originating in the investment of fortified places only, the practice of blockade had gradually been extended, with the growth of naval power, so as to embrace the entire seaboard of a belligerent State. As the customary law stood before the adoption of the reform which elicited the jubilant outburst just quoted, the investment of an enemy's ports, with a view to compel surrender, justified the stoppage of supplies by sea, and any attempt to evade a blockade was held to constitute a breach of neutrality. Against this far-going invasion of their liberties, neutral nations had repeatedly protested, and more urgently since the Napoleonic Wars, during which England confirmed her claim to be the undisputed mistress of the seas. The Russian Emperor had raised the validity of this claim with the Allies in 1801, but the Congress of Vienna tacitly recognized the existing status, " nor did the Congress so much as consider the propriety of subjecting to international discussion the practices and claims which that supremacy involved." [1]

There was no change until forty years later the Declaration of Paris, as accepted by all the Great Powers of Europe, laid down four important rules, viz. (1) that privateering is and remains abolished ; (2) that the neutral flag covers enemies' goods, with the exception of contraband of war ; (3) that

Sir A. W. Ward in *Cambridge Modern History*, ix. 654.

neutral goods, with the same exception, are not liable to capture under an enemy's flag; and (4) that blockades, in order to be binding, must be effective—that is to say, maintained by a force sufficient really to prevent access to the coast of the enemy. The definition last quoted, which still holds good, marked a decided advance, but it was weakened by its vagueness. Since it came into force it has provided abundant material for controversy, and occasionally, when the injured States were strong and stubborn, serious friction.

When the Powers by the Declaration abolished the ancient practice of privateering, by which belligerent Governments authorized vessels in private ownership to seize and confiscate enemy ships, the Government of the United States, represented by President Pierce, declined to accept the prohibition in the form proposed, and made the counter-proposal that the private property of belligerents at sea should be exempt from capture either by privateers or armed Government vessels—in other words, that commercial blockades should cease. This was going back to the attitude adopted by America when the first treaty with England was being negotiated after the War of Independence; for the American Commissioner, on Franklin's suggestion, then proposed the inclusion of an article which would have exempted from capture by the public or private armed ships of either belligerent State all merchant vessels, with their cargoes, employed merely in international commerce. The proposal was resisted and had to be dropped. In 1856 the same proposal, though favoured by Russia, France, and other Powers, and also by English merchants and shipowners, was again negatived by the British Government, on the plea that the existing practice as to commercial blockades was "essential to British naval supremacy," a claim which had never been formally admitted, though never openly challenged, either in America or Europe.

Nevertheless, following the trend of public opinion, President Buchanan, who succeeded President Pierce in 1857, advanced upon the latter's position, and now demanded that private property should not only be exempt from capture at sea, but should be free from molestation while entering or leaving commercial ports; and that blockades should be restricted to naval arsenals and towns invested by armies on land. " We must obtain the consent of the powerful naval nations," he wrote at the time, " that merchant vessels shall not be blockaded in port, but be suffered to pass the blockading squadron, and go out to sea."

In 1859 this demand was formally communicated to the European Powers, but once more the British Government met it with a definite refusal on the old ground. No parliamentary papers were published on the subject, but Lord John Russell subsequently informed the House of Commons (February 18, 1861) that the representations made by the American Government at the time were to the effect that

" the right of blockade as authorized by the law of nations was liable to very great abuse, that the only case in which a blockade ought to be permitted was when a land army was besieging a fortified place and a fleet was employed to blockade it on the other side ; but that any attempt to intercept trade by blockade, or to blockade places which were commercial ports, was an abuse of the right that ought not to be permitted."

It is one of the ironies of political history that a few months after the British Foreign Secretary made his belated statement this country was suffering acutely from the effects of a blockade which only became possible because of the position which had been systematically asserted by our own Government whenever attempts were made by others to abolish this crude method of warfare. In the meantime Lord Palmerston would appear to have veered somewhat towards the American view, but in 1860 President Buchanan dropped the question, with the result that when the American Civil War broke out the Federal Government blockaded the ports of the South with deadly effect. The closing of the cotton ports, which cut off Lancashire's supplies of raw material and plunged its operatives into want and privation, was thus virtually England's own act.

As Cobden said at the time : " We have imposed upon ourselves, as neutrals, the privations and sufferings incidental to a commercial blockade, because we assume that we are interested in reserving to ourselves the belligerent right which we now concede to others."

Further, as America had not signed the Declaration of Paris, she was also free to engage in privateering, and the Federal and Confederate Governments both obtained authority to issue letters of marque, though neither of them used its powers. All the Great Powers of Europe, however, prohibited the practice during the war, though owing to culpable official laxity, chargeable, by his own later admission, to Lord John Russell, the Foreign Secretary, vessels built in the Mersey were allowed to go to sea for service in the Confederate cause, and for this illegality committed by private profit-seekers the taxpayers of England were ultimately required to pay damages to the extent of three and a quarter million pounds, though nearly thrice this sum had been claimed.

So the position stood in 1862, when Cobden, the fight for Free Trade definitely won for a second time by the Anglo-French Commercial Treaty, took up the question of maritime law reform in a more systematic manner than hitherto. An event of the time seemed specially favourable to the new crusade, for Lancashire was then held, as by a vice, in the crushing grip of the cotton famine. Already the effects of the catastrophe, individual and social, were desolating. It was estimated that the working classes were suffering a loss in wages at the rate of twelve million pounds a year, and that the aggregate loss to employers and workers together in the end increased that figure threefold. Relief works were organized on a large scale by public bodies, and a million pounds were expended in this way in two years ; a national relief fund of two million pounds was also raised for the sufferers ; while North America sent to Lancashire food and clothing by the shipload. All this multifarious assistance, however, only mitigated without removing the terrible suffering, which yet was borne with heroic patience and fortitude from the knowledge that the States of the North, which had struck this hard blow, were fighting for the abolition of slavery.

The Civil War and the suffering which it occasioned in this country, and in a less degree in France, determined Cobden to work for such changes in maritime law as would " put an end to that system of warfare which brings this calamity home to our doors." Now as ever he was in favour of thorough-going measures. He saw that the entire existing system of sea law held together, so that " when once touched it crumbles to pieces." In order to help forward that process he advanced three fundamental demands :

1. The exemption of private property from capture at sea during war by armed vessels of every kind.
2. Blockades to be restricted to naval arsenals, and to towns besieged at the same time on land, with the exception of articles contraband of war (i.e. arms and ammunition).
3. The merchant ships of neutrals on the high seas to be inviolable to the visitation of alien Government vessels in time of war as in time of peace.

All these reforms he regarded as corollaries of the repeal of the Navigation and Corn Laws and the abandonment of colonial trade monopolies ; but it was against the practice of commercial blockade that he particularly directed his armoury of argument. His line of reasoning is set forth most fully in the Manchester speech and the letter to Mr. Ashworth already cited, but in his correspondence with Mr. Sumner in America, M. Chevalier in France, and others he returned again and again to the subject. Some of his illustrations and facts may have little relevancy to present conditions, but those who endorse the main principles of his political thought will agree that his case for sea law reform has gained rather than lost in force since his day.

As was his custom in dealing with international questions, he based his demands mainly on practical considerations, though those of equity and philanthropy naturally weighed strongly with him.

" Bear in mind," he told his audience of Manchester merchants in 1862, " that I am now arguing this matter only as it affects our interests. I do not come here as a humanitarian or philanthropist, asking my countrymen to give up a custom which is advantageous to them, out of homage to the genius of the age or because we are reaching a millennium ; but I ask it because, as an Englishman and as a public man, I have not and never have had any other criterion to guide me, nor any other standard by which to form my opinion, but the interests, the honest interests, of my country, which with God's blessing are the interests of mankind."

He faced at once the logical and practical conclusion, that if private property were to be exempted from capture on the open sea during war, commercial blockades would have to cease.

" To exempt a cargo of goods from capture when it happens to be on the ocean, but to say that it may be captured when it gets within three miles of a port—or, in other words, to declare that a cargo may be perfectly free to roam the sea when once out of harbour, but may be captured, if caught, before it gets three miles from land—is to propose that which cannot be practically carried into effect in negotiations or treaties with other countries. In addition, therefore, to the question of the exemption of private property, you have to consider the larger question of commercial blockades. I say it is the larger question, because the capture of private property at sea affects, necessarily, only the merchants and shipowners of the countries which choose to go to war ; whereas a commercial blockade affects neutrals as well, and the mischief is not confined to the merchants and shipowners, but is extended to the whole manufacturing population ; it may involve the loss of subsistence, and even of health and life, to multitudes of people, and may throw the whole social system into disorder."

Inevitably the blockade system could only be enforced or defended by naval Powers of the foremost rank, against which all weaker nations were helpless, and, impressed by the unfairness of this one-sided arrangement, he spoke of the " Blockade Laws " as " about as rascally an invention as the old Corn Laws." With his fondness for " homely illustration," he drew a hypothetical parallel from civil life :

" Suppose Tom Sayers lived in a street, and on the opposite side lived a shopkeeper with whom he has been in the habit of dealing. Tom quarrels with his shopkeeper, and forthwith sends him a challenge to fight, which is accepted. Tom, being a powerful man, sends word to each and every householder in the street that he is going to fight the shopkeeper, and that until he has finished fighting no person in the street must have any dealings with his shopkeeper. ' We have nothing to do with your quarrel,' say the inhabitants, ' and you have no right to stop our dealings with the shopkeeper.' The argument is just as good on a large scale as on a small one—for fifty million persons as for one."

Answering the plea that blockades enabled this country to inflict far greater injury upon an enemy than it suffered in return, he said :

" I want to know, in the wide range of the world, what conceivable injury you can do to any people that will equal the mischief which must be inflicted upon this region of Lancashire if the present state of things (i.e. the cotton famine) continues for another six months. It is in times of war, above all others, that you ought to have the freest access to the ports of those foreign countries on which you are dependent for your raw materials and your food. I can understand a great manufacturing country like this maintaining a large fleet for the purpose of keeping its doors open for the supply of that food and those raw materials ; but by what perversity of reasoning can any statesman be brought to think that it can ever be our interest to employ our fleet to prevent those indispensable commodities from reaching our shores ? "

Bad laws are like boomerangs : they have a way of rebounding to the hurt of those who apply them. A British Government had asserted the right of blockade against the wish of America, and, speaking in 1862 of the country which he knew so well, he could point to the tragic spectacle of a great industrial population doomed to bear the crushing weight of unemployment, impoverishment, and privation, as the direct result of its rulers' shortsightedness.

He was able to plead, however, that so strong were the practical objections to commercial blockades that in practice England, when herself proclaiming them, had never enforced them strictly, interest proving stronger than policy.[1] The blockades of France under the Orders in Council of 1807, of the North American coast in 1813, and of Cronstadt and the southern ports of Russia during the Crimean War were cases in point ; for the measures taken against those countries had either to be abandoned or relaxed because of the injury they were inflicting upon our own people and commerce. So he came to the conclusion that neither the British nor any other Government had a right to obstruct and suspend the commercial intercourse of the world for the sake of gaining an advantage over an antagonist with whom it might be quarrelling.

A subsidiary demand which Cobden put forward was the abolition of the right of visitation or search on the high seas, as being unsuited to an age of extended commerce, of steamships, and of posts. He contended that one great advantage

[1] This, of course, was the case during the Great War, one result being that large supplies of raw material and merchandise passed through neutral hands to belligerent countries.

of this change would be that it would simplify the question of contraband of war, and so obviate the danger of international disputes. He agreed that the definition of unlawful cargo might properly go beyond arms and ammunition, as the United States Government had proposed, but subject to this qualification he held that it should be a recognized principle of international law that the exportation of merchandise should cease to be regarded as a belligerent act. Exemption was introduced in the Franco-British Commercial Treaty of 1860 as regards coal, but he wished to apply it to the entire field of legitimate commerce.

His demand was, in short, for a wholesale jettisoning of the harassing hamper of obsolete maritime rules which still obstructed commerce in time of war and the adaptation of the law to the conditions and needs of modern times, by simplifying it, reducing its restrictive provisions to a minimum, and, in general, subordinating the interests of warring nations to the convenience of the nations which had the good sense to keep the peace.

He brushed aside with impatience, as a fallacy which could only obscure counsel, the notion that international maritime law was, like the Decalogue, a fixed and immutable code, incapable of revision and adaptation. On the contrary, it was merely a collection of precedents, largely proceeding from the English Courts, and arising out of circumstances of a kind which no longer applied. England, however, still blocked the way to serious reform, and he held her official attitude to be the less justifiable since she had taken her stand on the doctrine of Free Trade and stood before the world as the great protagonist of that doctrine. " We no longer intend, I hope, to fight the battles of everyone on the Continent, and to make war like a game of ninepins, setting up and knocking down dynasties, as chance or passion may dictate." Let England, therefore, adapt her maritime policy to that situation. With a generous gesture of faith he avowed his conviction that good will and trust on her part would be fully justified by the result.

" We have thrown away the sceptre of force," he said, alluding to the abandonment of restrictive tariffs and conventions which was involved by the acceptance of Free Trade, " to confide in the principle of freedom—uncovenanted, unconditional freedom. Under this new *régime* our national fortunes have prospered beyond all precedent. During the last fourteen years the increase in our commerce has exceeded its entire growth during the previous thousand years of reliance on force, cunning, and monopoly. This should encourage us to go forward in the full faith that every fresh impediment removed from the path of commerce, whether by sea or land, and whether in peace or war, will augment our prosperity, at the same time that it will promote the general interests of humanity."

It has been shown that in his campaigning on behalf of political reforms Cobden showed himself a master of strategy. It was a happy thought which led him during the American Civil War to make use of the cotton blockade as an argument for discrediting blockades altogether. As has been said, the blockade came home to the staple industry of North England with crushing force, but the cotton operatives of France likewise suffered in a less degree and also with less patience. He, therefore, did his utmost to enlist the influence of his friend Sumner in favour of the abandonment of this weapon, which wounded indiscriminately both friend and foe. When the affair of the *Trent* occurred (November 19, 1861), inflaming opinion in English circles hostile to the North, he urged that the two Confederates who had been illegally seized on that British vessel should be set free, but that the Federal Government should stipulate simultaneously for the abandonment of the old code of maritime law as upheld by England and the other European Powers and the adoption of the changes which have been explained above. He admitted that these changes would not be popular with the Government, but he believed they would be accepted if the lifting of the cotton blockade were offered as the price. Perhaps there was more hope than faith in a letter written to the same correspondent, wherein he said :

" We are, in ordinary times, two nations : a busy toiling multitude and a governing class. The latter would be most averse to this revolution in maritime law, by which the pretence for vast armaments would be annihilated. The favourite plea when we vote the Navy Estimates is that they are necessary for the protection of commerce. It would be useless, therefore, for you to propose these changes through the channels of secret diplomacy. It must be done publicly. I have said that in ordinary, quiet times we are ruled by a governing class. But when a sufficient motive is presented to induce the busy millions to exert their power they can always bring the aristocracy into subjection to their will. Now if it were publicly announced that you had made the above proposals to our Government, I will engage that our mercantile and manufacturing community will compel this Ministry, or some other, to accept them."

He bade Sumner not to be discouraged by the fact that his Government had failed to convert England on the subject in 1859. For " diplomatic arrangements," he wrote, with an oblique allusion to his successful negotiation of the French Commercial Treaty, " especially when they involve a novelty, are never made in such a way, *unless when an amateur diplomatist intervenes*, as to warrant us to hope that in a year or two so great a change . . . could have been accomplished."

It was his idea that the North should execute a " great strategic movement," which should " turn the flank of the European Powers, especially of the governing classes of England." " Recollect," he wrote, " how immensely you would gain in moral power by leading old Europe in the path of civilization. You owe it to yourselves and us."

When arguments failed he tried the effect of a mild threat, as when he warned Sumner that the world would not wait for cotton much longer and the Governments of Europe might soon be expected to " be knocking at your door," and even reminded him that Great Britain had a powerful navy. " There is always a desire on the part of Governments," he wrote, " to use such armaments by way of proving that they were necessary. France was the pretence, and now we have plenty of people who would be content to see this fleet turned against you."

Laboured argument of this kind was, in truth, unreal—a quite innocent mixture of polemical romancing and " bunkum " (to use a word often on his lips and pen, which he brought home from America [1]), and if Sumner had swallowed it he would not have been half as clever as Cobden thought him. In a confident moment he ventured the rash prediction that there would never be another blockade, since the world would not stand it. " Our recent doctrines," he wrote, " on which

---

[1] Carlyle may have helped to naturalize the word in this country. He used it in the *Latter-day Pamphlets*, originally published in 1850.

you have also acted, with reference to China and Japan, denying them the right of shutting up themselves from the rest of the world, are symptoms of the same tendency in men's minds." That, too, was a curious position to be taken, even in a good cause, by a public man who had for years been protesting in every degree of indignation against the claim of the European Powers to coerce Eastern countries into trading with them.

All such ingenious special pleading, done with the best intentions, was yet obviously foredoomed to failure. Then, as later, it was no ambition of America to drag " old Europe," or any part of it, out of the difficulty into which a self-inflicted handicap of the Declaration of Paris had landed it. The North stood on its just rights as asserted by the British Government, and so it happened that while the industrial population of Lancashire was suffering untold hardships and privations, because of silent factories and widespread unemployment, due to a blockade which but for the attitude of his own Government in 1856 would have been impossible, Lord Palmerston had to defend this instrument of force by the argument that England would have the right to apply it to some other country at a future date.

Not all of Cobden's arguments against commercial blockades in war have equal force in the present day ; yet his case has been greatly strengthened by the altered conditions of modern warfare, nor does the experience of the Great War prove the contrary. For, even granting that Germany's surrender after more than four years of stubborn fighting, in which at last she almost stood alone, was due less to political discontents at home, fomented by revolutionary elements in the population, than to the closeness of the blockade which Great Britain was able to impose owing to an overwhelming superiority of sea power, the success with which that country was so long able to feed itself and to carry on its industrial system by the aid of inventions, discoveries, and substitutes of all kinds was one of the wonders of the war.

Moreover, the application by Germany herself of a new, indirect, and deadly form of blockade in her submarine warfare, though it inflicted upon the people of these islands at most the pinch, and never the privation, of straitened food supplies, has revealed grim possibilities of the future. Aerial warfare likewise is still in the experimental stage, yet to its developments no limit can safely be placed. Unless these two abortions of military science are strangled in their infancy, it is more than likely that the value of commercial blockades in war-time, even to the most powerful of maritime States, may progressively decrease, until the practice ceases to be worth while.

Two other facts to be borne in mind are that the late war has directed the attention of all the larger Powers to the necessity of greater economic self-dependence, particularly in the matter of food supplies, and further that if in 1914 the German Navy had been either materially weaker or stronger, the war would have run a far more rapid course, and a commercial blockade might have played a quite insignificant part in the result. It is significant that while one school of naval experts calls for the prohibition of submarine and aerial warfare by international agreement, there are other experts whose confidence in the inability of maritime action to determine the issue of future campaigns has been so far shaken that they would scrap the large fighting ships at once.

Cobden advocated the reform of sea law not merely in the interests of free commercial intercourse, but because he saw in its inequity an obstacle to international understanding. Morley suggests that, recognizing the unlikelihood of any absolute cessation of war, all he wanted, or at least hoped, to do was to make it " less destructive to the interests and the security of great populations." If that was all he expected, his crusade against war and non-intervention would look something like a sham. It is certain—and a hundred avowals prove it—that he was inspired by a larger faith, and that, though conscious that that crusade would have to be continued far beyond his time, he never for a moment doubted a successful issue. Meanwhile, like a practical man, he was willing to accept sea law reform, and any other mitigation of the essential savagery of warfare, as instalments towards the final victory of reason and peace.

John Stuart Mill objected to Cobden's proposed alleviations of the maritime law in time of war on the ground that its effect would be to relax the public restraint upon Governments

M

disposed to enter upon hostilities. It is doubtful whether there is much reality in this objection. Imagination is the rarest of gifts, and in the past no nation has been led by the remembrance of the losses and misfortunes inflicted upon it by war to adopt measures to prevent its repetition. If nations have not yet proscribed war owing to the fact that by it their best manhood is decimated and their treasuries are impoverished, it is certain that they will never do it from a fear that, owing to the possible pressure of a commercial blockade, the cost of living might rise and the supply of breakfast bacon run short.

Perhaps to people of normal moral feeling the strongest argument against commercial blockades is the fact that they are aimed primarily at the non-combatants, so that their principal victims are women and children. How terrible the punishment which this weapon, when drastically used, can inflict upon a great civil population was shown during the late war. It is an objection hardly less strong that while an effective blockade inconveniences the rich little and last, it grinds the poor from the first. Fighting of such sort, whether it achieves its purpose or not, is neither magnificent nor is it chivalrous war.

At present no nation, whether maritime or not, is altogether satisfied with the state of international sea law ; yet mere denunciation on any side without the wish to improve and humanize the existing rules, legalized or prescriptive, with a view to adjusting them as far as possible to the interests common to all countries, would be a step backward. Moreover, whatever is done should have the assent of all maritime States, large and small, if not of civilized States generally, and such a condition points to action through the League of Nations.

As the status is at present the interests of some countries are directly opposed to those of others, and that is why, for example, the idea of abolishing submarines, which is largely favoured in Great Britain, is just as widely opposed in France and the smaller maritime States. For the nation which finds that it cannot be strong in defence in one way will try to be strong in another, and it will insist on choosing for itself the weapons which best meet its special circumstances and needs. The little maritime States which cannot afford to build men-of-war at ten millions sterling apiece know that the submarine is their only means of getting straight with their powerful and wealthy neighbours, and this inexpensive and effectual arm they will only renounce at a price.

The crucial question for this country, now as when Cobden wrote, is that of commercial blockades. Much of the hostile criticism which from time to time is passed on the British attitude on this question is wide of the mark. The common view that Great Britain maintains the right of blockade in violation of some existing international agreement is, of course, baseless. The practice is a relic of antiquity—perhaps a barbarous relic—which has been rather tolerated than formally sanctioned by international law, and continues simply because the Power specially interested in preserving it has hitherto refused to abandon its right. All that jurisprudence has so far done is to limit the exercise of the right by defining what shall constitute blockade. In its attitude on this question Great Britain has simply exemplified a political dictum of Bismarck which, because of its origin, has been systematically misrepresented, either in ignorance or malice, as essentially immoral. It was uttered in the Prussian Diet during the Constitutional conflict of over sixty years ago. The Budget was held up, and a long struggle found the Crown and the Lower House as far from agreement as ever, since the Constitution did not provide for an emergency of the kind. Then it was that Bismarck declared that in such circumstances, " inasmuch as the life of a State cannot stand still, conflicts become questions of power, and whoever is in possession of power will follow his own counsel." [1] That rule of conduct for States, when situations arise for which no solvent exists in law or custom, has in the past been applied—and to a certain extent it applies to-day—in the case of differences arising out of the defects and gaps in sea law. Here, too, in the absence of agreement the stronger Powers have " followed their own counsel," nor has their action in so doing necessarily involved any violation of legal rights.

[1] For giving utterance to that truism Bismarck has ever since been credited with the authorship of the doctrine that " Might goes before right," words which he never used. A succeeding speaker so interpreted his words, but unfairly, since the essence of the dispute was the question on which side did right lie.

Simply because of her unequalled naval power Great Britain is in a more favourable position than any other country to contribute to a common agreement on this question, and the call comes to her even more strongly now than in Cobden's day to give the world a bold and generous lead. A specially strong case would exist for the abolition of commercial blockades, as equally advantageous to Great Britain and the rest of the Empire, if prohibition were applied simultaneously to submarine and aerial warfare. With the proscription of blockades, however, the right of search for contraband would have to be further restricted. It will be recalled how the exercise by our Government of the right against American and German vessels during the Boer War led to strong diplomatic protests. How seriously America took the matter in 1900 is shown by the fact that President McKinley said in his message to Congress on December 3 :

" The war in Southern Africa introduced important questions. A condition unusual in international wars was presented in that while one belligerent had control of the seas the other had no ports, shipping, or direct trade, but was only accessible through the territory of a neutral. Vexatious questions arose through Great Britain's action in respect to neutral cargoes, not contraband in their own nature, shipped to Portuguese South Africa, on the score of probable or suspected ultimate destination to the Boer States."

On that occasion the British Government solved the difficulty by agreeing to purchase outright all goods shown to be the actual property of American subjects, though President McKinley regretted that there had been no " broad settlement of the question of a neutral's right to send goods not contraband *per se* to a neutral port adjacent to a belligerent area."

" C'est à la guerre comme à la guerre " is a maxim always sure to be popular with combatants who find themselves in a position of advantage. During the Great War the Allied Powers—in effect Great Britain—by sheer superiority of naval strength, and by no sanction of international law, closed the ocean to neutral commerce. Again protests were abundant and ceaseless, and in the case of the United States it was only the intervention of that Power as an active belligerent that put an end to a series of incidents which, in the absence of very careful handling, threatened more than once to provoke acute friction. In the event of Great Britain being involved in war there would still be a certainty of similar misunderstandings arising so long as the existing practice, so favourable to this country and so unequal in its effects for other countries, continues unchanged. Nine out of ten of such disputes might prove amenable to amicable adjustment, on terms more or less onerous, as in the past. It is the odd case which, perhaps owing to obstinacy on one side or the other, does not admit of such adjustment, that is dangerous, and when it occurs the only alternative to war is humiliating surrender. Meanwhile, it is well to bear in mind that the American protest of 1900 still stands on record, and that the challenge of an earlier President has never yet been met.

It may be admitted that a good deal of loose thinking prevails amongst those who contest as well as those who uphold the British claim to retain this right. While its defenders contend that our maritime primacy is used solely for the protection of the common rights of nations where otherwise they might be exposed to arbitrary invasion, its critics object that the claim involves a too exclusive regard for British interests and implies at all times a potential menace to other nations, particularly the weak ones. The fact is that, while we are thinking of British naval power in the light of present conditions, our critics are sometimes thinking of events that happened in the past. Cobden himself is open to criticism because of his habit of drawing general conclusions from exceptional incidents, though it may be contended in his defence that he wrote of things which happened in his own day and, as it were, under his eyes. Such were the blockade of the Piræus in 1850, the bombardment and partial destruction of Canton in 1856, over the discreditable affair of the *Arrow*, and the wanton destruction of the Japanese town of Kagosima in 1863, all episodes which the Governments concerned failed to justify even to the public opinion of the time.

But a navy is a singularly mobile instrument of punition, particularly useful for rough business—if it has to be done—in distant parts of the earth, and against races of inferior status ; and in such circumstances guns are apt to go off far more readily, and to do their work more effectively, than would be approved nearer home. It is unfair, however, to draw from historical events conclusions which the altered political circumstances and the suaver and more moral spirit of modern times do not justify. The best testimony to the honour of the British Navy, as the world is in justice bound to judge it to-day, is to be found in the clean record with which it emerged from the late war.

Nevertheless, remembering how directly such questions as right of search and blockade bear upon the problem of international peace, and how to preserve it, it would be wise to accustom ourselves to the expectation of early and important modifications. It is inconceivable that we can count long on the world's acceptance of claims of sea power and sea practice in war which to us may be self-evident, yet which continue to be asserted only because they have not as yet been actively contested. Where concessions of any kind are overdue it is always wise policy to anticipate the inevitable and make a virtue of necessity. Capitulation under pressure seldom deserves gratitude and still more rarely receives it.

CHAPTER IX

COLONIZATION AND EMPIRE

" There is no country which from its political and commercial circumstances, from its maritime interests, and from its colonial possessions, excites more envious and jealous feelings in different quarters than England does."— LORD PALMERSTON, June 1849.

" No peace can last, or ought to last, which does not recognize and accept the principle that Governments derive all their just powers from the consent of the governed, and that no right anywhere exists to hand peoples about from potentate to potentate as if they were property."—PRESIDENT WILSON, speech in the United States Senate, January 22, 1917.

COBDEN'S discussions of the questions of Colonization and Empire—for this distinction must be made—cannot be ranked with his more helpful contributions to political thought. For that fact the changed circumstances are chiefly responsible. In particular much of his argument on the colonial question, some aspects of which were so prolific in controversy in his day, has little relevance to present conditions, though from the historical standpoint it is useful as showing the remarkable transformations of national opinion which have taken place in the interval.

I. COLONIZATION.

When he began to write the colonies were the disregarded incumbrances of unsympathetic and somewhat surly step-parents. Of the two political parties, one did not value, while the other did not even want them. The taxpayer knew them chiefly as a costly and troublesome burden, needing a vast amount of attention, and saw no likelihood that they would ever be worth the effort and money expended on them. Statesmen, as a rule, wasted no sentiment on these undeveloped and sparsely populated territories, and, immersed in European

184 RICHARD COBDEN AND FOREIGN POLICY

quarrels as they were, the future of the Greater Britain beyond the seas but little stirred their imaginations. If, therefore, the attitude of Cobden to the colonies was one of apathy, it merely reflected the spirit of the time.

The somewhat contemptuous conception of the colonies which prevailed almost down to the middle of last century can, perhaps, be best explained by recalling the purposes to which they were put. Some of the largest of them, now powerful Dominions playing an influential part in the world's life, were then chiefly regarded as convenient dumping-grounds for our irreformable felons and the wastrel sons of families too genteel to keep their social breakages at home. When Cobden first wrote on the colonies transportation, revived in 1786, after a brief period of suspension, was still a prominent feature of the penal law, and down to 1834 the punishment for unpermitted return to England was death. It was to the colonies that the convicts were sent—first to Canada up to 1775, and, after its doors were closed, to Australia, Norfolk Island, Van Diemen's Land, South Africa, Bermudas, and elsewhere. The Cape of Good Hope succeeded in stopping the immigration of criminals in 1849. Australia ceased to take convicts in 1865, yet long after the law had ceased to banish to the Antipodes the worst of the home country's criminals the conventional method of treating harum-scarum young men who had gone wrong was to "send them to the colonies," and as Australia was farthest away they usually went there.

The view of the commercial world was hardly less intelligent, since it saw the colonies only from the material side. The spirit of the old " colonial system " still survived. True, the traditional motive of colonial possession, the maintenance of trade monopolies, which Adam Smith had so severely criticized over half a century before, was becoming discredited, but it had not been repudiated in practice. Privileges continued to be granted to certain of the colonies which cost the Mother Country dearly, but there was no longer notorious abuse ; for what was done in that direction was done aboveboard and as part of a recognized policy, or what passed as such. The trade of one colony was bartered against that of another. Thus the West Indies were given a monopoly of the sugar trade with Canada, and Canada in return received a corn and timber trade monopoly in the West Indies. Colonial trade in and out was still restricted by fiscal regulations, arbitrarily imposed by the home Parliament and determined as much by British interests in other parts of the world as by concern for the prosperity of the individual colonies affected.

At that time also the cost of Empire played a far larger part in the attitude of Colonial Secretaries and political parties than in the present day, when the House of Commons is readier to vote millions for carrying railways through tropical jungle than it would have voted thousands for transatlantic cables three-quarters of a century ago.

To Cobden it was obnoxious that the colonies should be used as instruments of commercial barter of a kind injurious to the public at large and prejudicial to the maintenance of friendly relations between Great Britain and other countries, particularly the United States and rising States in South America. He also combated the prevailing view according to which aboriginal populations existed simply to be exploited by the traders. Having been taught from earliest infancy that it was man's duty to subdue the earth, the white settler concluded that the subjugation of the natives was a part of the task, and at times he discharged it in very drastic fashion. A Committee of the House of Commons appointed to inquire into the state of New Zealand had laid down the doctrine that

" the uncivilized inhabitants of any country have but a qualified dominion over it, or a right of occupancy only, and until they establish amongst themselves a settled form of government, and subjugate the ground to their own uses by the cultivation of it, they cannot grant to individuals, not of their own tribe, any portion of it, for the simple reason that they have not themselves any individual property in it."

That doctrine, which practically made of the landless natives mere instruments of labour, was not everywhere applied in the crude form here stated, though it has operated in many parts of Africa down to the present time, and as late as April 16, 1926, it received practical endorsement by the Judicial Committee of the Privy Council in the Swaziland case.

Viewing all the circumstances, there was not much in the British colonial empire of Cobden's early days that was likely to excite pride or give promise of the destiny that awaited it. He saw the colonies, as most of his contemporaries saw them, as parasitic growths which only maintained a penurious existence by draining the financial strength of the Mother Country. He broke his first lance over the colonial question in his pamphlet of 1835, *England, Ireland, and America*, but later he discussed it freely in parliamentary and platform speeches, and in his correspondence. In the pamphlet he boldly challenged the entire system of colonization as then practised, and called for its abandonment. He wrote :

" Nothing, we believe, presents so fair a field for economical analysis, even in this age of new lights, as the subject of colonization. Spain lies at this moment a miserable spectacle of a nation whose own natural greatness has been immolated on the shrine of transatlantic ambition. May not some future historian possibly be found recording a similar epitaph on the tomb of Britain ? In truth, we have been planting, and supporting, and governing countries upon all degrees of habitable, and some that are not habitable, latitudes of the earth's surface ; and so grateful to our national pride has been the spectacle, that we have never for once paused to inquire if our interests were advanced by so much nominal greatness."

It was his lament that Great Britain had " about a hundred times the amount of territory beyond the seas to protect, as colonies and dependencies, that France has." Yet the colonial empire at that time was far less extensive than now, a large part of it had but lately passed under British rule, and its development had barely begun. In South Africa we had only Cape Colony and Natal, which had been taken from the Dutch. There was not a square yard of British territory in either East or Central Africa, and Egypt and the Soudan had not yet risen on the political horizon. The greatest of the colonial possessions was, of course, Canada, obtained by conquest from France ; while the colonization of Australia, begun in the last quarter of the eighteenth century, had made but little progress up to the second quarter of the nineteenth. The entire white population of British North America, the Cape, Australia, and New Zealand even in the middle of last century was under two millions.

It was, however, the financial argument against the maintenance of colonies that weighed with Cobden more than any other. He complained that far from the colonies being profitable to the Mother Country, they did not even " pay for their keep." Following Adam Smith's example he attacked a system under which English taxpayers were bled in order that the colonies might have peace and good government at a cheap price and be protected from external menace at no cost at all.[1] It was a bad bargain for the Mother Country, since the gain and advantage were all on one side, and he held that the arrangement was only possible because the colonies were governed from Downing Street, and because Downing Street was still the most treasured of the many pocket boroughs of the aristocratic class. His idea, therefore, was to give them self-government, and in that way relieve the homeland of all future financial liability. He wrote :

" We are told we must keep up enormous armaments, because we have got so many colonies. People tell me I want to abandon our colonies ; but I say, do you intend to hold your colonies by the sword, by armies, and ships-of-war ? That is not a permanent hold upon them. I want to retain them by their affections. If you tell me that our soldiers are kept for their police, I answer, the English people cannot afford to pay for their police. The inhabitants of those colonies are a great deal better off than the mass of the people in England—they are in the possession of a vast deal more of the comforts of life than the bulk of those paying taxes here ; they have very few of those taxes that plague us here so much—excise, stamps, and taxes, those fiscal impediments which beset you every day in your callings, are hardly known in our colonies. Our colonies are very able to protect themselves."

Had it been practicable he would have gone further and let the larger colonies have complete political independence at once. He appears to have adopted the argument for the rupture of the colonial tie which Adam Smith had put forward, though he did it without Smith's admission that not even " the most visionary enthusiast " could believe a policy of mere abandonment to be practicable. He wrote, almost paraphrasing passages in the *Wealth of Nations* (Book IV, chap. vii, part 3) :

[1] On the colonial question generally Cobden closely followed Adam Smith—so closely, in fact, that it is at times difficult to distinguish Cobden from his economic mentor. Compare on the financial aspect of colonization the *Wealth of Nations*, Book IV, chap. vii, part iii.

" We are aware that no Power was ever yet known, voluntarily, to give up the dominion over a part of its territory.   But if it could be made manifest to the trading and industrious portions of this nation, who have no honours, or interested ambition of any kind, at stake in the matter, that, whilst our dependencies are supported at an expense to them, in direct taxation, of more than five millions annually, they serve but as gorgeous and ponderous appendages to swell our ostensible grandeur, but, in reality, to complicate and magnify our government expenditure, without improving our balance of trade—surely, under such circumstances, it would become at least a question for anxious inquiry with a people so overwhelmed with debt, whether those colonies should not be suffered to support and defend themselves, as separate and independent existences."

Later, as a Member of Parliament, he lost no opportunity of advocating the limitation of colonial responsibilities by the widest possible extension of autonomy.   Thus he raised the question in the House of Commons on March 8, 1850, in the course of a speech on finance.   Therein he proposed the gradual withdrawal of imperial troops from the colonies in which the British race was likely to be indigenous and to remain paramount, leaving them to provide for their own internal defence ; but he excluded from this measure Gibraltar, Malta, Ceylon, and territories in which the African race predominated.   The Kaffir War of that year roused his ire against the colonists of the Cape, and he would have required them to bear the entire cost of keeping order in future.   " This must be done by first giving them the powers of self-government and then throwing on them the responsibility of their policy. They would then be very careful to treat the neighbouring savages with justice."

At that time suggestions of autonomy for the colonies found willing listeners in Parliament, for revelations of misrule, cruelty, and official illegality in some of the colonies, as in the notorious cases of Ceylon and British Guiana, and administrative extravagance in nearly all, had painfully impressed public opinion at home.   In 1849 Sir William Molesworth proposed in the House of Commons the appointment of a royal commission to inquire into the entire subject of colonial policy.   Lord John Russell, then Prime Minister, admitted the urgency of the question, but preferred that the initiative should be taken by the Government, and, the House supporting his attitude, the motion was rejected. A little later he promised constitutional government to Australia and the Cape, following the precedent already set in the case of Canada after the revolution of 1837.

It was in relation to Canada that Cobden carried his disruptionist sympathies farthest. To the end of his life he was wishful to see the Dominion loosed from the moorings which bound it to Great Britain, leaving it free to join the United States, or otherwise manage its affairs as it would. His visits to America in 1835 and in 1858 convinced him that amalgamation with the Union was Canada's natural destiny, and in 1849 he corresponded with Sumner on the subject. He accepted Sumner's claim that " nature has decided that Canada and the United States must become one for all purposes of free inter-communication," and even agreed that the question of union was one for the two countries alone to decide, adding somewhat in the Tooley Street tailors' dogmatic way, " I can assure you that there will be no repetition of the policy of 1776 on our part, to prevent our North American Colonies from pursuing their interests in their own way." At the same time he was in favour of leaving the question to be decided by " the natural play of events," that impersonal force in human affairs in which he placed so much faith, yet which so often failed to justify his expectations.

" If the people of Canada," he wrote, " are tolerably unanimous in wishing to sever the very slight thread which now binds them to this country, I see no reason why, if good faith and ordinary temper be observed, it should not be done amicably. I think it would be far more likely to be accomplished peaceably if the subject of annexation were left as a distinct question. I am quite sure that we should be gainers to the amount of about a million sterling annually if our North American colonists would set up in life for themselves and maintain their own establishments, and I see no reason to doubt that they might be also gainers by being thrown upon their own resources. The less your countrymen mingle in the controversy the better."

The reader who may be inclined to scoff at ideas so entirely contrary to the later trend of events must be called back to the fact that Cobden's attitude was by no means singular amongst responsible statesmen at the time. On the question of the costliness of the colonies Cobden was in line with Sir

Robert Peel, who, in a speech made in the House of Commons in 1849, deplored the heavy financial burden thus imposed upon the Mother Country, and admitted that the major part of the military budget was then caused by the measures needed for colonial defence. Even the policy of " cutting the painter " which he advocated in the case of Canada had many outspoken supporters in England. At that time the attitude of the home Government was altogether hostile to the extension of imperial responsibilities. Indeed, as late as 1850 this attitude received formal avowal when, in endorsing the annexation of the Orange River, the Privy Council besought the Queen to let that be the last British appropriation in South Africa, and recommended

" that all officers who represent or who may hereafter represent Your Majesty in Southern Africa should be interdicted in terms as explicit as can be employed, and under sanctions as grave as can be devised, from making any additions, whether permanent or provisional, of any territory, however small, to the existing dominions of Your Majesty in the African continent."

Fifteen years later a Committee of the House of Commons unanimously recommended the same policy of abstention in regard to West Africa, affirming that any further extension of territory or assumption of government, or new treaties offering protection to native tribes, would be inexpedient. The position then taken was confirmed when in 1867 the Governor of Cape Colony, Sir Philip Wodehouse, urged an extension of British sovereignty which would have brought into the Empire the entire region between that Colony and the Portuguese colony of Angola ; for the answer of the Colonial Secretary, the Duke of Buckingham and Chandos, was a definite refusal. All that was done at that time was to annex some of the small guano islands in the neighbourhood of Angra Pequena, and Germany later took the rest of the country.

The tide of anti-colonial sentiment was still to fall much farther before the turn came. Strange as the fact may now appear, Benjamin Disraeli made himself the spokesman of the colony-weariness which prevailed so largely in the middle of the century. With his gaze turned to the east, where he saw the star of England rising, he was prepared to make a wholesale

clearance of the "burdensome" colonies as "a nuisance."
"These wretched colonies," he wrote to Lord Malmesbury
in 1852 (August 13), "will all be independent, too, in a few
years, and are a millstone round our necks." By 1866 he had
definitely made up his mind that England was "really more
an Asiatic Power than a European," and that conception
implied that the pivot of empire would be India and no
longer the colonies. He wrote to Lord Derby in that year
(September 30) :

"It can never be our pretence or our policy to defend the Canadian
frontier against the United States. If the colonists cannot as a general
rule defend themselves against the Fenians they can do nothing. They
ought to be and must be strong enough for that. Pride and influence
we should exercise in Asia ; consequently in Eastern Europe, consequently also in Western Europe ; but what is the use of these Colonial
deadweights which we do not govern ? Leave the Canadians to defend
themselves ; recall the African squadron ; give up the settlements on
the West Coast of Africa ; and we shall make a saving which will, at
the same time, enable us to build ships and have a good Budget." [1]

While, however, the Liberals long continued to doubt the
advantage of colonies, Disraeli retracted his error, and the day
came when, with audacious forgetfulness of his own back-
sliding, he described his political opponents as men who, having
"failed to enfeeble the colonies by their policy of decomposition,
may now perhaps recognize in the United Kingdom a mode
which will not only accomplish but precipitate their purpose."
If Cobden erred, therefore, he did it in good company.
If he was short-sighted, so were most other British statesmen
of his day ; for down to the last quarter of the century these
accepted the Empire as a finished dominion and were determined not to extend it by so much as a square mile of new
territory. At that time of great transitions, when momentous
political changes were upsetting old traditions, Cobden believed
that "the independence of the New World" had "for ever
put an end to the colonial policy of the Old."
Towards the close of the American Civil War the question
of Canada came up again in the House of Commons in a different
form, for there was then talk of federating all the British North

---

[1] *The Life of Benjamin Disraeli*, iv. 476.

American territories. Cobden's correspondence shows that he was deeply interested in the proposal, yet while he thought federation desirable he regarded it as only a first step towards an amicable separation. This continued to be his attitude to the last. In a letter of March 20, 1865, his latest utterance on the subject, he wrote :

> " I cannot see what substantial interest the British people have in the connexion to compensate them for guaranteeing three or four millions of North Americans living in Canada, etc., against another community of Americans living in their neighbourhood. We are two peoples to all intents and purposes, and it is a perilous delusion to both parties to attempt to keep up a sham connexion and dependence which will snap asunder if it should ever be put to the strain of stern reality. Whatever may be the wish of the colonies will meet with the concurrence of our Government and Parliament. We have recognized their right to control their own fate, even to the point of asserting their independence whenever they think fit, and which we know to be only a question of time."

In that time of widespread faint-heartedness and self-distrust in ruling circles, the colonial idea and faith in the Empire owed more to the instinctive attachment of the masses of the people than to the cold counting-house calculations of the nation's political leaders. When the colonial reaction was at the lowest ebb Cobden was not slow to recognize this fact and to comment on it as a strange contradiction. In a letter to Bright written in 1845, when he had been hammering at the question for over a dozen years, he confessed disappointment that there was " as much clinging to the colonies at the present moment amongst the middle class as among the aristocracy," and that " the working classes are not wiser than the rest." Perhaps he had forgotten that to large and growing sections of the population the colonies were now more and more offering the homes and the future which the land of their birth denied them. While during the ten years 1820–9 the emigrants from the United Kingdom to British North America numbered 126,000 and those to the Australasian colonies 5,200, the numbers were 320,800 and 53,300 during the succeeding decade, and 428,400 and 126,800 during 1840–9.

Incidentally it may be recalled how vigorously Cobden protested against emigration when the effect was to starve the land which ought to maintain a much larger population. In a speech on the prevalent agricultural distress made in the House of Commons on March 13, 1845, he told the landowners : " If you had abundance of capital employed on your farms, and cultivated the soil with the same skill that the manufacturers conduct their business, you would not have population enough to cultivate the land, and yet . . . you are smuggling the people away and sending them to the Antipodes, whereas if your lands were properly cultivated you would be trying to lure them back, as the most valuable part of your possessions."

Except that it is chiefly the urban and industrial workers who form the majority of our modern emigrants, and that the choice of new homes is now far wider, there is as much truth in these words as when they were uttered over eighty years ago. It is also a deplorable fact that the standard of life in rural England generally has altogether failed to keep pace with the advance made in the towns.

II. Imperialism.

Cobden was not only opposed to the permanent retention of settled colonies, he was still more hostile to what has come to be known as Imperialism. Here, again, it is necessary to remember that most of his criticism of Empire was called forth by events and conditions peculiar to his day, and it should be judged from that standpoint. The British Empire has had no severer critic than this uncompromising exponent of the doctrine of non-intervention. He discountenanced all dominion which carried rule over alien races as opposed to every law of nature, and therefore hopelessly futile, and as likely to react injuriously upon the country which exercised it. Herein he was wholly of Abraham Lincoln's opinion that the Almighty has endowed no nation with wisdom sufficient to entitle it to rule other peoples.

While opposed to Imperialism of every kind and degree, the British occupation and government of India represented to him the worst evils incidental to the domination of alien races. As he put it in his dogmatic way, " We have attempted an impossibility in giving ourselves to the task of governing

N

one hundred millions of Asiatics. God and His visible natural laws have opposed insuperable obstacles to the success of such a scheme." Viewing the facts of the past and of his time, the whole system of Indian government was to him a " blood-stained edifice " which would " one day cave in like a house of cards."

It is no cynicism to say that seldom if ever has a nation undertaken the rule of inferior races disinterestedly and for their sole good, however the real motives behind the pretexts may have been cloked by subterfuge and moral unction. This is hardly less true for the modern age of annexation for the sake of minerals and oil than for the early epochs of civilization. The empires of antiquity—of Persia, Rome, Carthage, Greece —were the outcome of sheer lust of conquest, and their founders sought reward in glory, power, and gain—objects not the highest, yet at least frankly acknowledged. Modern Imperialism, by whatever name it has been called, has been commended to the democracies of Europe in one quarter by the need and advantages of extended commercial intercourse, in another by the need for outlets for superfluous population, in another by the call to evangelization and the advancement of civilization generally.

Cobden, tearing the veil from pretence, saw in his country's past relations with India only sordid ambitions and territorial greed, and its record spoke to him mostly of warfare and cruel oppression, varied by occasional rebellions in which the pent-up passions of the subject races found relief. Had he written and spoken half a century later his indictment of Indian rule would have been greatly modified, and much of it would have lost point altogether. When he entered public life, however, India was still governed by the John Company, and governed despotically ; for though the Governors-General (the first Viceroy dated only from 1858) were appointed by the Crown, they exercised far more power than the Crown at home. Of native representation and voice in the councils of government there was no suggestion, and only in the lowest grades were Hindus, and few of them, admitted into the public service of their own country. In the middle of the century the European population, dispersed amongst 150,000,000 Hindus, was estimated at 67,000 or 68,000, of whom 50,000 were the Queen's or the Company's troops, between 7,000 and 8,000 civil employees of the Company with their families, and the residue of 10,000 for the most part persons engaged commercially. Of a revenue of 20¼ millions sterling at that time 10 millions were spent on the military and about half a million on the naval force.

He added India to his political repertory somewhat late, for his first systematic essay on Indian affairs, the pamphlet entitled *How Wars are got up in India : the Origin of the Burmese War*, like his first recorded speech on the same subject, dates from 1853, though casual references to India occurred in earlier public utterances. Events which had occurred under his eyes gave point to the harsh censures contained in this writing. The record of the preceding half-century had been a dismal sequence of wars and local mutinies, soon to culminate in one of the most tragic episodes known to history. Of the wars, some were deliberately instigated for the purpose of justifying the addition of new territories to the sphere of British rule, and nearly all had that result. Scinde, the Punjab, Oude, and of lesser territories, hitherto under independent sovereignty, not a few, had fallen into the all-devouring maw of British dominion ; there had also been two wars (1824–6 and 1851–2) with Burma, a Naboth's vineyard lying temptingly on India's eastern frontier, resulting in the absorption of more than half of the ancient Kingdom of Ava ; while in 1838 began the first war with Afghanistan, precursor of half a century of trouble with the Ameer's wild, liberty-loving tribes, whose resolution alone spared their mountainous country the same fate.

Not fairly, perhaps, but not altogether unnaturally, it was episodes in India's life like these which chiefly impressed a man whose hatred of injustice was only equalled by his hatred of war, most of all war waged against weak and unwilling combatants ; they coloured his entire judgment of Indian government, and convinced him that it could not and should not last.

He came to closer quarters with Indian questions as a member of a Committee of the House of Commons appointed by Lord Aberdeen in 1853 to inquire into the government of the dependency. Before the Committee had got through half its task, however, the Government produced a measure dealing with the subject of investigation. Cobden, viewing the act as a deliberate snub for the Committee, absented himself from further attendance, since he would have regarded it as a mockery and a waste of time, and when Sir Charles Wood, the Secretary of State, introduced his India Bill he spoke in support of Lord Stanley's amendment, the object of which was to postpone legislation until the Government and Parliament were in possession of all the needed facts. The speech (June 27, 1853) was a powerful indictment of the entire system of Indian administration as he had discovered it for himself in the course of his work on the Committee, and it also contained a vigorous protest against the policy of wholesale annexation which was then being pursued by a forceful Governor-General. The amendment was defeated by the large majority of 182 (322 to 140), though the figures proved more the strength of party discipline than that the House of Commons thought strongly or deeply on the subject of debate.

In his speech he told an extraordinary story of how the great dependency was governed at that time. At the head of the junta known as the Indian Government stood, nominally at least, a body known as the Board of Commissioners. Below the Board, and sitting at Leadenhall Street, came the Court of Directors, whose power related only to " patronage "—the appointment of minor officials. Then there was a fictitious Secret Committee of three members, which proved on investigation to be the President of the Board of Control himself. Theoretically the President possessed almost absolute power ; he could declare war, annex territories, and determine the weal or woe of the uncounted and uncountable millions of the native population, uncontrolled by the British Crown, Government, or Parliament. " It is in the power of the President of the Board of Control," he told the House, " to sit down and write an order to annex China, and send that order to these three gentlemen (the Select Committee), and they are obliged to send the order to India for prosecution by the Governor-General."

That was the strict law of the matter, though in practice ultimate authority was exercised by the Governor-General, at that time Lord Dalhousie. Dalhousie was the *Mehrer des Reiches,* the " empire-augmenter," *par excellence* of last century.

He had laid down, and he faithfully followed, the principle that " In the exercise of a wise and sound policy the British Government is bound not to put aside any rightful opportunities of acquiring territory or revenue as may from time to time present themselves." To Cobden this policy was well designed to create a maximum of mischief, and he contrasted the non-annexation policy which Parliament had enforced upon the Colonial Office with the Indian Governor-General's power to annex when, where, and as he would at his own discretion. Dalhousie had declared, " We are lords paramount in India, and our policy is to acquire as direct a dominion over the territories in possession of the native princes as we already hold over the other half of India." His critic protested against the continual inroads upon native sovereignty as a dangerous extension of imperial responsibilities. For on the Dalhousie principle annexation was not a wrong to be apologized for, but a duty to be faithfully discharged.

In the same speech he earnestly emphasized the nation's direct responsibility for the government of India. The Company's rule was a fiction and a sham, and for the wrongs done in the dependency England must bear the blame. His views on the subject of non-intervention were so strong that he would have been willing to see the Company remain in full control had he been able to trust it, and certain that the responsibility which Great Britain had assumed in virtue of conquest and occupation would be properly met. Not satisfied on these points, he was opposed to the continuance of the system then in existence. The Imperial Government did, in fact, supersede the Company after the Mutiny of 1857. He also warmly advocated the generous admission of native Indians to the higher branches of the administrative service, a reform favoured by several earlier Governors-General, but not introduced until a later date.

Cobden never ceased to fear that the English character would suffer deterioration from contact with Asia and the different moral standards which were applied in dealings with backward races. This fear is the burden of many of his letters, particularly those written after the war with China in 1856 and the Indian outbreak of the following year. In one of these he wrote :

" Nobody has a greater horror, scorn, and detestation than I have for the doctrine of an irresistible law or destiny impelling to brute violence and injustice. That may be the law for wild beasts, but it is because we are something better than wild beasts that it ought not to be our law. . . . When a Government plants its power and authority among an inferior race (I don't like the word, but there are inferior climates for the development of man), the very superiority, whether intellectual, moral, or physical, leads to an extension of its power and influence over surrounding barbarism." [1]

He admitted that a form of ascendancy might be tolerable if it were moral and " the governing intruders " were capable of taking root with the indigenous population and amalgamating with it. As that prospect did not exist in tropical countries, climatic conditions alone forbidding it, the only safe thing both for West and East was to keep apart. If there must be interference it should be left to the missionaries, both religious and secular, who should try to inspire the native population with ideas of an improved social and political status and the desire for better government. But government should be their own affair. His advice was, " Don't attempt to govern them, or to exert your influence through the Government. Do, in fact, as St. Paul did."

The Mutiny of 1857 confirmed Cobden's worst forebodings. The first reflexion which the catastrophe forced upon him was that there had been something radically amiss with the relations of the governors and the governed in India, that English influence had been deteriorating, instead of elevating, that if England had really been engaged in a civilizing mission that mission had lamentably failed, and that we had reached the beginning of the end of our rule in the dependency.

" There is one thought ever recurring to my mind," he wrote when the news came to this country : " how is it possible that we, a Christian and a superior race, can have been for a century in close contact with this people and produced no better results than these ? Has not our conduct been such as to imbue the minds of the native population not

---

[1] In his *Journal* (p. 199) the Earl of Elgin, who early in 1857 had been dispatched as plenipotentiary to China, and who took thence a relief force to Calcutta, writes under date August 21 of that year : " It is a terrible business, this living among inferior races. I have seldom from man or woman since I came to the East heard a sentence which was reconcilable with the hypothesis that Christianity had ever come into the world. Detestation, contempt, ferocity, vengeance, whether Chinamen or Indians be the object."

only with hatred but contempt for us ? How can we account for these unnatural cruelties among our fellow-subjects in India upon any theory which is not a mournful reproach to ourselves as the conquering and dominant race ? "

When the hoarse cry was raised for crude, blind vengeance, for paying back the murderers in their own coin, and plenty of it, no more vigorous protests were uttered than his. He recognized that the revolt had to be put down, in justice to the peaceable section of the population, which was at the mercy of hordes of armed fanatics, but he feared that in the process " we shall familiarize ourselves with deeds of blood which may tend to make us a cruel and sanguinary nation." He voiced the opinions of most moral people, though not of all, when he wrote to Bright (September 22) :

" We seem in danger of forgetting our own Christianity and descending to a level with these monsters who have startled the world with their deeds. It is terrible to see our middle-class journals and speakers calling for the destruction of Delhi, and the indiscriminate massacre of prisoners. To read the letters of our officers at the commencement of the outbreak, it seemed as if every subaltern had the power to hang or shoot as many natives as he pleased, and they spoke of the work of blood with as much levity as if they were hunting wild animals."

Criticisms like these might almost suggest uncharitable exaggeration ; yet the experience of recent years should be sufficient to remind all of us into what extremes the lust for revenge can betray people who in normal circumstances would be incapable of base or inhuman thoughts. It may be recalled also how Lord Canning wrote from India to the Queen (September 25, 1857) deploring the evil spirit which was poisoning the public mind there. " There is a rabid and indiscriminate vindictiveness abroad (he said), even amongst many who ought to set a better example, and it is impossible to contemplate it without a feeling of shame for one's country-men. . . . The cry is raised loudest by those who have been sitting quietly in their homes from the beginning, and have suffered little from the convulsions around them, unless it be in pocket." Perhaps those who resent Cobden's plain speaking will think better of him when they remember that the passages quoted above occurred in private letters, and are told that, far from striking publicly any harsh note of discord at that trying time, he reproved the editor of the *Morning Star*, the organ of the peace party, of whose policy he had for some years been the unofficial inspirer, when he seemed to be trying to make party capital out of the Mutiny episode, bidding him " beware of allowing a tone of exultation over the Indian troubles to appear in your articles. I thought I perceived such a spirit in the *Star* article yesterday."

But the question which chiefly troubled him was—what next, and at the last ?

" But the future—what is in the distance ? " he wrote to Bright. " You know my opinion of old : that I never could feel any enthusiasm for the reform of our Indian Government, for I failed to satisfy myself that it was possible for us to rule that vast empire with advantage to its people or ourselves. I now regard the task as utterly impossible. Recent and present events are placing an impassable gulf between the races. Conquerors and conquered can never live together again with confidence or comfort. It will be a happy day when England has not an acre of territory in Continental Asia."

" No, there is no future but trouble and loss and disappointment, and I fear crime, in India," he wrote to another correspondent, " and they are doing the people of this country the greatest service who tell them the honest truth according to their convictions, and prepare them for abandoning at some future time the thankless and impossible task."

He put the question hypothetically, " Should Great Britain give education to India, or reform its criminals, or abate its crime, or moderate its religious bigotry and intolerance ? " And his answer was, " Physician, heal thyself ! " We had not yet done these things at home ; how could we hope to give to such a vast and backward population a high standard of morality when we ourselves lacked it ? He therefore accepted the alternative step, which was withdrawal. Yet he saw that this would need to be gradual, and that it could not be complete. It would be improper to resign authority in certain territories whose deposed native Sovereigns had left no descendants, since the possible native claimants might have no better right to hold it than the supplanting administration. He held, however, that this objection did not apply to recently annexed States like Scinde, the Punjab, Burma, and least of all to Oude, " that stolen piece of property," " the latest and worst of all our violations of right and justice," whose people were then fighting for their rights, " with as much title to the rank of patriots as was bestowed on Swiss or Dutch in their wars of independence."

When religious enthusiasts of the type who, in Byron's phrase, " pervert the prophets and purloin the Psalms," professed to see in the late barbarities another and louder call for the conversion of the Hindus, he energetically rejected so mechanical an interpretation of divine purpose. " Their doings," he wrote (October 14, 1858), " are enough to make atheists of us all—i.e. if we are to take them as the accredited exponents of Christianity." He " wanted to ask them point-blank, who told them that God gave us India in trust for religious purposes ? The presumption of that class is astounding." Let the evangelists pursue their work, by all means, but let them refrain from mixing up religion with politics. Once more, " Let them do as St. Paul did."

To the last he continued unconvinced that British rule had a long future in India. He believed that the difficulties would increase until all people, other than the interested classes, would begin to ask themselves seriously, " What benefit do *we* derive from the ' possession ' of India ? " and that the answer would be that its possession was the worst bad debt the nation had ever made. The great danger was lest by the time Great Britain became permanently disgusted and threw up the impossible task of ruling the country, the last traces of a governing class or of governing capacity would have disappeared, and that we should " abandon the nation, as Rome did our ancestors, to intestine anarchy and foreign conquest."

So distrustful, under the influence of the great tragedy of that time, did he become of the impossibility of a Western nation successfully governing Asiatics that he now ceased to take any practical interest in the reform of Indian administration, believing it to be incapable of betterment. Even when, the rising suppressed and peace restored, it was possible again to think over matters more quietly, his pessimistic outlook remained unaltered. In what appears to have been the last of his references to the question of Indian government he wrote (August 4, 1860) :

" I have no heart for discussing any of the details of Indian management, for I look on our rule there as a whole with an eye of despair. Ultimately, of course, nature will assert the supremacy of her laws, and the white skins will withdraw to their own latitudes, leaving the Hindus to the enjoyment of the climate to which their complexion is suited. In the meantime, we shall suffer all kinds of trouble, loss, and disgrace."

Viewed in the light of subsequent developments, and particularly of the remarkable growth of the imperial idea from the last quarter of his century forward, Cobden's attitude both toward the colonies and India may be disappointing to those who look to him for guidance in present difficulties. Yet to condemn him off-hand, without reference to time and circumstances, would be unfair. Justice requires that his opinions should be judged from the standpoint of his day, and above all in relation to the critical and unsympathetic view of imperial responsibilities which was then largely current, not merely amongst taxpayers who thought of Empire only in terms of pounds, shillings, and pence, but in parliamentary and governing circles. It has been shown that in relation to some aspects of the question he only put into plain language the thought of his time, and if in regard to other aspects he went beyond or entirely differed from his contemporaries it was because his logical mind was dissatisfied with abstract positions and half-measures, and because he never feared to draw from his principles the extreme consequences.

When an interpreter takes words out of a man's mouth it is a just rule that he should try to understand them as he understood them, and to avoid reading into them meanings which may not have been intended. Cobden is not a man who can be easily misrepresented except of set purpose. Words occasionally slipped from his ready lip or pen which would justify a critic in making points against him on the score of inconsistency. But in general he was so essentially clear, direct, and straightforward that there is little difficulty in following his teaching. And it must be frankly said that, in his way and for his time, he was a quite robust Empire-breaker. Perhaps to most readers of his utterances to-day it must come as a shock to find this practical man of affairs, who began life as a merchant and never lost the wide-minded merchant's outlook, and who prided himself on his native common sense, telling colonial and imperial enthusiasts that they had better abandon the oversea dependencies altogether and be content to send missionaries and teachers there instead. Had he had his way England would not have had so much as a back garden of a colony to which to migrate her surplus inhabitants, all of whom would have been advised to seek homes in less congested countries or to form independent oversea communities only attached to the Mother Land by the commercial and cultural interests common to the rest of the world. That this is no exaggeration of his pure and unadultered doctrine of Empire is shown by a passage like the following, taken from the first pamphlet :

" If ever there was a territory that was marked out by the finger of God for the possession of a distinct nation, that country is ours ; whose boundary is the ocean, and within whose ramparts are to be found, in abundance, all the mineral and vegetable treasures requisite to make us a great commercial people. Discontented with these blessings, and disdaining the natural limits of our empire, in the insolence of our might, and without waiting for the assaults of envious enemies, we have sallied forth in search of conquest or rapine, and carried bloodshed into every corner of the globe."

The truth is that to Cobden there were things more precious even than colonies and Empire, and such were justice and morality. Never did he acquit his country of the guilt of having acquired so large a part of its imperial patrimony by violent means [1] and of having so long exploited it for material advantage ; and his remembrance of these things largely determined his unsympathetic attitude to foreign dominion in general.

Nevertheless, it would be but little complimentary to a man of his liberal breadth of view to suppose that he would to-day have held on the colonial question, in the narrower sense, the opinions of sixty years ago. He was never slow to face hard facts, and to adjust his mind and action to new perspectives, insomuch that if he had a special weakness as a controversialist it was his habit of forming hasty conclusions

[1] A classification of the titles by which Great Britain came into possession of 75 different oversea territories, shows 30 as having been acquired by conquest, conquest and cession, or annexation, 20 by treaty cession (sometimes following forcible occupation), and 18 by settlement (*Whitaker's Almanack* for 1926, p. 459).

and generalizing too boldly on inadequate data. It would appear only reasonable, therefore, to assume that if his public life had begun and ended later in the century his attitude on this question might have been greatly modified. Like Bismarck down to the close of his career, he might still have been at heart a " no colony man " ; yet while he would certainly have been a foremost protagonist of the Dominion idea and the widest possible extension of self-government throughout the empire, it is probable that he would have talked less about secession.

We have seen that, following yet going a step further than Adam Smith, he looked for an amicable dissolution of partnership between Great Britain and the colonies. As fate would have it, there was a preference on both sides for his more habitual method of solving political difficulties, which was to " trust to the course of events," with the result of a happier development of the imperial relationship than either of these thinkers anticipated. The grant to the larger colonies of the Dominion status, which when made had come to be regarded as the most natural thing in the world, was an arrangement that offered all the practical advantages, while entailing none of the disadvantages, of political separation. At the same time it has been attended by a great and ever-growing augmentation of commercial intercourse within the Empire.

One may say, therefore, that since Cobden's day the colonial question has settled itself. British colonies hardly exist any longer in the sense in which the term was then understood ; the larger territories settled by the British races have become autonomous units in the Empire ; the lesser ones have long practically managed their own affairs ; and only the little communities, too weak to stand alone, have still to lean on the friendly arm of the Colonial Office. Better still, the modern idea is that each part of the Empire should be governed for itself and primarily in its own interest. The abuses of the old colonial system are so far behind us as to be forgotten, so that to-day few people understand what trade monopolies meant two or three generations ago. At the same time the principle of reciprocal liability is both recognized and increasingly applied in regard to imperial defence and its cost.

The principal change relates, of course, to the great British-settled colonies which Cobden specially had in mind, and which were almost the only ones which seriously counted at that time. All of these have long outlived both the old status and the old name : as Dominion or Commonwealth or Union their position is for practical purposes that of Federal States, enjoying almost unlimited independence in internal affairs, with just so large a right to be consulted on questions of imperial and foreign concern as they are disposed to claim, with separate diplomatic representation abroad where they ask for it, with the power to negotiate treaties of certain kinds with foreign States, and even with representation on equal terms with Great Britain in international congresses. The further extension of the rights of the Dominions now in course of negotiation will draw them more closely into the imperial councils. At a time when the elevation of the status of the High Commissioners of the Dominions, with this end in view, is being considered, it is interesting to recall the fact that these envoys are the lineal descendants of the old Colonial Agents, though with wider powers and functions. The North American colonies commonly appointed politicians or other persons of distinction, resident in England, to the office of Agent, and Edmund Burke at one time acted in this capacity for New York.

A measure of autonomy going so far might well have been welcomed by Cobden as preferable to the independence for which he believed Canada to be ready in his day. If, however, at this distance of time some of his opinions on the subject of secession sound unreal, it cannot be denied that he faithfully anticipated the present position of Great Britain in relation to all the self-governing commonwealths. We want them to remain in the Empire, strengthening its fabric, deepening the attachment of the British races to the Crown as the symbol of its unity, because convinced that union will make for their good as well as ours, and by its example and influence will contribute to the peace of the world. Yet no longer merely material ties, but in a far larger degree voluntary attachment, rooted in a consciousness of common interests, common ideals, and a common indebtedness to civilization, binds together this great world-wide partnership of equals. If and when, however, any one of the partners should be convinced of its ability to stand alone and go its own way in the world, and believe that its welfare would be best served by so doing, then, in Cobden's

words, there would be " no repetition of the policy of 1776 on
our part." It would be a parting of regrets—on one side
certainly, on both sides probably—but not one of anger or
resentment, and the door of exit would thereafter remain ever
open for the comrade's return.

It would be impossible to press the " relativity " theory
in an equal degree in favour of Cobden's opinions on the subject
of Imperialism in the wider sense. Here, too, some of his
apprehensions have proved baseless and some of his predictions
have been falsified, yet there is no justification for supposing
that his objection to the rule of Oriental races by Western
Powers would ever have been modified. Granting that the
idea of Empire to-day connotes responsibility to a degree it
never did in the past, yet the great moral advance of public
opinion on this question visible in many countries, and pre-
eminently in our own, would have failed to reconcile him to
the enormous extension of the British dominion which has
taken place since his time. No less sturdily than then he would
to-day have rejected the plea of a mission of civilization as
justifying the arbitrary subjugation of native populations.
Much of the later colonizing enterprise of European Powers,
however, whatever the pretexts advanced on its behalf after
the event, has been an unintelligent scramble for territory.
But land-hunger never made forcible expropriation honest,
whether committed by Governments, Chartered Companies, or
Irish Land Leagues. Apart from the claims of morality, to
which he never gave a too conspicuous place in his argument,
believing that, as nations still were, more practical appeals
often carried his causes farther, he would have seen in these
indefinite extensions of the Empire only a foolish increase of
liabilities, risks, and dangers.

Lord Rosebery was regarded as an imperialist of the
forward school, yet he was not unconscious that greater
Empire means greater peril. In 1896, just after he ceased to
be Foreign Secretary, in reminding his countrymen that in the
course of twelve years additions had been made to the British
Empire, in part by himself, to the extent of two and a half
million square miles—an area equal to two-thirds of Europe—
he warned them that the effect had not been to make them
and this country more popular with the rest of the world.

The fact that from that time successive statesmen of all parties have repeatedly disclaimed the idea of further extensions did not prevent new acquisitions, camouflaged by the phrase " mandate government," from taking place when the opportunity offered during and after the Great War. To pretend that an Empire with an area of thirteen million square miles was not large enough or complete in 1919 is tantamount to a claim that it never will be large enough or complete. Ever since Imperialism was given a new start about half a century ago, no opportunity of adding to our dominion has been lost. It is even doubtful whether there exists a British statesman to-day who, in spite of all recent increases of our territorial responsibilities, would dare to repeat the words uttered many years ago by the late Mr. Bonar Law [1] in the House of Commons—that the British Empire was sufficiently extensive, that there was no need for any addition to it, and that our business was to develop what we had.

The fact is that, owing to wars and foreign interventions and an insatiable craving for territory wherever it can be obtained, we have so overloaded ourselves with debt and liabilities of all kinds that to-day our resources, not only in money but in administrative power, are mortgaged up to the hilt, insomuch that the Prime Minister, voicing the apprehension of thousands of his countrymen, had recently to confess a " dread at the heart " as he reflected on the late holocaust of so much of the finest flower of our young manhood. Still we are able to make the proud boast that we have the greatest Empire the world has ever known ; but we have also the greatest national indebtedness in history. Still we can claim that our navy remains the strongest afloat ; but we have also the most and the greatest oversea liabilities and risks. And the irony of the situation is that while our power at sea is bound to diminish relatively to that of at least two other maritime States, our imperial liabilities and risks will for that reason increase in the same or a greater proportion.

Upon no imperial question would Cobden have been less likely to modify his opinions than upon British rule in India.

---

[1] He repeated the disclaimer in the House of Commons so late as February 20, 1917, when declaring that Great Britain in the late war was ' not fighting for additional territory."

That rule has not collapsed as he predicted, but, with whatever degree of success, has continued to hold its ground, until to-day it is responsible for the welfare of an oriental population, of divers races and religions, numbering not one hundred and fifty, but three hundred millions. Yet if the East, like the Alpine glacier, moves slowly, so that a generation in its life is but as a Western day, it moves with inexorable sureness. During the late war the electrifying doctrine of self-determination was proclaimed *urbi et orbi* by rhetorical politicians prodigal in phrases, and a large body of such opinion as finds public expression in India is to-day calling for the fulfilment of the hopes then aroused.   If as yet British rule in the dependency is unshaken it is more definitely challenged than ever before, and many present signs seem to point to a growing recognition of the challenge as inevitable.

At the same time Cobden's argument that the government by Western nations of oriental races, however backward, is wrong because it is against nature is unconvincing.   There is a possible alternative to working against nature even in such a matter, and it is to work with her ; and in the regard shown for native traditions, sentiment, and idiosyncrasies this has long been the aim of British administration, whatever its shortcomings in earlier times.   Even to-day there is no evidence whatever of any general dissatisfaction with that administration, which has done for the Hindu population a hundredfold more than, unassisted, it could have done for itself.   It is notorious that there are exponents of nationalist opinion who, while in their public utterances advocating the vague policy of " India for the Indians," are not slow to declare in private that the withdrawal of the British would be a calamity for the country, and is the last thing in the world which they would like to see.

Yet the assumption that the agitation for practical autonomy will grow in strength, which is the only safe one, does not imply the acceptance of a policy of " scuttle," which Cobden himself repudiated, or even suggest the possibility of yet talking about time limits ; but only the recognition of the duty to leave India to herself as soon as she can safely dispense with our help and protection.   It is probable that, for a far longer time than either we or our Hindu *protégés* think, we shall continue to bear the heavier share of the burden of government, and that in circumstances of increasing difficulty and discomfort. But that fact only the more clearly points to the duty and expediency of pushing forward the work of educating the masses of the population and building up the system of local administration with greater energy than heretofore, in preparation for the time, however distant it may be, when India will be ripe for complete political autonomy, which, after all, must be the purpose and end of any rational conception of a " trust of civilization." No Englishman of his time urged this duty with greater earnestness, or anticipated its full discharge with greater satisfaction, than Cobden.

CHAPTER X

THE EASTERN QUESTION

" As we are drifting fast towards war, I should think the Cabinet ought to know where they are going."—LORD ABERDEEN to the Earl of Clarendon, June 7, 1853.

" I am aware that I am opposing the present current of public feeling, but where is the man of sense, courage, and honesty who will deliberately say that the truth ought not to be spoken because it does not flatter the preconceived impressions of the hour ? "—COBDEN on the Crimean War.

" No respect I have for men who form a Government, no regard I have for going with the stream, and no fear of being deemed wanting in patriotism shall influence me in favour of a policy which in my conscience I believe to be as criminal before God as it is destructive of the true interests of my country." —JOHN BRIGHT on the Crimean War, October 1854.

COBDEN'S attitude on the question of East European policy deserves to be recalled for two reasons : because it was ultimately endorsed by the nation generally, though only after two generations had passed away, and because the Eastern Question, as it developed in his day, is even yet only partially solved. Referring to a debate on the subject which took place in the House of Commons on August 16, 1853, Sir James Graham, who was at the Admiralty in the Aberdeen administration, wrote to Lord Clarendon : " We have a standing fight between Cobden and Palmerston —the former the champion of Russia and Christianity, the latter the sworn ally of Turkey and Mahomedanism. Both made very able speeches in opposite senses ; but both pushed their doctrines to an extreme. Cobden, in the long run, will have England with him, but the Derbyites were enchanted with Palmerston and cheered him to the echo." [1] Cobden was right, and England " in the long run " did accept his views, but conviction came slowly, and first bitter experiences

[1] *Life and Letters of the Fourth Earl of Clarendon* (by Sir Herbert Maxwell), ii. 16.

were necessary—two years of stubborn war with Russia, followed by over a generation of armed peace with the same Power.

Upon no question of foreign politics did the people of this country take sides more passionately during the greater part of last century than upon this. Twenty years before the Crimean War, and probably earlier, Cobden had made definite choice between the two Powers which disputed for influence in the East of Europe. He discussed Russia's attitude to Turkey and England's attitude to both of these Powers in his first political pamphlet, *England, Ireland, and America* (1835). At the time it was written the nation was suffering from one of its earliest attacks of Russophobism. The prejudice against Russia, which Palmerston shared, was fomented by politicians and journalists, who represented her as an insatiable Power, bent not only on appropriating Turkey in the Near East, but on extending her conquests beyond the Indus and supplanting British rule in the Far East. The nation was bidden to nip this nefarious design in the bud, by attacking and disabling the suspect enemy in Europe, while he was still not invulnerable.

In his counter-blast, Cobden boldly declared that even if Russia were to subjugate Turkey it would be a good thing, and England in particular, as a mercantile country, would gain rather than lose in consequence. " Our sole aim," he said, " is the just interests of England, regardless of the objects of other nations." Warning his countrymen against the danger of allowing appeals to their emotions to override calm and sober judgment, he contended that the Eastern Question, as it had been formulated, was one with which this country had no concern, and that if Russia and Turkey came to blows the British Government should resolutely refrain from entering the quarrel, and be content to accept the result, whatever it might be. With singular foresight he wrote :

" Russia, and no longer France, is the chimera that now haunts us in our apprehension for the safety of Europe ; whilst Turkey for the first time appears to claim our sympathy and protection against the encroachments of her neighbours ; and, strange as it may appear to the politicians of a future age, such is the prevailing sentiment of hostility towards the Russian Government at this time in the public mind, that, with but few additional provocatives administered to it by a judicious Minister through the public prints, a conflict with that

Christian Power in defence of a Mahomedan people more than a thousand miles distant from our shores might be made palatable, nay, popular, with the British nation."

It is easy to see, after the event, how wise British statesmen of that time would have been had they orientated national policy in the direction of Cobden's doctrine, and endeavoured more and more to limit England's liabilities in Europe, instead of deliberately increasing them, with results of which we are still digesting the bitter fruit nearly a century later. The Crimean War was still on the knees of the gods, but already forces were in train which were directly making for that great political crime, even at a time when England was still smarting from the wounds received during the long and exhausting struggle with France. Cobden saw the dangers ahead and warned his countrymen of them. There were ruling statesmen of his day who likewise saw, or at least suspected, them, but they preferred to wait on events.

In the following year he returned to the subject in the pamphlet bearing the title *Russia* and published anonymously. It is recorded that on its appearance Lord Durham, then British ambassador in St. Petersburg, was so much impressed by the sanity of the writer's views that when he next returned to England he procured a meeting with Cobden, of whom he predicted, " Mark my words—Cobden will one day be one of the first men in England." In this pamphlet his views on the Eastern Question and Great Britain's attitude thereto are set forth in greater detail. Holding it to be the duty of a nation to review and modify its foreign policy from time to time, just as it reviews and modifies its domestic policy, according to circumstances, he discussed the question whether the " States system" which was suited to the international affairs of Europe a century before equally suited the changed conditions of that day. This question he answered negatively, advancing as reasons " the rise and paramount commercial importance of free America, the downfall of the colony system, and the application of the doctrines of free trade." He pleaded, therefore, that " the mighty influence which such changes are now exercising over our destinies ought to be duly studied and appreciated by those who, as statesmen, are permitted to regulate the external affairs of this commercial empire."

Coming to the practical point of his argument, he contended that no longer Turkey, an effete and hopeless Power, but Russia, as representing in Eastern Europe, in however inadequate a way, Christian civilization and the spirit of progress, should be recognized as the natural heir to the European patrimony of the Caliphate. He was ready even then to welcome Russia's formal occupation of Constantinople, and from such occupation he predicted commercial consequences of immense importance for the world. He discounted the idea that Russia would or could be a danger to British power in the Far East, and as for her alleged aggressive designs he maintained that reproof came with a bad grace from his own country, since for every league of territory annexed by Russia during the preceding hundred years England had taken three. Further, on the question of the right to expand, there could not be one law for England and another for the rest of the world ; what was legitimate for this country must be equally permissible for any other.

Cobden never modified his low estimate of Turkey or his conviction that ages of unchanging misgovernment, oppression, and cruelty had disqualified her for the custody of alien populations. On the contrary, his visits to the East only strengthened the antipathy to Mahomedan rule to which the study of history had led him.

His constant appeals to his countrymen not to pin their faith to the Sultan's empire, or to assume its integrity to be for Great Britain a vital interest, had little result at the time. Those who did not need to be convinced acclaimed his sagacity, but they were an ineffectual minority. The nation at large preferred Palmerston to the Manchester manufacturer, and when in the middle of the century the rupture came which Cobden had foreseen, it plunged with enthusiasm into a long and disastrous war.

Public controversy and clamour apart, what were the political and diplomatic events which led up to that catastrophe ? The Treaty of Adrianople (September 14, 1829) closed a sixteen months' war between Russia and Turkey in which, after many fluctuations of fortune, the Tsar's armies set up the standard of victory in that ancient capital of Islam. By that treaty Greece gained independence, Russia acquired new territory in the Caucasus, together with a modified protectorate over the Danubian principalities of Moldavia and Wallachia (later forming Roumania), and the Straits were thrown open to the merchant ships of all nations.

From that time Russia and Great Britain went more and more apart. His success in beating the Sultan both in war and diplomacy encouraged the Emperor Nicholas I in the belief that the Ottoman empire was hastening to its fall, and as early as 1844 he endeavoured to draw this country into an agreement for its division. This invitation was declined, ostensibly on the just plea that if the status of Turkey had to be reconsidered it should be done by the common assent of all the Great Powers. The real reason was the old determination to maintain the integrity of Turkey as a bulwark against Russian expansion in the direction of the Mediterranean. Yet at that time England had no immediate interest in either Asia Minor or Egypt. The construction of the Suez Canal was only begun in 1859, and the highway to India was the broad ocean. In January 1853 the Tsar again raised the question. Turkey, he said, was unquestionably a "Sick Man," and it was expedient to delay no longer the disposal of his dominion. He suggested that Great Britain might take Egypt and Crete ; he would prefer Constantinople. He was acutely displeased that his advances once more failed to receive encouragement.

When a rupture occurred it was over a narrower issue, originally affecting only Russia and France. Hidden away in the archives of the French Foreign Ministry was a treaty of 1740 by which the Sultan recognized France as the rightful protector of the Holy Places in Palestine. The treaty had been forgotten, and the obligations incurred under it had never been discharged. At a later date the Porte, true to its traditional propensity for making mischief between rival Powers, granted to Russia rights which conflicted with those already conceded to France. This it did by the Treaty of Kutchuk-Kainardji, concluded in 1774, by which the Sultan gave Russia an undertaking that he would " protect constantly the Christian religion and its churches," and placed the Greek church in Constantinople under Russian protection. By prescription Russia had come to interpret these provisions as

conveying to her a general right of protection over the Greek
Church throughout Turkey. There was here material for
conflict between the Latin and Greek Churches and their
patrons, and the crisis came in 1850. In that year Louis
Napoleon, as President of the French Republic, wishing to
please the Roman Catholics, formally claimed the custody of
the Holy Places, basing his action on the treaty of 1740. The
Sultan complaisantly acquiesced, but Russia protested and
counter-claimed on behalf of the Greek Church.

The question of the Holy Places might not have caused
insuperable difficulties had not the Tsar advanced the further
demand that Russia should be recognized as the protector of
all Greek Christians in the Ottoman empire. With this demand
the Porte refused to comply, herein following the advice of
the British Ambassador, Lord Stratford de Redcliffe, who had
not waited to obtain his Government's instructions. Three
Christian Powers were now involved in the dispute, two on
Turkey's side and one against her. In July 1853 a conference
of ambassadors was held in Vienna at which a compromise
was proposed. This was accepted by Russia, but not by
Turkey, again owing to Stratford's crooked action, for while
officially he had to counsel compliance, privately he urged
resistance.

Whether Russia's claim was strictly tenable or not, it was
at least arguable that the undertaking given to her by the
Sultan seventy years before, that he would " protect constantly the Christian religion and its churches," gave to
Russia by implication as clear a right to intervene in Turkey,
on due cause shown, as was given to Great Britain in relation
to the Christian races of the Sultan's Asiatic dominions by the
Cyprus Convention of June 4, 1878. Even Lord John Russell
spoke of the Russian claim as one " prescribed by duty and
sanctioned by treaty," and Mr. Gladstone likewise recognized
its strength.

In May Russia had thrown troops over the Pruth and
occupied the Danubian Provinces, by way of " pledge," and
as she refused to withdraw them the Porte declared war in
October. Diplomacy for a time tried to hasten the end of the
struggle, but from the beginning England's participation was
hardly less certain than sixty years later, when Germany,

Russia, and France seemed hurrying into hostilities in July 1914. For Lord Palmerston, the strong man of the Aberdeen Cabinet, was heart and soul with Turkey, and he had a capable accomplice in Constantinople in the person of the wilful ambassador—"the real Sultan," as Lord Clarendon called him at the time.

"I thought that we should have been able to conquer Stratford," Lord Aberdeen had written to Sir James Graham in the previous autumn, " but I began to fear that the reverse will be the case, and that he will succeed in defeating us. . . . To contend at once with the pride of the Emperor, the fanaticism of the Turks, and the dishonesty of Stratford is almost a hopeless attempt." Nevertheless, Aberdeen did not insist on the ambassador's recall, even though the Queen suggested it ; perhaps he feared that the Cabinet would break up if Palmerston's *protégé* were to be disowned. At that time Stratford was declaring in private letters that there must be a war, and that, in order to succeed, it "must be a comprehensive war on the part of England and France"—again an anticipation of the summer of 1914, when M. Isvolsky was manœuvring for "my war" in the embassies and clubs of Paris.

While thus Stratford was doing all that was necessary to stiffen the Porte in opposition to Russia's demands, at home Palmerston threw his influence in the Cabinet on the side of active intervention. Aberdeen believed in moral, Palmerston and Clarendon in material, pressure. So it was that the Cabinet was hopelessly divided, with the result—which was within an ace of being repeated in almost identical circumstances in 1878—that England, in Aberdeen's mournful and now historical phrase, "drifted into war." The very phrase was an implicit admission that the war was a blunder and a crime, and should never have occurred. Such, indeed, is the well-nigh universal verdict of historians and statesmen at the present day.

Cobden, like his friend John Bright, abhorred equally the war and the alliance in which England fought. "It is a war," he said, "in which we have a despot for an enemy, a despot for an ally, and a despot for a client." Writing later to Bright, he declared his willingness "to incur any obloquy in telling the whole truth to the public as to the share they have had in this war, and it is better to face any neglect or hostility than allow them to persuade themselves that anybody but themselves is responsible for the war " (October 18, 1854). Obloquy both he and Bright experienced in abundance. Throughout the two years that the war lasted these two brave men, who barely a decade before had rendered to the masses of their countrymen so magnificent and unselfish a service, drew upon themselves storms of popular passion and abuse of a violence hardly equalled before in English political life, and all because they dared to speak the truth as they knew it. It even happened that their effigies were burnt in the public streets of industrial towns to which their policy of Free Trade had brought prosperity and a higher standard of social life. In the House of Commons Lord Palmerston deemed it decorous to speak of Mr. Bright, who in dignified words had reproved his references to the war, as " the honourable and reverend gentleman," and to suggest that Cobden and his party should be confined in a madhouse. Even Disraeli protested against the " patrician bullying of the Treasury bench," and reminded Lord Palmerston that as the leader of the House he was expected to hold the language of a gentleman (July 16, 1855).

The widespread animosity against Russia at that time may have been deepened by her late co-operation with Austria in suppressing the Hungarian revolution, which was no business of hers, but apart from that stimulus the war without question was immensely popular. For those were the days when sturdy patriots, after bravely singing " Britons never shall be slaves," could still without compunction proceed to hire defenders of their liberty to do the necessary fighting at a shilling a day. The nation was weary of peace—" Why do they prate of the blessings of peace ? We have made them a curse," Tennyson wrote in *Maud* while the struggle was in progress—and the prejudice against Russia which had been fostered so diligently and so long by a virulent political coterie, backed by a powerful Press, had prepared the way for the conflict. Every influence and interest, social and political, was on the side of Turkey and against her antagonist—the Court and Parliament, the newspapers, the classes and the masses, and even to a large extent the Church, though Cobden notes as significant that " the Church of England clergy have from the first given more encouragement by their correspondence to Bright and myself than Dissenting ministers." *The Times* called attention to the striking fact that while in England the war spirit was held in check by the Government, in France Louis Napoleon had to justify before the people every warlike step he took.

When in the autumn of the first year of hostilities there was a notion of organizing a public demand for peace Cobden questioned whether there were " ten men in the House or a hundred and twenty outside, excepting the Quakers, who were to be relied on." A meeting was arranged at which he was to speak, but a letter written by him just before the day shows how profound were the rifts caused by the war not only in public but in private life. " I have an invitation from —— to go to his house," he said, " but have advised him to let me take shelter in an inn rather than carry discord into his domestic circle." If the Government " drifted " the nation literally rushed into the war.

To the last, Cobden and Bright stood out against the fierce tide of clamour and calumny, heroic figures, serene and unperturbed, never overwhelmed, never daunted or shaken. They likewise refused to regard the war as merely a Government's blunder or a diplomatist's adventure. The nation had sanctioned it, its heart was in it, and with the nation would rest the responsibility for the consequences. Exposed to every manner of abuse and insult, for the only reason that they would not go with the unthinking crowd, well might these men have replied to their accusers in the words used by Socrates when he faced his judges and the cup of hemlock :

" I have been condemned . . . because I did not choose to say to you the things that would have been pleasantest for you to hear, weeping, and lamenting, and saying and doing other things which I affirm to be unworthy of me, as you are accustomed to see others do. But neither did I then think fit to do or say anything unworthy of a free man, nor do I now repent of having thus defended myself. I would far rather have made the one defence and die, than have made the other and live."

The revelation of the nation's temper, fickleness, and intolerance at that time was a sore trial to Cobden's faith in human nature. He grieved most of all because it seemed to prove that the work of peace to which he had given so much of his life had not made the headway he had supposed.

" I am as much satisfied as ever," he wrote to Bright (September 14, 1854), " that we have followed a right course on the war question. It must be right for us, because we have followed our own conscientious convictions. But in proportion as we are devoted to our principles must be our regret to see so little prospect of their being adopted as the practical guide for our foreign policy. It is no use blinking the fact that there are not a score of men in the House, and but few out of the ranks of the Friends in the country, who are ready to take their stand upon the principle of non-intervention in the affairs of other countries. This is no reason why we should hold our peace ; but it shows that we have to begin at the beginning, by converting to our views that public opinion which is at present all but unanimously against us."

" You ask when *our* turn will come," he wrote to the same a little later (October 1), and he answered, " When common sense and honesty are in the ascendant." What horrified him greatly was the indecent manner in which pious people persisted in dragging into the war controversy the Deity and religion. He wrote :

" Scenes have evidently been enacted there (the Alma) after the battle which our most criminal population of the metropolis itself would have shuddered to take part in. And yet our ' religious ' people call God's blessing upon these doings ! Why, they have only to become sufficiently general and widespread to make this earth a hell. Faugh ! it is enough to make the very heathen and infidel shudder for the dangers of those who mock a Christian's God with such blasphemous cant."

At the beginning of 1855 he was eager, as a Member of Parliament, to make his views known to the people of Leeds, and he asked a well-known local politician to arrange for a meeting. The reply came that " the leading reformers " were opposed to his visiting the West Riding at that time. Cobden was too proud and also too combative to take the threat of a boycott meekly, and he accordingly ignored the self-constituted guardians of the public conscience of Leeds and made his own arrangements. Not only had he his meeting, but he was given a patient hearing, for he had secured what he expected in a Yorkshire town—" a rational audience."

The war frenzy had not then reached its climax, and as soon as he felt convinced that his power to do good was exhausted he discontinued public expostulation as a waste of effort. Why try to argue with people who are suffering from dementia ? Better wait until reason returned. Herein he showed a restraint which Bright—as he believed, unwisely—did not imitate.

For a long time the war went ill, and the patience and staunchness of the people who wanted victory and glory at the price of a naval parade were put to severe trial ; for cholera, dysentery, and inclement weather worked havoc amongst the Allied forces, and Sebastopol refused to fall. The Ministry itself was paralysed by division in counsel, impotence in decision, vagueness of policy, half-heartedness, resignations one day followed by returns the next, ignorance of the enemy's strength and resources and the geography of his country—handicaps fatal to the efficient conduct of a campaign a thousand miles away. A war carried on in such circumstances, whatever its ultimate outcome might be, was sure to be prolific of blunders, scandals, and consequent disasters. As usual, before and since, gross miscalculation of the difficulty of the task undertaken was the principal cause of the long postponement of success.

The death of the Tsar (March 2, 1855) and the negotiations between the representatives of the Great Powers, including Russia, which took place at Vienna a little later seemed to open the way for peace, but Gortchakoff declined to accept the restrictions which England sought to impose on Russia's naval strength in the Black Sea, and the conference broke up in June. Palmerston, who had succeeded Lord Aberdeen as Prime Minister, preferred it so, for he wanted a fight to a finish—a knock-out blow. He had victory of a sort, but it cost the nation a needlessly heavy penalty in life and treasure, for another year was to pass before hostilities were formally suspended.

Before the door was again locked and barred against peace Cobden deemed it opportune to make another appeal in the House of Commons (June 5, 1855). He criticized the Government for pressing conditions on Russia which not only offended her honour, but were niggling and without practical purpose.

Then he dealt with the broader question of the policy of undertaking to protect Turkey against encroachment, and warned the nation that the task would commit it to indefinite expenditure by compelling it to emulate the Continental Powers in the maintenance of great armies. Coming to the question of responsibility for the war, he said :

" I will never truckle so low to the popular spirit of the moment as to join in any cry which shall divert the mass of the people from what I believe should be their first thought and consideration, namely, how far they themselves are responsible for the evils which may fall upon the land and how far they should begin at home before they begin to find fault with others."

Prussia, which was then husbanding her strength for trials of her own known to be near at hand, has often been reproached unreasonably, chiefly in European histories written from any but a European standpoint, because she still remained neutral and declined to earn the permanent hostility of her powerful next-door neighbour by attacking her—a nation of sixteen millions against one of sixty millions. Cobden justified her attitude and charged the allies with the unconscionable selfishness of trying to drag that country into a war in which it felt no concern, without offering it any guarantee whatever of after-security. He also administered a much-needed rebuke to the patriots who did their fighting by proxy and stayed at home to cheer :

" I say that if the English people had the conscription, as they have in Prussia, so that when a war was declared every man in the country would be liable to be called out, and every horse and cart might be taken for the purposes of the army, we should be more chary how we called out for war. Our pot-house politicians would not then be calling out for war with Russia, but we should have a Government who would take a more moderate tone than this does, for it would require those sacrifices that bring home the miseries of war to the people."

Such plain speaking told slowly but effectually. Long before the war was over many people who had welcomed it had begun to suspect that Cobden and Bright were right and the nation's official leaders and guides wrong. Sir James Graham, who predicted Cobden's sureness of judgment in 1853, made this admission to Bright, adding his regret that England had allowed herself to be drawn in. The awakening came more slowly to the populace, which ever judges war not by its purposes or justifications, but only by its results—so much or so little cost, glory, territory. It wants for itself elation and the swell of pride, and that given it readily concedes to the actual fighters—all that are left of them—their fill of fame. Only on occasion and, as it were, by accident does it even trouble about responsibility either before or after : the end will crown, or not crown, the work. But this war brought no elation or pride or glory in which the non-combatants had a right to share, but only loss, suffering, impoverishment, and disenchantment.

After the abortive conference of Vienna there was a growing eagerness, both in this country and France, to know what results the long-drawn-out campaign was going to achieve. England sorely wanted a revival of her interrupted prosperity, while France looked for prestige at least, and Louis Napoleon was impatient for " compensations." What troubled Cobden was the future. He feared a peace which might only prove an armed truce between the combatants, leaving the Eastern Question a standing source of discord and friction. Avoiding all discussion of the origin of the war, he sought a common ground upon which both war men and peace men, if reasonable, might meet and confer. With that end in view he began towards the end of 1855 another pamphlet, the fifth of these writings, which he described as designed to " give some facts about Russia, with a view to prevent the self-confidence into which people fall of humbling that Power on her own soil," and it appeared in the following January with the title *What next—and next* ?

All sorts of penalties were being proposed for the stubborn enemy as soon as his armies capitulated. The writer pointed to the impossibility of striking Russia in so vital a place as to coerce her into a humiliating surrender. Where Napoleon tried and failed disastrously, the Allies could not hope for success. The idea of an invasion of Russia was to him sheer madness, while the policy of crippling her financially or economically was folly. Because after to-day there is always a to-morrow he urged a settlement based on moderation and regard for the enemy's *amour-propre*. In this pamphlet occurs the noble challenge, wrung from him by the spectacle of time-servers too cowardly to face the frowns and obloquy of an ignorant populace :

"I am aware that I am opposing the present current of public feeling, but where is the man of sense, courage, and honesty who will deliberately say that the truth ought not to be spoken because it does not flatter the preconceived impressions of the hour ? "

The Five Points in which Cobden formulated his programme have more than a historical value, and may be recalled with profit even to-day. Incidentally they afford an intimation of the spirit in which his generous international mind would have approached the problems of peace at Versailles in 1919. The measures which he proposed were the following :—

1. The withdrawal of all British troops from Russia, always " the grave or prison of armies, dynasties, and even of empires," on the ground that the invasion of her territory was a political and strategical blunder.

2. In determining the terms of peace only such demands should be made as were consistent with Russian national honour, and independent of promises and guarantees.

3. Prussia and Austria should keep watch on Russia's western frontier, if so disposed, as the natural barriers to Muscovite aggression in that direction, as was the purpose of existing treaties.

4. If Russia had really to be regarded as the menace to Europe which she was represented, the British Government should approach all Continental States with a view to the formation of an alliance to ward off any act of hostility by the common enemy. If they refused he would draw the conclusion that our own alarms were baseless, and would have our Government wash its hands of the thankless task of fighting for the liberties of Europe.

5. Finally, anticipating Bismarck's historical phrase about the Pomeranian Curassiers, he " would not risk the life of a single Englishman or spend another shilling for the chance of the barren triumph of extorting pacific pledges from the Russian Government, and having come to this determination there would no longer be an obstacle to peace."

Before the pamphlet appeared Austria had been accepted as mediator between the belligerents, and the proposals put forward by her as the basis of an armistice having been approved by the Allies (who since the preceding May had included Sardinia) and accepted by Russia, negotiations for definite conditions of peace were opened in Paris in February 1856, and these were embodied in the treaty of March 30. By this treaty the contracting Powers undertook to respect the independence and integrity of the Turkish Empire, and three of them—Great Britain, France, and Austria—gave a reciprocal pledge, collectively and severally, that they would treat any infraction of that or any other part of the pact as a *casus belli*, while the Sultan granted independence to the Danubian provinces subject to his suzerainty, agreed to the neutralization of the Black Sea, with slight reservations in Russia's favour, and " promised "—but no more—to give to the Christian races under his rule equal treatment with Mussulmans. The treaty also freed the Danube to the ships of all nations, and restored the pre-war territorial status in Asia Minor as between Russia and Turkey.

It was a slight atonement for the crime of a needless war, which is estimated to have cost 600,000 lives, that Turkey, so long the political anarchist of Eastern Europe, was brought within the ambit of international law, and that the Powers agreed upon certain ameliorations of the Sea Law. For not one of the territorial provisions of the Treaty of Paris was faithfully observed ; most of them were openly violated ; and in particular the guaranteeing Powers ignored their " collective and several " pledges to stand surety for Turkey's independence. This Cobden had foreseen.

Worst of all was the fact that Turkish misgovernment went from bad to worse. Cobden relates how, before the war began, he was implored by " some illustrious men not to oppose it, since it was likely to tend to the emancipation of the downtrodden communities on the Continent." He refused to believe this, and his distrust was confirmed. Not only was the Treaty of Paris redeemed by no generous gesture of emancipation, but for twenty years the Porte strove in every possible way to evade the obligations which it had incurred towards the Christian races under its rule, niggardly though these obligations were. More insurrections, more wars, more battues of helpless Christian communities, and more international conferences were necessary before the stubborn will of Ottoman despotism was broken. On the whole it was more through their own efforts—by rebellions sometimes successful but oftener suppressed by massacre, and by bloody wars, fought against terrific odds—than through the intervention of the Powers, most of whom had no heart in the humanitarianism for which the world gave them credit, that these races gradually won their liberties. Five years after the Crimean War *The Times* wrote of it : " That ill-starred war, those half million of British, French, and Russian men left in the Crimea, those two hundred millions of money wasted in the worst of all ways, have discharged to the last iota all the debt of Christian Europe to Turkey. Never was so great an effort made for so worthless an object. It is with no small reluctance that we admit a gigantic effort and an infinite sacrifice to have been made in vain." Events more than justified this lament.

Although the strong anti-Russian animus abated as the war fever passed away, many years were still to pass before any widespread transformation of national opinion took place in England. Cobden's attitude on the Eastern Question, however, never changed. He re-stated it forcibly in a letter to Bright dated March 18, 1861, when France was attempting new aggression in Syria. That action he regarded as indefensible, but he added :

" Our Government violates the principle of non-intervention toward the Turk every day; and every statesman in Europe, with the sole exception of Palmerston, recognizes the unavoidable fall of Ottoman rule at an early day, and the necessity of providing or recognizing some other mode of governing Turkey. If the Great Powers will allow the Greeks outside of the present Turkish Empire to give their fellow-countrymen, or at least their co-religionists of the same language and race, material aid, they will soon succeed, with the aid of the other Christian sects, in driving the Turks beyond the Bosphorus, and ere long in securing possession of the coast of Asia Minor and Syria."

It has been shown before that as a controversialist Cobden now and then contradicted himself. It is noteworthy that in the same year he submitted to Louis Napoleon a formal programme for the treatment of Turkey, to be carried out jointly by Great Britain and France. It consisted of the following measures :

" That neither of them would take a hectare of territory from Turkey in Europe ;

P

"That the same policy should be enforced on Russia and Prussia and Austria;

"That then the doctrine of non-intervention which had been applied to Italy should be adopted towards European Turkey;

"That the Christians should be allowed to drive the Turks back into Asia;

"That the Greeks had a right to repossess themselves of their ancient capital of Constantinople; and no foreign Power had a right to stand between them and the recovery of their rights from their Mahomedan conquerors."

The Emperor, fond though he was of political adventures, particularly when he could pose as a sort of *deus ex cathedrâ*, does not appear to have been enamoured of this novel scheme, which combined intervention with non-intervention, coercion with suasion, and made deliberate provision for an indefinite amount of war and bloodshed. In his reply he suggested that Austria might be allowed to take Bosnia and Herzegovina in exchange for Venetia, but he reminded Cobden that it had been the policy of Russia to prevent the formation of a Greek empire at Constantinople. So the matter dropped.

By this time Cobden, his sanguine spirit undismayed, believed that sympathy with the Turk was already out of date even in the House of Commons. He wrote to M. Chevalier in June 1862:

"There will be no Crimean Wars for us in defence of the Turks. Should a Slavonic or Hellenic Garibaldi arise to wage war with the Ottoman oppressor, British public opinion will instantly leap to his side, and then our Foreign Office will instantly turn its back upon its old traditions, as it did in the case of Italy. There is no demagogue like our high officials for flattering and bowing to the popular passion of the hour."

Here his characteristic optimism once again overreached itself. We know how little justification existed for any such confidence. When the Turkish atrocities in Bulgaria came to light in 1876, a generous wave of indignation swept over this country; yet so uncertain is the temper, so inflammable are the emotions of an ill-informed populace, that during the Russo-Turkish War which followed there was a renewed outburst of Russophobism, recalling the more violent phases of the frenzy of 1854. With Turkey's defeat the participation of Great Britain in the struggle seemed for a time almost inevitable ; and if Lord Beaconsfield's threat to declare war in the event of Russia's occupation of Constantinople had been carried out it is probable that the greater part of the nation would have been behind him. The danger passed away, and the Congress of Berlin, which determined the conditions of peace, proved as tranquil as the House of Commons when discussing the Post Office Estimates, though the resulting treaty excised not a few slices of the Turkish empire. With the death of England's greatest Minister for Imperialism in 1880 the anti-Russian bias ceased to be a party cult, and the Eastern Question, as hitherto understood, soon afterwards took new, larger, and more momentous forms. Before that happened, however, Lord Salisbury, the statesman who more than any other re-orientated British foreign and colonial policy during the last quarter of the nineteenth century, had begun to call in question the Palmerstonian tradition. The first doubts forced themselves on his mind during his experience as the British plenipotentiary at the futile Constantinople conference of the winter of 1876–77. He then came to the conclusion that the Turk was utterly hopeless, and his suspicion that a change of ground was necessary became a settled conviction when, released from Beaconsfield's influence, he became altogether his own man. Later came his public avowal of the belief that in championing Turkey against Russia this country had " backed the wrong horse."

A real reconciliation between Great Britain and Russia began only with the conclusion of the treaty of August 1907, which adjusted all territorial questions between the two Powers in Central Asia. The exigencies of the Great War carried the reversal of policy so far that, when the fruits of the expected victory were being divided, both British and French objections to Russia's presence at Constantinople, to prevent which one war had been fought and another threatened within the space of twenty-four years, were suddenly found to be so unsubstantial as not to be worth mentioning. The question whether the disastrous result of the war means the permanent abandonment or merely the postponement of that old ambition is one more suitable for curious speculation than for profitable discussion.

Looking back it can be seen how, from the second quarter of last century forward, the Christian races, then still wholly or partially under Turkish rule—those of Greece, Servia, Roumania, Bulgaria, Montenegro—one by one gained complete independence, until at the close of the late war it seemed that little remained but to wind up the Sultan's empire in Europe by amalgamating the remaining subject territories with adjacent organized and more or less stable States. To-day all that remains of Turkey north of the Narrows is the greater part of Thrace, lying eastward of a line running from Constantinople to Adrianople, including both of these cities, while Asiatic Turkey has been reduced to the northern part of Asia Minor by the severance therefrom of the now independent or mandated territories of Syria, Palestine, Iraq (Mesopotamia), and the Hejas.

All this steady progress of the ideas of nationality and political liberty in the Near East is but the logical result of the Russian policy which Great Britain, alone or with France, so long obstructed and threw back. The great miscalculation of successive Russian Emperors and Governments was the assumption that the misgoverned and disaffected peoples whom they sought, for a time successfully, to bring under their influence could be permanently satisfied with anything less than the full control of their own destinies. The anticipations of Cobden have been fully justified by events. Not only did England in the end come over to his side, as Sir James Graham predicted, but posterity in general has affirmed that he was right and his opponents wrong. The verdict of Morley carries the weight not only of his biographer, but of a practical statesman : that the forced overhauling of the Turkish empire by the Treaty of Berlin—with which must now be associated the Treaties of Sèvres and Lausanne—has convinced later generations that " the two chiefs of the ' Manchester school ' saw much farther ahead in 1854 and 1855 than men who had passed all their lives in foreign Chanceries and the purlieus of Downing Street." [1]

[1] *Life*, ii. 153.

CHAPTER XI

THE FRIEND OF AMERICA

" Let the alliance between England and America be re-baptized by a policy worthy of both. The laying of the first stone of that temple of Humanity which we all foresee is a labour well worthy the co-operation of the two worlds."—JOSEPH MAZZINI, in *Life and Writings*.

" When they spoke of Anglo-American relations they . . . thought of the two nations as having the same language, the same outlook on life, the same ultimate standards, the same instincts of right and wrong, the same feeling of what could be done and what could not be done. Such a relationship between two great world Powers was unique in human history. Was it not pregnant with hope for the future that at a time when so much seemed in flux the two countries were in substantial agreement as to the sort of world, the sort of social life, even the sort of international relations that they desired ? " —MR. HOUGHTON, American Ambassador, May 28, 1926.

AMERICA never had a warmer admirer or a truer friend in the British Isles than Richard Cobden, and during the critical years of the Civil War, when feeling ran dangerously high at times on both sides, no Englishman did as much as he and Bright to smooth over difficulties and to keep the cup of bitterness from running over. It was with a certain degree of justification that these comrades-in-arms in so many good causes, the one representing Rochdale and the other Birmingham in Parliament, were called " the two members for the United States." Living at a time when great prejudice against Americans, encouraged by writers otherwise capable of a larger outlook, still existed, Cobden was the first leader of English public opinion whose judgments of that kindred people were marked by generous sympathy and a sincere desire to efface the memory of old misunderstandings.

Independently of its influence on contemporary thought, nearly everything he said about America and the Americans still has interest for its own sake, and much of it is particularly opportune at the present time, when the two nations are thrown upon one another as never before, and stand before the decision whether they shall face together and accomplish for the world, as they alone can, a work of peace and civilization which otherwise may remain long unfulfilled.

Cobden seemed to have an instinct for attaching himself to unpopular causes and people. The foreign nations on whose behalf he specially employed both voice and pen were the Americans, the French, and the Russians; and when he entered public life, and for a long time afterwards, all three, politically speaking, were in the bad graces of large sections of his countrymen. His heart was early set upon promoting an intimate and cordial understanding with America, and his work to that end was the more meritorious since it was one of immense difficulty, for the memories left by the rupture of the preceding century were still vivid on both sides. His admiration of the Americans was unbounded, though he criticized as well as praised them. Perhaps a consciousness of affinity influenced him in this, for he had all the most marked of that people's characteristics—a fresh and independent outlook; an instinctive distrust of conventions and traditions; abundant self-reliance, energy, and enthusiasm; and, above all, love of freedom as the indispensable basis of an intelligent and progressive citizenship. Had he not been so good an Englishman he would have made one of the best of Americans.

He visited the country twice, being drawn thither by a conviction that it had much to teach the slower-going and more conservative homeland. It is testimony to his early interest in America, however, that his first pamphlet, *England, Ireland, and America* (1835), in which he said so much that was true and timely for his day, was written before he knew the country at first hand. Perhaps with Canning's dictum in mind [1] he there advanced the opinion that the New World was destined to dominate and determine the commercial policy, and ultimately the political development, of Great

---

[1] Canning's famous saying of December 1826, now indiscriminately applied, referred, of course, to his recognition of the independence of the South American colonies of Spain at a time when there seemed a fear that both Spain and her American empire might pass under French influence. It ran: "I resolved that if France had Spain it should not be with the Indies. I called the New World into existence to redress the balance of the Old."

Britain and the Old World generally, and he deplored the apparent absence of any suspicion that a process so momentous had already begun. He confessed to irritation that British statesmen, Press, and public should be troubling themselves about little States like Portugal, Belgium, and Bavaria, and that political pamphleteers should be successfully endeavouring to work up an agitation against Russia and her alleged designs in the east of Europe, when the urgent duty of the time was to watch and study the great republic of the West, whose progress meant vastly more for England, for good or ill, than the affairs of the rest of the world together.

" It is to the industry, the economy, and peaceful policy of America," he wrote, " and not to the growth of Russia, that our statesmen and politicians, of whatever creed, ought to direct their anxious study ; for it is by these, and not by the efforts of barbarian force, that the power and greatness of England are in danger of being superseded ; yes, by the successful rivalry of America shall we, in all probability, be placed second in the rank of nations. Nor shall we retard but rather accelerate this fate by closing our ears or shutting our eyes to all that is passing in the United States."

His advice to statesmen at all times was : Cherish your friends, if you have any ; but at least pay your rivals the compliment of watching and studying what they are doing in the world, and how they are doing it. Asking how the superior advancement of some modern States had been gained, he answered that it was by commerce and not by force of arms—in other words, by that policy of " peaceful penetration " which, at a later date, was to acquire so large an importance in other directions. He wrote :

" Thus the power and civilization of maritime Italy succumbed to the enterprise of Spain and Portugal ; these again were superseded by the more industrious traders of Holland ; who, in their turn, sank into insignificance before the gigantic growth of the manufacturing industry of Great Britain ; and the latter Power now sees in America a competitor in every respect calculated to contend with advantage for the sceptre of naval and commercial dominion."

Next to the advantage of a high-grade population, educated, inventive, energetic, and self-reliant, America owed her favourable position to the wisdom of her statesmen, in refusing to entangle her in the political affairs of the rest of the world, and her consequent freedom from external wars and the incumbrance of national indebtedness. With this happy immunity he compared the position of his own country, which, because of its constant foreign aggressions and fightings, was then struggling under the burden of a debt of 800 millions sterling, an amount exceeding that of the public debts of the rest of the world, while owing to the same cause its expenditure on State establishments and services, civil, military, and naval, was many times larger than that of its menacing rival.

It is interesting to note that more than twenty years later another political seer of still greater fame came round to Cobden's view of America as the centre of gravity of the future, and similarly warned Europe of the fate which a career of warfare was preparing for her. Addressing his constituents at Aylesbury in 1859, Disraeli said :

"The day is coming, if it has not already come, when the question of the balance of power cannot be confined to Europe alone. You have on the other side of the Atlantic vigorous and powerful communities, who will no longer submit to your circumscribed theory of authority. The Australian colonies, though now in their youth, but in the youth of giants, have already, as it were, drawn their colossal shadow over Europe. And it is for old Europe I lament, that she is exhausting her energies and her resources in these wars. I could wish that she would rather prepare for that awful competition which in coming times she must encounter."

The pamphlet appeared early in 1835, and in the succeeding summer he crossed the Atlantic, being absent from England three months. His expectations were more than confirmed by what he saw and heard. Here was a people to his mind— alert, strenuous, enterprising, progressive, self-respecting, and, crowning virtue, educated and loving education. Such a nation deserved success, and was bound to have it increasingly. He summed up his impressions in a letter to his brother Frederick, wherein he wrote :

"Great as was my previous esteem for the qualities of this people, I find myself in love with their intelligence, their sincerity, and the decorous self-respect that actuates all classes. The very genius of activity seems to have found its fit abode in the souls of this restless and energetic race. . . . All is done in pursuit of one common object, the economy of time. You know I predicted, when leaving England for this continent, that I should not find it sufficiently to my taste to relish a sojourn here for life. My feelings in this respect are quite altered. I know of no reasonable ground for an aversion to this country, and none but unreasonable minds could fail to be as happy here as in England, provided friendly attachments did not draw them to the Old Country."

In his second pamphlet, on Russia, published in the following year, he went out of his way to emphasize what he had written before and during his American travels :

" The writer reiterates the moral of his former work by declaring his conviction that it is from the West rather than from the East that danger to the supremacy of Great Britain is to be apprehended—that it is from the silent and peaceful rivalry of American commerce, the growth of its manufactures, its rapid progress in internal improvements, the superior education of its people, and their economical and pacific government, and not from the barbarous policy or the impoverishing armaments of Russia that the grandeur of our commercial and national prosperity is endangered."

Yet he was no weak flatterer of other countries ; impressed though he was by America's progress, and by the handicaps which, in his view, England was creating for herself owing to her propensity for costly wars and foreign adventures, he never lost faith in his native land :

" What ! shall we consign Old England, then, to ruin ? " asked this most English of Englishmen. " Heaven forbid ! Her people are made of tough materials, and he would be a dastardly politician that despaired of them even yet."

He visited America again during the winter of 1858-9, and his estimate of her people rose, if possible, higher than before. Again he admired the restless energy and spirit of mastery visible on every hand, but not less the " orderly self-respect which is the great characteristic of the masses." Everywhere he found that avenues of prosperity were open to industry and talent, so that it was possible for every man of resource and will to be his own master if he would. He wrote home : " It is the universal hope of rising in the social scale which is the key to much of the superiority that is visible in this country." He also formed a high opinion of American statesmanship, and was convinced that, grave as were some of the national problems, and pre-eminently the problem of slavery, it would successfully solve each difficulty in turn, since it had the unique advantage of freedom from foreign embarrassments.

In the course of his oversea travels he made lasting friendships, and by means of the resulting exchange of letters and in other ways he kept in close touch with American life and politics. Chief amongst his correspondents was the Charles Sumner mentioned in earlier pages. Never did his belief in the greatness of America's future or his faith in the sagacity of her statesmanship become weakened. What troubled him unceasingly was the indifference of European countries to a nation which was bound to exercise so large an influence upon their life and fortunes. When visiting Greece, enchanted though he was with the country and its people, he reflected with misgiving on the fact that half the educated world of Europe gave more thought to the feuds and bickerings, the geography and topography, of " the Lilliputian States " of antiquity than it bestowed on " the modern history of the South and North Americas, the politics of the United States, and the charts of the mighty rivers and mountains of the New World." To the last America was to him a bright and un-exampled illustration of a country where wealth multiplied and men did not decay, where energy and enterprise were exercised in an atmosphere of freedom, where education was valued and encouraged as a great national asset, where ability and intelligence received recognition ; above all, as a country whose Governments and people had the good sense to keep aloof from foreign interventions and to concentrate attention and effort upon their own internal concerns. The year before his death, when the Civil War was nearing its close, he could still write, in a letter to his friend M. Chevalier, " It is quite clear that America stands on a different footing from the Old World, and that its powers, whether in peace or war, are to be measured by a different standard."

The war between the North and South (April 1861 to June 1865) brought him into still greater prominence as an authority on American questions. The tragedy never ceased to horrify him, for he had deemed the American people too rational to fall into Europe's vicious ways ; and while retaining all the old respect for the North, as the spiritual part of the Union, his attitude towards the war was for some time one of outspoken hostility. The arrogance and clumsiness with which the Southern States had raised the question of secession disgusted him, and he wrote to Sumner (February 28, 1861) : " They have gone about the work of dissolving the Union with less gravity or forethought than a firm of intelligent drapers or grocers would think necessary in case of a dissolution of partnership." Nevertheless, at the outset, viewing the question at issue as solely one of the claim of the Confederate States to set up house for themselves, his strong sense of liberty and his deep detestation of force as the arbiter in what he regarded as a merely political dispute disposed him to take the side of the seceders. Before the first shot was fired he wrote to Sumner, " If I were a New Englander I would vote with both hands for a peaceful separation." Perhaps, too, his sympathies were influenced by the fact that the Southern States were wedded to Free Trade, while the North was Protectionist.

Like most public men in this country he failed at first to realize that the principle at stake was more vital, and admitted of no compromise. For the South claimed not only the right to secede—itself a claim incompatible with the Act of Union—but the right to give formal sanction and a new life to the institution of slavery, and thus to render void and of no effect a fundamental provision of the Declaration of Rights.

Bright, with swifter and clearer intuition, at once grasped the fact that slavery was the true issue, and that failure to respond to the challenge of the South would imply tacit approval of a vile wrong and throw back everywhere the cause of human progress. Thus some time passed before the old comrades found their rightful place, which was side by side. " Our friend Bright," Cobden wrote in January 1862, " will not hear of anything against the claims of the North. I admire his pluck, for when he goes with a side it is always to win."

Cobden was then still unconvinced that the North would succeed in forcing the South back into the Union. So also were many other men of distinction, like Earl Russell and Gladstone, the former Foreign Secretary and the latter Chancellor of the Exchequer. In November of that year Gladstone predicted the complete failure of the North, since Jefferson Davis and his associates had " made an army ; they are making a navy ; and they have made what is more than either—they have made a nation." Not to the last did Cobden reconcile his soul to the " brutality and havoc," " the vulgar and unscientific and endless butchery," which the struggle involved, or retract his confession, made in 1863, that had he at the commencement had in his hand the negro's fate he would have " refused him freedom at the cost of so much white men's blood and women's tears." Nevertheless, when the North made emancipation the battle-ground, he saw that the struggle must be carried to the bitter end, and that the Union, too, must be maintained. " To restore the old Union, slavery and all," he wrote to Sumner on August 7, 1863, " will be to cover with shame the partisans of the North throughout the world and justify the opponents of the war everywhere. It would leave the question still to be settled by a similar process of blood by another generation."

From that time the North had no more devoted champion in England than Cobden, and the only question which troubled him was whether the Federals would have resources and staying power sufficient to bring the struggle to a definitely successful close. He even urged, in letters to Sumner, that the negro should be required to help in " fighting his own battle," and early in 1864 he looked forward to " a hundred thousand coloured men under arms before midsummer." In such a warm-hearted humanitarian and moralist this idea of setting blacks to fight whites, which the North refrained from doing, can perhaps only be explained by the assumption that there was more of " the old Adam " in him—and he confessed to much—than he imagined.

No Englishman also rendered more useful service to his own country in those critical years than he, by his efforts to curb irrational passions, to keep the Government on the right and safe path of neutrality, and to smooth over the many delicate causes of misunderstanding and friction which from time to time threatened to embroil England in the struggle.

There was great need at that time for the well-informed counsels and sobering influence of men like Cobden and

Bright.   For the majority of the ruling classes, and most of all
the die-hards of Toryism, perpetuating the ideas and traditions
of Lord North and the Duke of Wellington, were with the
South.   It was not that they approved slavery, but that
they disapproved republicanism, and had neither forgiven
nor forgotten the fact that the rebellion of 1776 originated
in the democratic spirit of the North, and honestly believed
that but for a trumpery dispute over a few chests of tea the
United States would still have been under the British Crown
—and the right thing, too.   Both political parties were divided
in sympathy between the two sides, but with the difference
that while amongst Liberals hostility to the North was the
exception, amongst the Tories it was the rule.

The Government hedged, not always creditably.   Openly
its policy was one of neutrality, but its sympathies were
strongly with the Confederates, and, if not given practical
form, were sufficiently obvious to stiffen Southern resistance
and for a time to make more difficult the task of the Federal
Government and its armies.   Encouragement, however, which
went no farther than words, and therefore cost nothing, did
the South no good, and it came to value it accordingly, with
the result that before the war ended England was equally unpopular with both sides.   On the other hand, the unlettered
masses of the people, slow to understand or heed the juristic
bearings of the dispute, but recognizing by unfailing instinct the
great moral and human issues which it involved, were ardent
supporters of the Federal cause.   No more remarkable transformation of popular feeling is known to history than that
which took place in the industrial towns of the north of
England during the first year of the war.   For a time the
general attitude there was apathetic, and a mere struggle to
coerce a number of unwilling States back into the Union would
have failed to the last to move the labouring classes.   When
the blockade of the Southern ports, by creating the cotton
famine, brought to a standstill Lancashire's staple industry,
and want and suffering entered into the homes of the operative
population, indifference gave place to resentment that the
North should be so callous and domineering.

This temper disappeared directly it was realized that the
war was one to strike the fetters from the slave.   The publica-

tion of Lincoln's proclamation of emancipation of September 22, 1862, fired the imagination of a generation to which the name of Wilberforce was still more than a memory. Everywhere popular meetings were called to express sympathy with the new crusade against slavery, and discontent and grumbling were silenced in Lancashire's grass-grown streets. Impressed by the changed attitude of public opinion, the Government itself took alarm, and for a time kept under more careful control the disposition, hardly repressed hitherto, to give to its neutrality a bias in favour of the South.

More than ever Cobden hoped that the North would come out of the struggle victorious, for he wanted America to be strong. He wanted this for the reason that Canning did in his time—in order that European Powers might not be tempted to carry their propensity for intervention across the ocean—but also in order that the Americans might continue to serve the world as a shining example of a nation which prospered by refraining from foreign adventures. When men who had been amongst the stoutest defenders of Lord Palmerston and intervention tried to throw upon the North responsibility for the war, he retorted that it was the first time they had shown any horror of bloodshed. The last country in the world, he reminded them, that had any right to criticize and protest was England, seeing that she was perpetually at war.

Nothing could have been fairer than his action in endeavouring to mediate between this country and the North. With no sacrifice of patriotism, and no disregard of legitimate British interests, he yet preserved a judicial spirit such as few, if any, men in office showed in their positions of greater responsibility. In his eagerness to maintain unimpaired the past good relations with America he even, on occasion, went out of his way to pay a compliment to the " old dodger " of Downing Street, who so far had not intervened, and incidentally to give his countrymen credit for a little less intelligence than they possessed.

" The English people," he wrote to Sumner at the end of 1861, " have no sympathy with you on either side. You know how ignorant we are on the details of your history, geography, constitution, etc. There are two subjects on which we are unanimous and fanatical—personal freedom and Free Trade. In your case we observe a mighty

quarrel : on one side protectionists, on the other slave owners. The
protectionists say they do not seek to put down slavery. The slave
owners say they want Free Trade. Need you wonder at the confusion
in John Bull's poor head ? He gives it up ! Leaves it to the Government. Which Government, by the way, is the most friendly to your
Government that could be found in England, for, although Palmerston
is fond of hot water, he boasts that he never got us into a serious war.
As for his colleagues, they are all sedate, serious men."

That he was seriously prepared to give Palmerston and
the aristocracy so handsome a vote of confidence must be
doubted. The letter was just a characteristic example of his
occasional habit of special pleading and of his strategical
dialectic, not entirely disingenuous yet pardonable, since it
was for the sake of his country and of peace.

Yet his friendship for the North did not blind him to the
many mistakes made by its Government, officials, and war
leaders, and he was specially severe in his condemnation of
acts done in its name, though not always with its authority,
in contravention of international law. At a public meeting
held in Paris official representatives of the North invited the
Emperor to join in a war against England, in order to avenge
Waterloo and St. Helena ; while in America men in high position talked as though Canada were already a new State in the
Union, and, confident of the ultimate success of the Federal
cause, threatened retaliation against those in that British
colony who had dared to sympathize with the seceders. Cobden
did not take such affronts patiently. At a time when there
seemed a real danger that England might enter the fray he
wrote to Sumner :

" Everybody tells me that war is inevitable, and yet I do not believe
in war. But it must be admitted that there are things said and done
on your side that make it very difficult for the advocates of peace on
this side to hold the field. . . . When grave men (or men that should
be grave) compliment Captain Wilkes for having given an affront to
the British Lion, it makes it very hard for Bright and me to contend
against the British Lion party in this country."

In the affair of the *Trent*, which is referred to here, a
choleric Federal captain had arbitrarily boarded a British
mail steamer and carried off two Confederate envoys, with

their secretaries. It was an illegal proceeding, and Lincoln soon complied with the demand of the British Government that the prisoners should be given up, though Mr. Seward, his Secretary of State, unkindly reminded Lord Clarendon that Wilkes had only followed British precedent. But indiscretion and illegality were not confined to one side. Lord Palmerston showed how his sympathies ran when, referring publicly to the Federal reverse at Bull Run, he uttered his gibe at the " unfortunate rapid movements " of the Northern force on that occasion. During the war England sold arms and ammunition to North and South indiscriminately, but the Confederate States were, in addition, provided with British-built vessels, which were readily adapted to warlike purposes. With his old blindness, John Bull, already nettled that naval operations were being carried on without either his participation or his permission, applauded the enterprising firms who thus sent privateers to prey on the commerce of the North, never dreaming that a heavy bill of costs might come one day home to him, as it did eight years later.

If England did not intervene, though France at one time was willing to share that responsibility with her, Cobden was convinced that the reason was less unwillingness on the part of the leading Ministers, or the aristocratic classes and the " educated mob of the clubs " behind them, than fear of the consequences. He was quick to observe how the ruling classes at home reacted to the oscillating fortunes of war. When the North had bad luck and its prospects seemed gloomy they were jubilant, and prematurely celebrated the fall of the Republic and the discomfiture of democracy. He notes, however, how that temper changed to one of almost servile deference directly the Federal Government, mobilizing vast unsuspected resources in men and material, mastered the situation and dispelled the last uncertainty of victory. The reflexions to which this undignified *volte-face* led him were exemplified in a letter to an English friend written on February 23, 1865 :

" Shall I confess the thought that troubles me in connexion with this subject ? I have seen with disgust the altered tone with which America has been treated since she was believed to have committed suicide or something like it. In our diplomacy, our Press, and with our public speakers all hastened to kick the dead lion. Now in a few months everybody will know that the North will triumph, and what troubles me is lest I should live to see our ruling class—which can understand and respect *power* better than any other class—grovel once more, and more basely than before, to the giant of democracy. This would not only inspire me with disgust and indignation, but with shame and humiliation. I think I see signs that it is coming. *The Times* is less insolent, and Lord Palmerston more civil."

To Sumner also he wrote on March 5 of that year : " It is nothing but your great *power* that has kept the hands of Europe off you." His one source of pride was that " the common people of England were true to the cause of freedom." These letters, among the last that came from the great patriot's pen, were written at Midhurst during his last illness. He did not live to see the restoration of peace, for his end came on April 2 and that of the war on May 26.

In nothing did Cobden's clear foresight and sound political intuition more excel than in his recognition of the value of America's good will and of her importance as a factor in modern world history. During the late war Mr. Walter Page wrote, amongst many other memorable things, " British-American friendship is the greatest asset left to civilization." But Cobden said that more than two generations before ; he also lived up to his words, for the need for the cordial reconciliation of these two branches of a great family was one of the most cherished articles of his political creed. Those, therefore, who in this country to-day think on this question as Cobden and Bright did may well remember with gratitude that no Englishmen did better or more lasting work as mediators between the two nations than " the members for the United States " of sixty years ago. There was, admittedly, a material side to Cobden's interest in America, in his conviction that the only commercial and naval rivalry which Great Britain had then to fear would come from that direction ; but he was far more attracted to her as the emancipator who, he hoped, would one day destroy the feudal traditions which kept so large a part of Europe in bondage to retarding political traditions, and break everywhere new paths for a broader and more diffused civilization.

Writing to Sumner in the last year of the Civil War, he said : " I agree . . . that you are fighting the battle of liberalism in Europe as well as the battle of freedom in America. It is only necessary to observe who are your friends and who your opponents in the Old World, to be satisfied that great principles are at stake in your terrible conflict." The close of that struggle left the British ruling classes more rather than less prejudiced against America than before. How far is it different to-day ? Unquestionably the Americans are known better and esteemed more highly than before by thoughtful Englishmen, but the change of temper has been least noticeable, if noticeable at all, in the classes which Cobden, with rhetorical exaggeration, was wont to accuse of " clinging to the ideas of the Middle Ages." For it remains no less true now than then that, in the last resort, the relations between nations are determined far more by political affinities than by any other considerations. All the world over Liberalism gravitates to Liberalism and Conservatism to Conservatism, however these distinctive tendencies of thought, or their analogies, may be named. It is no accident that in the past the friends of England in Germany and the friends of Germany in England had to be sought mainly in the popular parties, whether Liberal or Labour, or that the late alliance between autocratic Russia and republican France, while welcomed by the military and aristocratic classes in both countries, never won the deep attachment of the masses of the people in either.

Mankind in the mass matures slowly, and traditional habits of thought, prejudices, and tempers persist most stubbornly in caste-bound societies. Cobden wrote in 1856 that " there is always a latent instinct at work in the breasts of our aristocratic ruling class which seeks to estrange the two countries as much as possible, and to render the Americans the object of dislike, fear, or suspicion to the English people." Even after a war which brought the two nations together in a unique comradeship, which should once for all have broken down the old barriers, these words are still true. So long as America's help was needed the traditional antipathy was kept under control, so far at least as external signs went, but it was not thrown off, and it is doubtful whether to-day the attitude of Great Britain to America is, on the whole, as friendly as that of America to this country. Amongst what are known as " the classes " there has been, on our side of the Atlantic, a marked deepening of the old prejudice and dislike. Those who doubt this have only to note the ill-natured comments upon America, American statesmen and policy which appear from time to time in the columns of the London journal which claims to be the special mouthpiece of this section of society.[1]

As we have seen, what most drew from Cobden admiration for America were her abstention from foreign entanglements and her settled policy of concentration upon her own affairs, and he believed that European nations would sooner or later imitate her example. Since then America has repeatedly been drawn into treaty transactions with European Powers, mainly of a commercial kind, and she has even done a little fighting and annexation on her own account. Thus in 1898 the Hawaiian (Sandwich) Islands were annexed to the Union, and as a result of a war with Spain Porto Rico, the Philippine Islands, and an island of the Marianne Group were acquired by cession and certain rights of intervention were obtained in relation to Cuba, henceforth made independent of Spanish rule ; while several of the Samoan islands fell to America by the tripartite division of 1900.

The Great War, however, was the first instance of America's armed participation in the quarrels which have made the European Continent a bear garden for centuries, and it is probable that it will be the last. For the more the Americans, settling down to their old life, have reflected on the diplomacy which they now know preceded the war and the events which

[1] A war-time experience bearing upon this question may here be recalled. During the early part of the struggle certain American correspondents were in the habit of keeping me informed of hostile public criticisms of the Allies and their aims, and to these I was accustomed to make such newspaper replies as the circumstances called for. On one occasion there came to me a copy of a leading American review containing an article recalling the traditional attitude towards America of certain classes of the British people and their Governments, and predicting that, in spite of the pleasant things that were then being said about Americans, the old spirit of hostility would return in the same quarters directly the war was over. The historical case against this country was so ably stated and so well grounded in fact, that, feeling that no effective answer would be possible without a certain amount of equivocation, I wrote to my correspondent to that effect, and referred the article to one of the official propagandist organizations which had then got to work. Later I was informed that a rejoinder was prepared by a writer whose versatility in controversy, and still more whose scholarship, I have never ceased to admire.

have followed it—the provocative peace treaties and the methods of their execution, the further militarization of the Continent, the deliberate endeavours of impoverished States, both old and new, to accelerate and complete their ruin by squandering their resources upon " bloated armaments," the ugly attempts to carry on this suicidal policy by evading national debts, and all the other signs of a determination to continue in the old evil ways—the stronger have become their conviction that intervention in Europe was a dangerous departure from time-honoured tradition and their resolve not again to turn from the safer and more prudent path of neutrality. They are conscious now, if never before, that in such an association they would be mated with Powers whose diplomatic system they do not understand, whose diplomatic language they cannot speak, and whose diplomatic jugglery they have no wish to imitate or learn ; above all, with Powers some of which have not yet begun to believe in international right or, if they believe in it, have done so much international wrong in the past that their capacity and will to make a new start in a more decent way of life are paralysed.

For Europeans, and for ourselves in particular, it should be a humiliating reflexion that of the Great Powers which came out of the war successfully only America has honourably kept the pledges with which she entered the struggle. In his message to Congress of April 2, 1917, President Wilson said : " We have no selfish ends to serve. We desire no conquests and no dominion. We seek no indemnities for ourselves and no material compensation for sacrifices we shall freely make." To her honour America has staunchly kept her plighted word ; for she came out of the war with clean because empty hands. She has not only paid her own war bills, but she has helped to pay the bills of most of her war associates ; and though, when Germany's colonies were being divided as the prize of war, she might reasonably have asserted the right to add that country's share of the Samoan islands to her own, even that small advantage was renounced.

The irrational accusations against America of a spirit of exploitation and egoism because she has not cancelled the whole of the European debts come in the main from two quarters —in this country from people of the type whom Cobden tried in vain to cure of the belief that a British interest must necessarily be a world interest, and who during the early months of the war indulged in daily abuse of America because she failed to side with the Allies at the start ; [1] on the Continent from militarist politicians who have been foiled in their hope of seeing the late belligerent nations freed from the incubus of debt, in order that they might continue to arm for further warfare in the old pagan way. If, as has been stated, the enforcement against Great Britain of the whole of her debt was intended as a gentle reminder of the million square miles of mandated territory which have been added to British rule, we have no right to complain. Still less cause for complaint has France, which is able to support a larger army than before the war, has created the most powerful air fleet in Europe, is now engaged in increasing her navy, and has been able to lend hundreds of millions of francs to Poland and her other allies for expenditure on munitions of war made in French factories. Let us honestly admit that America decided justifiably and most wisely to put her own interpretation upon her debtors' pleas for indulgence, and even to appraise for herself their ability to meet their obligations ; and that the conclusion to which her Government came was the true and right one—that nothing but the hard discipline of straitened resources will ever bring Europe to its senses and, by forcing economy on armaments, give to the cause of peace even a dog's chance of life.

So far, then, the expectations which Cobden built upon America as the country which would, by its example, lead British and European statesmanship into wiser ways have not been fulfilled. Yet more than ever before the importance of Anglo-American friendship needs to be emphasized, for the one reason, if for no other, that amongst the larger Powers America to-day is practically England's only safe, straightforward, and disinterested friend. To be candid, she is also a friend with whom we cannot afford to fall out. Cobden used to contend

---

[1] Anyone whose duty took him in and out of London six days out of seven at that time will recall the average City man's attitude. Compelled to hear, morning after morning, the same wrathful reproaches against America because she still hesitated to " come in " (though she was then better serving the Allies by remaining out), I ventured on one occasion to put the mild question, " Why should she ? " upon which a florid-complexioned *vis-à-vis* silenced me with the convincing rejoinder, " *Well, we're in !* "

that the danger of serious naval rivalry should bring home the value of American co-operation even to those whom higher considerations failed to influence. The same argument holds good to-day. Wise politics is three parts interest to one part sentiment : and dislike it as we may, it would be folly to ignore the fact that if America were disposed she could so build ships against us as to rob of meaning for ever our claim to naval supremacy. Rivalry of that kind would be the most senseless and disastrous known to history, but there can be no doubt as to which Power would be exhausted first. Every consideration of prudence and safety points to the cultivation of a closer association with America, at whatever sacrifice of European ties and supposed interests, nearly all of which consist of liabilities unbalanced by assets of any kind.

The critical question is whether America could be induced to respond to overtures in that direction. Perhaps the wide perspectives which such a prospect might open up would appeal to her. The British Commonwealth of Nations, viewed as an agency of civilization and a bulwark of order and progress, has proved a splendid achievement ; but the closer co-operation of the Empire with America in a partnership of peace, in virtue of those moral affinities which are the strongest bonds of international union—a common background of history, and identity of language, ideals, and largely of religion—might do more in a single decade for the world's good than the League of Nations, as at present organized, is likely to do in a generation. What such a partnership would entail on our part must be shown in the final chapter.

Those who are convinced of the urgent need for the closest possible association of the British and American peoples— and amongst the thoughtful sections of our population the number is rapidly growing—cannot but rejoice that the cause has received so strong and cordial a friend and advocate in the new Professor of American History at Oxford. The need was forcibly stated in the following words of his, spoken on May 28 last :

" America and Britain were not alike, and never would be alike, but the demands of a dangerous present and a most uncertain future required that they should not allow their differences, past or present, to divide them. They could not doubt one another and serve the world supremely. They must stand together, not because of blood-kinship, but because they measured by the same spiritual standards."

It must be the sincere hope of all who think like Professor McElroy that the movement for a true and lasting fellowship between the two nations, assuring to them the moral leadership of the world, far from adding to the tale of Oxford's "lost causes and impossible loyalties," will enjoy increasing success, and create a new bond of fruitful sympathy between that ancient seat of knowledge and enlightenment and the modern world. Perhaps there will yet fall to Oxford the honour and fame of establishing the first Chair of International Under-standing and Peace in the Empire.

CHAPTER XII

THE MECHANISM OF FOREIGN POLICY

" English policy is to float lazily down stream, occasionally putting out a diplomatic boat-hook to avoid collisions."—LORD SALISBURY.

" In each Government I have visited I have found stubbornness, determination, selfishness, and cant. One continually hears self-glorification and the highest motives attributed to themselves because of their part in the war. My observation is that incompetent statesmanship and selfishness is at the bottom of it all. It is not so much a breaking down of civilization as a lack of wisdom in those that govern, and history, I believe, will bring an awful indictment against those who were short-sighted and selfish enough to let such a tragedy happen."—COLONEL HOUSE, on his European tour of 1916 (*Intimate Papers of Colonel House*, ii. 164).

COBDEN'S lack of sympathy with so much in the British foreign policy of his day led him to criticize severely its entire mechanism. Here, again, his judgments were largely coloured by his hostility to Lord Palmerston, whose proneness to foreign intervention and whose violent methods of making his country's influence felt abroad he so vigorously condemned. Not only the Foreign Office, however, but the parliamentary system under which these things were possible came beneath the lash of his censure.

He was in political life for nearly a generation ; he was an active member of four Parliaments for an aggregate period of some twenty years ; and his estimate of the House of Commons, at no time a high one, appears to have gradually fallen to the zero point. He was aghast at its satisfaction with its own ignorance of foreign affairs, its readiness to accept as truth everything that secretive Ministers told it, and its general lack of independence. In his view the duty of a Member of Parliament was not to echo the sayings and applaud the doings of his official leaders, however eminent they might be, but to subject both to conscientious examination ; like the vigilant watch-dog, it was his business to protect the national house from harm, whether from within or without. He typified his ideal parliamentarian in his own person, for no member went his own way with a stronger sense of self-responsibility and a completer disregard of conventional party ties, or so audaciously challenged every claim to justify opinions or policies by appeal to authority. Let every man be persuaded in his own mind, but first let him be sure of his facts. He held that upon all questions of public policy, domestic as well as foreign, the nation, through its Legislature, should have, if not always the first, in every case the last and decisive, word.

Perhaps the most spirited of his many assertions of the function of legislators who aspire to be something more intelligent than mere gramophones and purveyors of other people's opinions was made during the general election of March 1857, which confirmed Lord Palmerston's hold upon the country for the remainder of his life. There were circumstances which gave special point to this vigorous utterance. In the previous month (February 26) he had introduced in the House of Commons a resolution, which Lord John Russell supported, condemning the war with, or more truly on, China over the *Arrow* episode, and so moved were the House and the nation by the wrong which had been done that it was carried, though only by a majority of fourteen. Lord Palmerston treated the vote as one of no-confidence, and at once dissolved Parliament. In the ensuing election both the Prime Minister and his supporters resorted to every sort of strategy that promised to discredit the patriotism of the men who had dared to assert the honour of their country, with the result that Cobden, Bright, and many other advanced Liberals were repudiated at the polls, and a compliant House was returned. It was in the course of a speech which he made at Manchester on behalf of the candidature of Bright, then laid aside by illness, that Cobden said (March 18) :

" Well, now, there is a great question involved in this, which I think the people of this country ought to take very much to heart. Do you want the members of the House of Commons to look after your rights, and watch the expenditure, and to guard you from getting into needless and expensive wars ? (' Yes.') Well, but you are not going the right way to work about it, . . . for I am told that those members who joined in that vigilant care of your interests, and voted according to the evidence before us on the question of that war, are all to be ostracized, sent into private life, and that you are going to send up there men—to do what ? To look after your interests ? No, to go and do the humble, dirty work of the Minister of the hour. In fact, that you are going to constitute Lord Palmerston the despotic ruler of this country. ('No, no!') Well, but if he is not checked by Parliament—if, the moment Parliament does check him, he dissolves Parliament, and, instead of sending up men who are independent enough to assert their and your rights, you send up mere creatures of his will, what is that but investing him with the powers of a despot ? Ay, and let me tell you that it is a despotism of the clumsiest, most expensive, and at the same time most irresponsible kind on the face of the earth ; because you surround the Minister with the sham appearance of a representative form of government ; you cannot get at him while he has got a Parliament beneath whose shield he can shelter himself."

He anticipated misgivings common in later times when he warned his audiences that the gravest danger-spots in national life were the intersessional periods when, temporarily relieved from parliamentary control, Governments and Ministers were apt to run wild. It was then that " all the mischief is generally done in our foreign relations." The warning was the more opportune in his day since Parliament was not yet the hard-worked machine which it became later, so that its sessions were of far shorter duration than now ; with the result that for the greater part of the year the country was practically under Cabinet government and there was no check upon the strong-willed Minister who from 1830 forward succeeded to the Foreign Office, Parliament after Parliament, with the regularity of clockwork.

Enough has been said already to show that his measure of Governments and the governing class was far from complimentary. He once wrote to Bright : " The more I see of the rulers of the world the less of wisdom or greatness do I find necessary for the government of mankind." From that sweeping generalization he did not exclude his own caste-bound country. What was the use of privileged orders, or Governments recruited from them, if they had no greater foresight and sagacity, and sometimes even less, than ordinary people ? For that he held to be the fatal defect of aristocracy. Of the branches of that still ruling order he preferred the Tories to the Whigs ; he found their Governments to be more honest, and their parliamentary rank and file "more civil in inter-course." In later life he was wont to say that there was more true Liberalism in the young "hopefuls" of the Tory party in the House than in the Free Trade manufacturers of Lancashire who had been spoiled by prosperity. The same thing has often been said since.

On the point of Ministerial honesty in general, however, he held strong reservations. Long observation had convinced him of the deteriorating influence of office upon men who were naturally upright and conscientious ; he saw how it had a tendency to emasculate character, to undermine fidelity to principle, and to encourage the easy cynicism which tolerates things known to be wrong. In the early part of Mr. Gladstone's official career he suspected that the moral fibre of that rising hope of the revived cause of " Peace, retrenchment, and reform " had been weakened since he held no longer the independent position of the private member, and he said hard things of him because, while making eloquent speeches in disapproval of wasteful expenditure on armaments, he did nothing to abate the evil. " There ought," he once wrote, " in the interest of conscientious men, to be another verse added to our Litany, and in addition to praying the good Lord to deliver us from ' battle, murder, and sudden death,' we ought to pray to be preserved from the temptations of the post of a Cabinet Minister." When in 1859 he declined his second invitation to join a Ministry, his reason was less the apparent inconsistency of accepting office at the hands of a statesman (Lord Palmerston) whose policy he had been publicly censuring for over twenty years than the fear of sacrificing his independence, or, more exactly, the knowledge that an independent mind would be out of place in a piece of official mechanism which could only function efficiently if all its parts worked in unison. Morley's verdict on his decision was probably correct : " If Cobden had taken office at midsummer he would certainly have been out of it by Christmas."

It was his constant complaint that Governments and Ministers were seldom straightforward in their dealings with the House of Commons and the country, and so shaken did his faith in official statements and assurances become, that he ceased at last to accept as true the word of any Minister unless it could be authenticated by independent testimony. It was when he was nearing the close of his career that he made the saddening confession :

> " My maxim has been to distrust the Treasury bench at all times, and never to admit myself wrong in a controversy with the Government until I have better evidence than their assertions. Old Saddletree's example in *The Heart of Midlothian* is worth remembering. When hard pressed by an opponent in an argument who asked, ' There, can ye deny that, Master Saddletree ? ' he replied, ' No, but I'm not going to admit it, neither.' "—(July 27, 1861.)

It was for the diplomacy of foreign policy that he reserved his most searching criticisms. He was entirely out of sympathy with the official mechanism, and much of what he said on this subject applies to the present day. The Foreign Office was then, as it is still, a water-tight compartment of the vessel of State. It was an autonomous Ministry, which cold-shouldered all other Government Departments— an *imperium in imperio*, which made its own policies and executed them with but little regard for parliamentary or public opinion. An impenetrable veil of secrecy shrouded the entire subject of foreign affairs. Momentous acts of policy, critical decisions, even armed enterprises were undertaken on the sole authority of the Cabinet, or even of the Foreign Secretary alone, and presented as accomplished facts to the Legislature, whose approval or disapproval after the event was seldom more than a matter of form, since what was done could not be undone. As Palmerston said to Cobden, when in 1859 trying to overcome his objections to entering the Cabinet : " It is in the Cabinet alone that questions of foreign policy are settled. We never consult Parliament until they are settled." He might have added on his own account that on some important occasions he did not consult his colleagues beforehand.

In one of his pamphlets Cobden illustrated the *modus operandi* of official secrecy by some awe-inspiring words spoken in his hearing to a hushed and humble House of Commons by the Secretary of the Admiralty when calling for a large increase of the navy. Challenged to explain why the increase was needed, all the oracle would say was that the Government had arrived at the determination " that it would be better under existing circumstances not to enter into any particulars with respect to that course," since it " must necessarily be in possession of secret and important intelligence, and must necessarily be the fitting and only judge how far that intelligence ought to be communicated to the House." Mystifying utterances of that kind were specially characteristic of the Foreign Office whenever the House of Commons ventured to ask for information, even on questions of the utmost moment. Evasion was the recognized system, whatever Governments were in power, and as yet no opposition had been strong enough to overcome it.

Nevertheless, there were times when his sanguine temperament seemed to assert itself even on this question, for he had a singular capacity for mistaking signs for proofs. In 1851 he professed to believe that the end of clandestine negotiations and all duplicity in diplomacy was near. Emboldened by the work which Kossuth, the Hungarian liberator, was then doing on the same lines as himself, he wrote to Bright :

" My own opinion is that we are on the eve of a revolution in the diplomatic world ; that the old *régime* of mystification and innuendo and intrigue cannot survive the growth of the democratic principle ; that diplomacy must be a public and responsible organization ; and nobly again has Kossuth assailed this stronghold of the hierarchical spirit. In fact, he comes here preaching the main principles enunciated at our Peace Congress, but preaching them better in a foreign tongue than I could do in my own language. One of my reasons for hoping much from Kossuth's agitation here and in America is that it will tend to unveil Foreign Ministers and put Foreign Offices in order."

It was a vain hope. Within three years he was to witness, in impotent grief, a long and disastrous war into which his country was betrayed owing to diplomatic bad faith and conflict of purpose between the Prime Minister and the wayward Home Secretary. A year after the Crimean War ended he told how at the opening of the session (1857) the country was engaged in two wars in the Far East, with China and Persia, yet in neither case had Parliament been consulted beforehand. Official papers had been published in regard to the war which Sir John Bowring had provoked with China over the affair of the *Arrow*, since feeling on the subject was strong in both parties ; but when a demand was made for information concerning the Persian enterprise the answer given was that it would be " contrary to the public interest " to lift the veil ; in other words, it was right to wage war but wrong to tell the country why.

No Foreign Secretary of the century made the business of his office so much a personal affair, and took such wide liberties in transacting it, as Lord Palmerston, who at last began to ignore the Crown itself and was sharply pulled up for so doing. It was still a well recognized constitutional principle at that time that no important decisions on matters of public policy might be taken by the Foreign Office before the Queen had, in Lord John Russell's words, received " the most frank and full detail of every measure " proposed for adoption, and because Palmerston showed an increasing disposition to act on his own authority the rule was put into written form in 1850. It was his breach of this rule, in officially recognizing on his sole responsibility the *coup d'état* of December 2, 1851, which renewed for ten years Prince Louis Napoleon's tenure of the Presidency of the second French Republic, that led to Palmerston's early dismissal early in the following year. It was but a short eclipse, however, for Palmerston was at the Home Office as a member of Lord Aberdeen's Cabinet formed in December 1852, and for nine of the ten years 1855 to 1865 he was Prime Minister. The more he was idolized as the strong man of his day, the more he magnified his office, until he practically usurped sovereign powers.

One of the shifts to which the Ministerial wire-pullers of the Palmerstonian epoch were fond of resorting when money was wanted for armaments was the manufacture of French invasion scares. The ruse had been introduced in this country long before it was carried to greater refinements in Germany by Bismarck, who may have learned his skill from the older statesman. Distractions of the kind were a godsend to Palmerston, covering up many ragged ends in his foreign policy and giving him welcome breathing spaces in which to straighten out inconvenient tangles. The method pursued was simplicity itself. The Government gave the word, and great was the company of the preachers who thereupon proclaimed, on the platform and in the Press, the impending danger to the commonwealth. More than once Bright protested in the House of Commons against the demoralizing effect of this method of creating what was falsely represented as "public opinion." At the time of one of these scares Cobden went down to Manchester in order to allay the alarm which had spread to his constituents. His best exposure of the cry of "Wolf!" on that occasion was contained in the fact that the fleet which would have had to repel any danger of the kind was at that moment cruising leisurely in the east of the Mediterranean.

"So I assure gentlemen in the provinces who join in the cry," he added, "that they are only being heartily laughed at for their pains, and that the Government, which may profit by the cry, is by no means a sharer in the panic. And this is one of the worst parts of the panic —that the Government do manage to tide over a session and gain time when they can find silly people through the country who will occupy their fellow-citizens by such a cry as this."—(January 27, 1853.)

The hollowness of that particular scare was demonstrated only a year later, when the Government which had professed to believe that the French meditated a sudden piratical descent upon Britain's shores joined France in a war against Russia. Yet those early Victorians were hardly more credulous than a later generation, for most people of mature years will recall the newspaper scares which created so much trepidation on parts of the east coast of England when similar attacks from across the North Sea were said to be imminent ; though simultaneously the same fears of nefarious English designs were entertained in Germany.

Not less the base "Hidden Hand" conspiracies of our own day had an exact counterpart in the middle of last century, in the alleged sinister influence on British policy of the Prince Consort, an influence never seen though declared by the knowing ones to be everywhere felt. Cobden's sympathies were more French than German, but he poured scathing satire upon the childish fictions and cowardly innuendoes on this subject which were periodically disseminated by a certain section of the London Press, inspired, as he and many others believed, by Lord Palmerston. It was certainly a cause of suspicion that while Aberdeen and Russell felt it their duty to defend the Prince Consort from these underhand attacks, Palmerston never disclaimed either sympathy or association with them. As his disappointment with British foreign policy grew, owing to the continual and disturbing interventions of Lord Palmerston, his opinion of the Foreign Office proportionately declined until he persuaded himself that its entire system was " calculated to breed and perpetuate quarrels."

Of professional diplomatists in general he had formed a low opinion even before he negotiated the French Commercial Treaty of 1859–60 as an " amateur," but that experience left him still more disillusioned. He complained chiefly that they busied themselves about little things, were steeped in " old and musty traditions," thought so much of their ornamental functions as spokesmen of Courts to Courts, and did so little to conciliate and bring together the peoples whose relations, for good or ill, were so largely in their hands. He was incensed as he thought of the valuable work which might be done by men of the right sort, in smoothing international difficulties and preserving the peace of Europe, if they would but view their positions from a strictly utilitarian standpoint. Yet even when a serious crisis occurred diplomacy higgled over forms and phrases while all the time the sleuth-hounds of war were straining to be free. His special knowledge of commerce and industry added weight to his further complaint that British ambassadors systematically ignored those great interests, though in so large a degree the foundations of national prosperity.

He saw only one secret of a sober and pacific foreign policy, and it was to bring foreign affairs into the light of day and under the completest possible parliamentary control. In working for this end his first difficulty was to convince his popular audiences of a consciousness of their impotence in relation to their most vital interests. So long as he was agitating against the Corn Laws he was able to count on understanding and sympathetic hearers ; but when, later, he dealt with less concrete issues, like international relations, the origin of wars, the conditions of peace, disarmament, and arbitration, he found himself confronted by a Chinese wall of ignorance which for a time blocked the way to advance. " The people want information and instruction," he was always writing to his political associates, and as a Member of Parliament he never wearied in bringing home to his constituents the importance to them of every aspect of foreign policy. Again and again in his platform speeches he would turn aside in order to make it clear to his hearers that the greatest of home questions was, in reality, the foreign question, since this determined their material welfare in all sorts of ways. At times he felt a great disgust as well as a great pity for the simple credulity which resulted from ignorance of foreign affairs. He spoke of the British public as " a big baby " in its readiness to be amused with Lord Palmerston's " rattles and straws," and as a very glutton in gullibility.

Strong feelings may have tempted him to indulge in censures disproportionate to the shortcomings justly attributable to the diplomacy of his time, yet no man had a greater right to unburden his mind on this subject. For he was an outstanding example of the beneficent influence which even a private individual, endowed with the qualities of sagacity and sympathy, was able to exercise as an emissary of his country in the service of international conciliation. No statesman of his generation better understood the main currents of Continental thought, had a firmer grasp of the sound principles of international relations, a wider and more intimate knowledge of the modern history and the actual life of the nations which it was the special interest of Englishmen to know, or a judgment of finer balance and temper ; and perhaps none had in an equal degree his open-mindedness and his altogether un-English freedom from prejudices. It was the combination of all these qualities that set him apart amongst the British statesmen of his day.

One illustration of his clear perception of the signs of the times may serve. He was one of the very few contemporary statesmen who took Prussia seriously and realized the importance of the German unity movement which was steadily growing from the middle of the century. Most of them superciliously disregarded both of these coming factors in European history, though fate was unrolling before their

R

eyes a scroll scored with infinitely momentous characters. Baron Bunsen, the Prussian envoy to England, wrote in 1849 : " It is quite entertaining to see the stiff unbelief of the English in the future of Germany. Lord John (Russell) is merely uninformed. Peel has somewhat staggered the mind of the excellent Prince (Consort) by his unbelief, though he has a statesmanlike good will towards the Germanic nations and even for the German nation. Aberdeen is the greatest sinner. He believes in God and in the Emperor Nicholas." [1] In June 1862, Bismarck himself, then Prussian envoy in Paris, visited London, and, writing to his wife of the impressions he formed, he said : " It was very pleasant there, but the Ministers know less about Prussia than about Japan and Mongolia, nor are they any cleverer than our own."

Lord John Russell, more open-minded than most public men of his day, has left it on record that it was not until 1860, forty-five years after he entered parliamentary life, twenty-five years after he first became a Minister, and fourteen years after he formed his first Cabinet, that he began to study the German question seriously. In that year he wrote to the Prince Consort, confessing that he had " hitherto been very unwilling to enter at all into the intimate politics of the German Confederation," and asking for " some clue " as to what British policy in regard thereto should be. Disraeli, responsive as he was to atmosphere and environment, and willing to learn all that foreign diplomats could tell him about the problems of their countries, never ceased to regard Prussia as a *quantité négligeable* until the Danish war of 1864 told another tale. Only a year before he avowed his conviction that " Prussia without nationality, the principle of the day, is clearly the subject for partition."

For the astounding ignorance on the German question which prevailed in Ministerial and all political circles at that time the intelligence officers stationed at so many of the German Courts, who should have known the facts and did not, were largely to blame. The Prince Consort put his finger on a weak spot in the diplomatic system of the day when he complained that its agents did not take trouble to inform themselves, and even despised efforts of the kind. So it

[1] *Life of Bunsen,* ii. 189.

continued even after Germany had become an Empire and the strongest military Power in Europe.

Another defect of the mechanism of political life to which Cobden called attention, though without effect, was the whittling down of the constitutional doctrine of Ministerial responsibility, a doctrine invaluable if applied in any effectual form, but a dangerous delusion when allowed to fall into desuetude, as it has been in this country. For any practical value it had, the doctrine was scotched, if not altogether killed, even in Cobden's day, and he deeply regretted it. There were a dozen occasions when he would have rejoiced to see it put in practical operation in the sphere of foreign affairs. He would have given much if it had been possible to bring home responsibility to the Ministers who in 1864 nearly embroiled England in the war over the Elbe Duchies, and who, by allowing Denmark to believe that the force of this country would be at her disposal in the event of a breach with Prussia, led her into disaster.

" The natural solution," he said in the course of his last public speech, " in a case like that, in our constitutional form of government, is this—the nation must find some vicarious sufferer who shall be made to pay the penalty of this national blunder. In ancient times, a Minister that had got the country into a mess would have had his head cut off. Now he is decapitated in another way. He is sent away from Downing Street into the cold shade of the Opposition, on the left-hand side of the Speaker."

Cobden died in the spring of 1865, but had he lived a little longer he would have seen with disgust how Earl Russell (as Lord John became by succession in July 1861), who, as Foreign Secretary, was chiefly responsible for the discredit and humiliation which a policy of bluster brought upon this country in the Danish affair, escaped even the mild official form of execution. For when Palmerston, too, died in October of the same year it fell to Russell to form his second Administration, with Lord Clarendon as his Foreign Secretary.

So slow is the advance towards a genuine system of popular government that Cobden's indictment of the mechanism of British foreign policy, though dating from sixty and seventy years ago, might almost stand for the present day, except that certain of the sinister tendencies then visible have hardened in the interval. The Foreign Office still goes its own way, a political pontificate in a country which is supposed to enjoy free institutions, still jealously maintaining the tradition of secrecy in regard to its transactions, still exemplifying the anomaly that in constitutional life the servant may be, in some ways, far greater than his lord. Until recently it also continued to be the only public Department staffed from a limited class and to some extent on the dynastic principle; for there is now open competition, special nominations have been abolished, and a committee of selection has replaced the unfettered choice of the Foreign Secretary and his private secretary.

While in most matters the position is little different from what it was in Cobden's days, one development is quite modern. The publication of the dispatches which passed between the Russian Foreign Office and its Ambassador in London during the years immediately preceding the late war brought to light the fact that foreign diplomats were accustomed at that time to identify the higher permanent officials of the Department with special sympathies—with France or Russia or Germany, as the case might be. It is not enough to say that personal preferences of the kind, even if they were held, could not influence the action of these or any other officials, for few people will doubt that: the real danger is that the mere assumption of their existence, however arising, would be bound to cause suspicion and bad feeling in one quarter just because it created satisfaction and elation in another. Political sympathies and personal bias in any direction are assumed, as a matter of course, to be altogether barred in the British Civil Service, which in this respect, as in all matters of personal probity, does in general enjoy a reputation nowhere excelled. But in a Department like the Foreign Office, so much of whose work is of an extremely delicate character, and affects international relations so profoundly and in so many directions, the wholesome rule of absolute official impartiality—one might almost say impersonality—should be emphasized so strongly as to afford no excuse for the slightest misapprehension.

More serious than any matters of form and etiquette, however, is the fact that the tendency in public administration during recent years to expand, not the rights of Parliament, but the powers and claims of the Executive and the official hierarchy behind the scenes, has been specially pronounced in relation to foreign affairs. Even in the middle of last century Cobden regarded as a travesty of popular government the disproportionately unequal voice enjoyed by Parliament in decisions involving the issue of peace or war ; for, as he put it, the rule of the Constitution at that time " gave to the Court the power of declaring war, and to the Commons the privilege of providing the expenses." But this rule has since been further modified to the nation's disadvantage. In recent years we have seen how secret agreements for warlike co-operation with a foreign Power, having all the moral and binding force of a military alliance, though not set down in a formal treaty, have been made behind the back both of Parliament and of all but a few chosen Cabinet Ministers, so that when a Continental war broke out Great Britain suddenly and unexpectedly found herself committed to participation as a matter of duty. It even happened during that war that on the authority of a single Minister a slice of British territory was offered to a Continental State as the price of its military co-operation, though the transaction did not mature in that way.

Largely owing to the growing claim of the Foreign Office and its parliamentary heads to independence and freedom from control the attenuated theory of the " continuity of foreign policy " which lingered within living memory has disappeared. National interest would be best served if foreign affairs, in every relation, were kept as much out of party controversy as the business transactions of the Post Office or the Office of Works ; yet so long as the Foreign Office continues to be a law to itself there can be no hope of seeing foreign policy put on such a footing as will afford common ground for all parties to meet upon, and so give that assurance of moderation and steadiness of purpose which is so essential for an Empire whose first and greatest interest is peace.

To be just, the same exaggeration of Ministerial powers is visible in other directions, as in the repeated promises by individual Ministers of huge amounts of public money without prior reference to the House of Commons, though it took that

Chamber centuries of disputing and bartering with Sovereigns and peers before it succeeded in asserting exclusive control over national expenditure.

All such restrictions of the powers of Parliament are not merely inconsistent with any genuine conception of democratic government, but they open up possibilities of great danger ; for if they are to be regarded as precedents they are certain to be multiplied and extended, until in the end we may find ourselves in the clutches of a Ministerial and bureaucratic dictatorship compared with which the most drastic kind of Socialism yet advocated would be mild and almost beneficent. Yet now as in Cobden's day the House of Commons itself, still lacking either the dignity of a Senate or the independence of a Parish Council, is chiefly to blame for its own impotence. One has only to read Cobden's criticisms of the Foreign Office of his day in order to imagine the fight which he would have made against its continued claims. In the present flaccid state of parliamentary and public opinion, however, not one but half a dozen Cobdens will be needed before there can be any hope of bringing that oligarchic Department into line with the general principles upon which national affairs are managed in other directions.

Much that Cobden says about the disingenuousness associated with diplomacy likewise holds good still for Europe, and even for our own corner of it. It is of the essence of officialism in general that it tends to make cynics of even good men ; for it discourages candour, represses spontaneity, tempts to evasion, sophistry, and the equivocation that " lies like truth," and by indulging in obscurity of language encourages crookedness of thought. In the sphere of foreign affairs, owing to the atmosphere of secrecy and suspicion which pervades it, all these defects are magnified, so that it has come about that not merely the accepted language of diplomatic intercourse but its moral currency is regarded as alien to the usage and instincts of normal men and women. Nothing contributed more to make Bismarck a cynic than his early experience of diplomacy, of which he said that the most malicious of democrats had no idea of the charlatanism which it concealed.

Ferdinand Lassalle said on one occasion that lying was

" a European Power," and the late war proved it to be one of the great ones. Doubtless with certain notorious incidents of the struggle in mind, the Prime Minister, in his manly address to the students of Edinburgh University on November 6, 1925, deplored the fact that " with war and the preparation for war go the stratagems of diplomacy, the dropping of the code of morals, a holiday for truth, and an aftermath of cynicism. . . . In the arena of international rivalry and conflict, men have placed patriotism above truthfulness as the indispensable virtue of statesmen." But that is not the worst, for so far is deception countenanced in high affairs of State that it is practised in time of peace as well as of war, and, most pitiful of all, by men, honourable in all other relations of life, who do not seem to perceive the shame involved in the deliberate perversion and suppression of facts so long as these things are done merely officially.

Not without reason did the American inspirer of the Covenant of the League of Nations affirm, at the head of its preamble, the need for " open, just, and honourable relations." But that need applies not only to dealings between Governments but to the relations of these to their own Legislatures and peoples. We have seen how, owing to the systematic policy of secrecy and deception pursued in relation to foreign affairs in his day, Cobden never knew whether official statements on any question represented the whole or only part of the truth, or none at all, insomuch that he came at last to doubt the word of any Minister until it had been confirmed by independent testimony. When political reputations can sink as low as that there is something terribly amiss with the state of Denmark. And yet it cannot be maintained that candour and straightforwardness are to-day more cultivated in parliamentary relations than when Cobden lived. Even in the simple matter of answering questions the evasions, equivocations, trimmings, and suppressions of facts which are constantly resorted to stare in the face anyone who knows from experience how these things are done.

It is difficult to believe that either the nation or the House of Commons would again be willing to accept without searching investigation of the facts, and ample time for making it, any future justifications for war that might be put forward on purely official authority. Never in modern history was public faith in Governments and their assurances so rudely shaken as in the late war. Not only in France and Russia, but in this country, the official justifications for the war which were advanced at the outset were not the real and true ones, nor were the aims and purposes first avowed those which were actually pursued, some openly, others in the form of secret agreements, as soon as the nations had been set to work on the horrible business of killing each other. It is not likely that the deception practised on our own nation by the men in power, who had for years been binding it by invisible cords to France and Russia, whose Governments and diplomatists, as the world now knows, were bent on a war with Germany as soon as British military and naval co-operation could be counted on with confidence, will be either forgiven or forgotten by the generations now living.[1]

Nor is the diplomacy of our day any more able than in the past to rise to the height of great crises calling for the display of straight, strong, sagacious counsels. When this country was drifting into the Crimean War, the Earl of Clarendon wrote to Lord John Russell, " I verily believe that if two or three sensible people, meaning honestly and having real power to treat, were to meet together for an hour, the whole thing might be settled " (October 1, 1853). But they did not meet, and the war came. Was not that the position in 1914 ? The Great War found the statesmanship of Europe, as represented by its diplomatic machinery, insolvent, and just as incapable, in the severe testing time of need, of preserving peace as it had been of checking the forces which for years had been making for catastrophe.

No more tragic records exist in political literature than those which tell of the weak, halting, futile conversations, some of them so transparently insincere as to verge on frivolity, which took place between the Foreign Ministers and ambassa-

---

[1] Writing to President Wilson just before the war (May 29, 1914) from Berlin, which he visited in the course of a European tour of inquiry, Colonel House said : " The situation is extraordinary. It is militarism run stark mad. Unless someone acting for you can bring about a different understanding, there is some day to be an awful cataclysm. No one in Europe can do it. There is too much hatred, too many jealousies. Whenever England consents, France and Russia will close in on Germany and Austria." —*The Intimate Papers of Colonel House*, i. 255.

dors of the Great Powers during the three weeks which preceded the outbreak of hostilities. There they were, a dozen or a score of them, all supposed to be eminent in their special business of politics and diplomacy, hurrying and scurrying to and fro like a flock of bewildered sheep, exchanging all the conventional lispings and banalities of official intercourse, stickling about words, forms, formulas, precedents, and miserable etiquette, when all the time millions of human lives and the future of civilization were at stake.[1]

Few people capable of impartial judgment can have re-read in cold blood, at a later date, the terrible indictment of ineptitude and futility which is contained in these records without coming to the conclusion that the war should not and would not have happened but for the fact that the hands of some of the negotiators were tied fast, and that two of our Allies were not averse to it.[2] While the struggle was still in progress, though nearer to the end than the world suspected, I was in the company of the late Viscount Bryce, but lately returned home from the splendid work which he had done for this country and for Anglo-American good will during his tenure of the embassy in Washington, and the conversation turned on diplomacy in relation to the fateful month of July 1914. After emphasizing his opinion that the war might have been avoided, he said in a voice vibrating with intense feeling, " I would hang every diplomat on a lamp-post." Of course, the words were not meant to be taken literally, yet they unquestionably betrayed the outraged spirit of a high-minded statesman, who was conscious of the tremendous responsibility which rests upon the representatives of a calling which he had just ceased to adorn, and who knew from experience the large possibilities, as well as the limitations, of their influence, when seriously and conscientiously exercised.

Mention has been made of Cobden's complaint of the disdainful indifference of contemporary diplomats to British

---

[1] " The outbreak of the Great War is the condemnation not only of the clumsy performers who strutted for a brief hour across the stage, but of the international anarchy which they inherited and which they did nothing to abate."—G. P. GOOCH, *History of Modern Europe*, p. 559.

[2] Later (December 23, 1920), Mr. Lloyd George spoke of the war as "something into which they (the men 'at the head of affairs') glided, or rather staggered and stumbled, perhaps through folly; and a discussion, I have no doubt, would have averted it."

economic interests, and of their disregard of the public opinion of the countries to which they were accredited, and Morley endorses his strictures.[1] The first part of this indictment has been greatly weakened, though only in quite recent years, and owing to persistent outside pressure.[2] It is greatly to be feared, however, that public opinion has still for the average diplomat as little interest as half a century ago, when the British ambassador in Berlin entirely failed to recognize the strength, or even the existence, of the colonial and naval movements which were then taking hold of the German nation. On both of these questions he consistently gave the Foreign Office information which was inadequate because it was based altogether on official opinion, with the result that when Bismarck took up the question of colonization early in the 'eighties Lord Granville fell into blunder after blunder owing to ignorance of the fact that behind the German Chancellor there was a powerful national impetus which compelled him to take action, at first even against his will.

In that case the mischief done was irreparable, for the opposition offered by the British Foreign Office to Germany's appropriation of territories in Africa which had never been occupied or claimed, and were at the time as much no-man's-land as the North or South Pole, left behind feelings of resentment which never entirely disappeared, and formed the groundwork of much later suspicion.

How little the average diplomatist, closed as he is to any influences except those of his circumscribed professional circle, knows about the movements of public opinion outside was illustrated when, relying on Court and official report, Sir George Buchanan, for over seven years ambassador in St. Petersburg, gave the Foreign Office the assurance, as late as February 18, 1917, that the Russian nation intended to continue the war to the bitter end. " The majority of the nation," he wrote, " including the Government and the army,

---

[1] *Life*, ii. 243.

[2] I recall from my own experience an incident of under twenty years ago illustrating the typical attitude of diplomatic officials abroad to commercial questions at that time and later. Having to consult a certain British legation in the course of some official work, conversation turned on such questions, upon which the *chargé d'affaires*, pointing to a pile of papers at his side, burst out in petulant tones: " Here the Board of Trade keeps sending me these forms to fill up. Why does it bother me? What have I to do with trade?"

are at one in their determination to fight it out to a victorious finish ; but there the national unity ends." [1]

What was the truth ? Already when he thus wrote St. Petersburg was honeycombed by insurrectionary movements ; only a fortnight later there were shootings in the streets and mutiny in the barracks, the Socialists were in practical control, and even the Duma was kicking at authority ; while within a month revolution had broken out, and soon afterwards the Russian fighting machine lay shattered in pieces. The collapse had been predicted long before by Russians, both in that country and in this, familiar with the real facts, but their warnings, not being official, did not count. Towards the end of the year, when the Bolshevists were in full power, the same authority, echoing still the chatter of a feeble camarilla, urged the military expedition against the Red Army which proved so futile and costly a fiasco, and later he prided himself on having done it. [2]

A British diplomatist of this generation, recalling his past chiefs and colleagues, remarks that " by the side of scholars, of thoughtful statesmen, of accomplished linguists," he had " met with pompous mediocrities, and indeed sometimes, though rarely, downright nonentities." [3] No stronger reproach has ever been made against the most important of our Departments of State than is contained in the second half of this sentence, and if the explanation lies in the fact that, as an eminent statesman has said, " diplomacy is the most aristocratic of professions," the remedy is obvious. It may be an arguable contention that, in these days of telegraphs and aerial posts, diplomatic agents of the old type are obsolete, and that the most valuable qualification to be required of modern ambassadors and envoys is that they shall have an exceptional knowledge of the countries and peoples to which they are accredited, and be assiduous collectors and faithful reporters of full, true, and impartial information. Until that lower conception of the diplomatist's status and function is accepted, however, it will probably be agreed that for the higher diplomatic positions, charged with so much responsibility and

---

[1] *My Mission to Russia*, ii. 56.   [2] *Ibid.*, ii. 256–57.
[3] Sir Horace Rumbold, *Recollections of a Diplomatist*, i. 107–8, a work which well illustrates the lighter sides of the diplomatist's life.

offering opportunities for such beneficent and far-spreading influence, only the best men available can be good enough, and that in this department of State service there should be no place at all for either "nonentities" or "mediocrities." [1] The time may come when the best men will be both sought and obtained, but before it does not a few traditions of the Foreign Office will have to be jettisoned, and an end will need to be put to all appointments due to favour or justified merely by the mechanical principle of seniority.

Mr. Baldwin has been calling the nation to the greater exercise of the old Roman virtues of *pietas* and *gravitas*. Of *pietas* our diplomatists have no lack—let not that credit be denied to them—but *gravitas* is a characteristic which more than any other disqualifies for the diplomatic service. One of the ablest, and on European questions incomparably the best informed, of British diplomatists of modern times, Sir Robert Morier, failed to receive his deserts because he took his profession too seriously for the Foreign Office tradition, and because his way was blocked by the higher claims of privilege. In refusing to appoint him Permanent Under-Secretary for Foreign Affairs, Lord Derby wrote that he "*feared* Morier had one defect for that particular position—he was too much in earnest, and earnest men with ideas and great abilities were sometimes unsafe men." Another reason why Morier was overlooked was that a politician was wanted for the position.

No State officials are more in the public eye than the members of the diplomatic service, yet how few ambassadors and envoys, of the multitude who flit about the political stage from decade to decade, leave behind them even the barest memory of their names and service to the commonwealth ! When half a dozen are recalled as having during the present generation established the title to be regarded as statesmen, with how many more would it be possible to enrich the record ? All cannot be well with this most responsible department of State affairs so long as this can be said.

To-day, as in Cobden's time, however, the great grievance

---

[1] For an amazing and barely credible illustration of diplomatic tact in an incomparably delicate and critical situation the reader is referred to the Spring-Rice and House interview as narrated in *The Intimate Papers of Colonel House*, ii. 74–7.

against the Foreign Office is its tenacious will to secrecy. The revelations concerning the clandestine agreements which preceded the Great War and alone made it possible—the perfected military agreements with France, and the complementary naval agreement which was being negotiated with Russia up to June 1914, but was not completed [1]—served for a time to concentrate public attention upon the more dangerous features of what has come to be known popularly as the " old diplomacy." Granting that the phrase is vague, and rather invites a definition than offers one, it is not the phrase but the substance behind it that matters, and the public mind is in no uncertainty as to what the phrase connotes. It means precisely the diplomacy which was so obnoxious to Cobden and his school in their day—the policy which keeps Parliament and the nation in the dark about their own affairs, and allows a single public Department, or even its head alone, to form momentous and far-reaching decisions without so much as " By your leave." If the House of Commons and the nations are still, on the whole, abysmally ignorant on the subject of foreign affairs, the main cause is this mischievous policy of secrecy. Even Lord Rosebery after filling the office of Foreign Secretary in two Cabinets, those of 1886 and 1892, and being himself Prime Minister, confessed in a speech made at Glasgow just before the war :

" It is extremely difficult for us who know nothing about foreign policy but what we see in the newspapers to form any accurate judgment as to what that foreign policy may be. . . . What is seen on the stage of foreign policy is but a small part of the whole. By far the greater portion is what takes place behind the scenes, and as we ordinary mortals are not admitted behind the scenes, not even to the door of the green-room, our knowledge of foreign policy must be based mainly on speculation."—(January 13, 1912.)

I recall also how about the same time a well-known and universally esteemed member of the House of Commons poured out to me a long lament over his inability ever to

---

[1] In Lord Grey's political *apologia*, *Twenty-five Years*, this agreement is still described both in the text and index as " alleged." But why " alleged " ? It would be interesting to have Mr. Churchill's and the late Prince Louis of Battenburg's opinions on the point—better still, to be told what certain naval experts at the Admiralty at the time thought about the agreement.

obtain a plain answer to a plain question on any important subject put to the Foreign Secretary, and his amazement that the House of Commons, by conniving at its own efface-ment, encouraged this policy of secretiveness. The truth is that in the hands of a Foreign Secretary who has held his office long enough to be habituated to its traditions, the House of Commons is as clay in the hands of the potter. It was so in Palmerston's day, and it is so to-day.

Because of the Great War " democracy " has been accused of " failure "—failure, presumably, to maintain the peace. But democratic government, if that is what is meant, has never yet existed in any true sense, and the best theoretical democracy conceivable would fail so long as Governments continue to work in the dark and to trickle out to the Legisla-ture and the nation information on vital matters only sufficient to confuse without enlightening them. The war was in part the result of secret diplomacy, and the territorial arrangements which have made the peace treaties a source of infinite danger were likewise the result of clandestine agreements. The entire mechanism of foreign policy, as it exists in Europe to-day, is not only undemocratic and anti-national ; it is inconsistent with any rational and moral principle of foreign relations ; and under it there can never be a guarantee of permanent peace, since at present no one knows at any time what subterranean influences may be at work making for misunderstanding and mischief. Looking back upon our own modern history it will be seen that only on rare occasions, when public opinion has been so strongly expressed that it could not safely be ignored, and the House of Commons has made a firm stand, has the Foreign Office, before adopting critical decisions, fully taken the nation into its confidence. And while at times—as conspicuously in 1880—it has happened that an unpopular policy in foreign affairs has received con-demnation at the polls, such disapproval has at best arrested further mischievous action after harm enough had been done.

The League of Nations has made a half-hearted start on a path which will have to be travelled far before the victory for open diplomacy and the establishment of straightforward relations between Governments and nations is won. On the whole the provisions of the Covenant on this subject are more noteworthy for what they omit than for what they contain. For example, the requirement that treaties concluded by members shall be registered with the League is a laudable step in the right direction, but it is unfortunately notorious that several members have failed to keep their word in this matter. At registration, however, the Covenant cannot stop. Treaties by which military or naval alliances are concluded or aggressive action of any kind against other Powers is contemplated should be rigidly prohibited as contrary to the comity of nations; for every such arrangement, let the pretexts be what they may, is a provocation and a challenge to other nations to do likewise. Further, all treaties, whatever their purpose, should be of limited duration, and subject to periodical revision, with a view to their adaptation to changed situations, so that in future Governments and Parliaments may not unexpectedly find their hands tied by old pledges undertaken in different circumstances. If the secret negotiations between Great Britain and France which led to the adoption of a definite plan of campaign, to be carried out in certain contingencies on Belgian soil, had been disclosed at any time before 1914, the continuance of the Belgian neutrality treaty would have been recognized by the world at large as a farce. Writers in neutral countries have maintained that before Germany violated Belgian territory it had already been violated in spirit by two of the other contracting Powers.[1]

All that the Covenant says on this subject is that " the Assembly (of the League) may from time to time advise the reconsideration by members of the League of treaties which have become inapplicable, and the consideration of international conditions whose continuance might endanger the peace of the world." What is really needed is that all treaties which contain provisions liable to give rise to disagreement owing to lapse of time, or in any way affecting the interests of third parties, should contain their own guarantee against becoming a source of danger, and the most effective guarantee, next

---

[1] Amongst the documents found by the Germans in the Belgian State archives in Brussels in 1914 was one recording a conversation which took place in April 1912 between the British military attaché and General Jungbluth, wherein the former, referring to the Franco-German crisis over Morocco in the preceding year, said that inasmuch as the Belgians " were not in a position to prevent the Germans passing through our (Belgian) territory, Great Britain would have landed troops in any event."

to full and immediate publicity, would be to restrict their duration to a short period, so as to ensure automatically their frequent reconsideration.

Whatever may be done for the cause of peace in this domain by international action, however, there are some constitutional safeguards of a kind which cannot safely wait, and which no nation which pays due regard to either its interests or its dignity will any longer forgo. It is the duty of our own country, as the home and birthplace of constitutional government, to give Europe a lead in asserting in effectual form the principle of full parliamentary control of foreign policy. Such control does not mean that every sort of communication between one Government and another should be publicly divulged in every detail, still less that while matters remain in the stage of negotiation everything that is being done should be trumpeted from the Treasury Bench or the Press. It does mean, however, that foreign policy should be open to the full light of day, and in particular that no treaty, convention, pact, agreement, or understanding, formal or informal, written or verbal, which imposes on the nation obligations or liabilities of any kind shall be concluded without the prior knowledge and assent of the two Houses of Parliament, meeting in joint session in case of disagreement.

The British public fondly believes that it possesses already the right to approve or, to use the customary word, "ratify," treaties.[1] It does not. If on occasion Parliament exercises this limited function, it is by the special favour of the Foreign Office and the Government of the day ; and even then it is at best empowered to say whether it agrees to accept as it stands, without addition, omission, or amendment, a treaty already concluded, or to reject it altogether. But the Government which has entered into the treaty, having a majority at command, has only to pass round the word that rejection would be viewed with disapproval, and at the call of the division bell the docile Ministerial flock swarms into its fold without so much as the barking of the watch-dogs of the Whips' office. Besides, at present Parliament can always be deceived by the addition to the published treaty of secret provisions, as was the case with the Anglo-French convention of 1904, and may,

[1] Strictly speaking, ratification is the final action of the Sovereign.

for aught the world knows, have been the case with other treaties which have not come into full operation.

Not only should the Legislature have a clear constitutional right to be consulted before treaties of the kind named are concluded, but its power to approve, alter, or reject such treaties at discretion should be unqualified. At the same time, in order to prevent conflict between personal conviction and party loyalty, it would be reasonable that the defeat of a Government in divisions over treaties should not in future involve resignation. How far the party spirit might be banished from the domain of foreign affairs altogether, with a view to greater restraint, stability, and continuity in foreign policy, is another question, which will be considered in the last chapter. If the Foreign Office insists on maintaining that there are some arrangements which cannot be concluded if they are made public, well and good ; the nation must then say with equal decision that it will do without such arrangements ; and, judging from past experience, it is probable that both its safety and its honour will be better protected as a result. It will be remembered that when asked in the House of Commons whether the purpose of the clandestine Abyssinian agreements concluded between this country and Italy at the end of 1925 had been communicated to the ruler or Government of the State affected, the Foreign Secretary replied in the negative, and pleaded in support of this secrecy that " the communication to the Abyssinian Government during the course of protracted negotiations with Italy of information regarding their progress would not have contributed to their successful outcome " (August 2, 1926). Precisely, and for that very fact the transaction stood from the first self-condemned.

The objection that to give Parliament power to modify a treaty would entail delay is without point in view of the fact that the Foreign Office—once called by Lord Clarendon, before he became its head, " that Temple of Procrastination " —has seldom been in a violent hurry to complete international negotiations or, indeed, to do anything at all. Three years ago a dispute with the United States Government, relating to claims for compensation on account of land expropriations in the Fiji Island, was settled by arbitration after negotiations which had lasted since 1876, yet the Under-Secretary for

Foreign Affairs could boast of the result, achieved after forty-eight years of delay, as a triumph of the arbitral principle ! It is worth while adding that Germany had a precisely similar dispute with our Government, but Bismarck, being a forceful statesman, insisted on a settlement being arrived at thirty-six years ago.

Moreover, if a treaty is necessary at all, it is surely common sense that it should be made as satisfactory and water-tight as possible, though more time be needed to ensure this. Even if it could be shown that ratification as now exercised proves sufficient the existing practice is in most cases none the less a travesty of any true idea of democratic government, and, worse still, it does not cover the exceptional case, which is the case that is likely to prove a source of danger, and potentially of disaster. Bitter experience has taught the nation and Empire that they may be committed to a great war, costing them a million lives and six thousand million pounds sterling of debt, in virtue of a sort of " gentleman's agreement " of which they knew nothing until it was too late to repudiate it.

Nothing that has occurred since 1914 has modified my opinion, published at the time, that as the European situation had been allowed to develop England could not have remained out of the war. But to make that admission is not to condone the deception which was practised upon the nation, nor does it weaken my conviction that without the British pledge of armed co-operation France and Russia would never have given to the *entente* a provocative tendency and entered upon a policy of " encirclement " as regards Germany, with the humanly certain result that the Great War would not have happened in our day. Sir Austen Chamberlain went farther in his speech in the House of Commons on February 8, 1922, when he said of the secret commitments incurred prior to 1914 towards France by the British Government, or a part of it, " if . . . our obligations had been known and definite it is at least possible, and I think it is probable, that war would have been avoided in 1914."

It is unnecessary to tell in detail the story of how from 1905 forward a friendly relationship between statesmen on both sides was allowed, under cover of secrecy, to develop into a practical alliance between the nations they represented. The story has often been told in part, but for all the facts already available—and many more will yet be known—it is necessary to co-ordinate the data contained in the collections of British, French, Russian, German, Belgian, and other official dispatches which have been published since 1914.[1] Not least important is the French official record of the three years of conversations and dispatches between the Foreign Ministries of France and Russia and the ambassadors of these countries in St. Petersburg and Paris respectively which culminated in the conclusion of the Franco-Russian military alliance of December 31, 1893. For exactly the same astute and unceasing pressure was exercised by the Quay d'Orsay upon the British Foreign Office until it had gained the objective followed from the first, and the innocent and well-meaning Anglo-French *entente* of 1904 had developed into formal and momentous military engagements.

How the first negotiations with France struck a clear-thinking, undiplomatic mind is shown by the remark made by Sir Henry Campbell-Bannerman when the friendly " conversations " began to take a military character. He wrote to Lord Ripon on February 1, 1906: " I do not like the stress laid upon joint preparations. It becomes very close to an honourable undertaking. *But let us hope for the best.*" It was, of course, a definite undertaking in honour from the first, though the nations concerned were compromised and pledged without their knowledge. Lord Loreburn, an ex-Lord Chancellor, stated the truth bluntly when he said that we went into the war of 1914 " in a Russian quarrel because we were tied to France in the dark."

How will it be with the future ? Speaking of secret diplomacy, Kossuth once put the matter paradoxically when he said : " Diplomacy tells us that the dinner is prepared and eaten, and we (the people) have nothing to do but to digest the consequences." But a nation which has any decent respect for itself will refuse to tolerate its present position of

---

[1] While this book is in the press the first volume of *The Roots and Causes of the Wars* (1914–18) by John S. Ewart, K.C., the Canadian jurisconsult, has reached me. It contains a masterly study of the origins of the Great War, and of the real, as distinguished from the professed, motives of the Governments which engaged in it.

half-citizenship. All through the war, with the disclosures as to the origin and course of the clandestine negotiations which bound it to participate fresh in memory, the nation took it for granted, in the easy and slip-shod way it has a habit of doing, that secret diplomacy of that kind had had its day, and that for the future everything done by our Foreign Secretaries and their Department would be open and above board. For a time there seemed a real hope that a new beginning was to be made. For the Labour Government of 1924 set an example by formally introducing the principle that no agreement of any kind should be concluded before the House of Commons had had an opportunity of expressing an opinion upon it. Yet one of the earliest acts of the succeeding Government of Mr. Baldwin was to dissociate itself from this reversal of Foreign Office traditions, and there exists to-day no pledge or promise that can serve as a definite safeguard against the repetition of the wrong done to the nation in 1905 and the following years.

In March 1925 the Labour Opposition invited the House of Commons to adopt a motion affirming, plainly and unequivocally, the principle of open diplomacy and treaties,[1] but the Government resisted the motion, and on a party division it was rejected by 255 votes against 133. During the discussion an ex-Under-Secretary of State for Foreign Affairs even asked the House :

" Why should the Secretary of State for Foreign Affairs be stripped of all authority any more than his colleagues at the Colonial Office or the India Office ? The only possible way to safeguard parliamentary control over all these offices was to leave responsibility for taking decisions to an executive officer who must give place to others as soon as he ceased to have the confidence of the House."

Argument of that sort might be used just as validly for abolishing self-government altogether. Those who reason

[1] The motion ran : " That no treaty shall be ratified and no diplomatic arrangement or understanding with a foreign State involving, directly or indirectly, national obligations shall be concluded without the consent of Parliament, and no preparations for co-operation in war between the Naval, Military, or Air Staffs and the Naval, Military, or Air Staffs of a foreign State, shall be lawful unless consequent upon such arrangements or understanding, and this resolution shall be communicated to all States with which this country is in diplomatic relations and to the League of Nations."

thus assume that Parliament exists simply in order to provide offices for a few of its members. The millions of the nation say : " A plague on all your musty rules, conventions, and traditions, the entire hamper of which does not weigh with us against one man's life or one woman's tears ! What we want is peace, and to that end the right to control and check the actions of our supposed servants—to say what shall be done before it is done beyond recall, so that if harm results we shall have ourselves to blame. Of what use to us are votes of censure passed on unpopular Ministers ? All that happens is that these men are given other offices or are sent to the House of Lords, there to be out of further mischief, while we and our children are left to pay the penalty of their blunders and follies."

At times the eagerness with which the Foreign Office tries to evade and frustrate the claim to open diplomacy and full and effectual parliamentary control shows a spirit almost of desperation. Witness the recent speech of Sir A. Chamberlain at the London Guildhall (March 26, 1926). After saying that " foreign affairs used to be the mystery of the few, they have become in these days the affair of all," he proceeded to warn the nation that there were limits beyond which its curiosity could not be satisfied or encouraged :

" The claims of democracy to control, to be informed as to all the events of importance, to have, *perhaps*, prior knowledge of all possible commitments, to preserve to the democratic organs of the State their predominant influence over public affairs, may clash sometimes with the work of the League of Nations, and unless those necessary rights of the democracy in democratic States are handled wisely and used with discretion, you will find that Geneva, instead of opening a new chapter of conciliation, repeats the old story of irreconcilable claims, of the clash of national pride, of points of honour, and all the consequences to which those lead."

That sounds a dangerous doctrine, for the implied suggestion that the League of Nations should have a knowledge of the foreign policy of a nation which is denied to the nation itself would involve an indefensible invasion of national rights, and the League would not deserve to survive a week if it made such a claim. What our Foreign Secretaries will not do is to emancipate themselves from the superstitious obsession that in external relations secrecy means safety. There is in reality nothing so impolitic and dangerous.

It is important that the nation should clearly understand the position. The Foreign Office has re-established its right to resort to secrecy at its discretion, and to dole out to Parliament just such information on any given decision or issue as it may please, and that after the event. It is a position which most people believed that it had formally, if unwillingly, renounced, but they were mistaken. The result is that there exists to-day no guarantee against a repetition of such clandestine agreements as those of 1905–14, which ended as the country knows to its bitter cost. Even so temperate an authority on foreign policy as Lord Parmoor, who held the office of Lord President of the Council in the Government of Mr. Ramsay MacDonald, appears to have no great confidence that perfect faith will be kept with the country in future. " The risk," he said a few months ago, " was not that any sane man would advocate, directly, a policy of aggressive warfare He feared specious phrases or *formulæ* intended to capture the national imagination, and often shrouded under a veil of inaccurate information." Yet the demand for open diplomacy and the recognition of the unqualified authority of Parliament in this domain, though foiled for the moment, cannot be abandoned, but must be prosecuted with intenser effort until this long-protracted struggle with privilege has been carried to a successful issue.

It has been necessary to state the facts with unequivocal frankness, since the issues involved for the nation are momentous beyond estimation ; yet at least it has been done without personal animus or conscious lack of charity. By all means let us, as soon as possible, call oblivion on the past, lamentable as is the legacy which it has left us, since what has been done is beyond recall or remedy. But first let us be perfectly sure that the future will not be a repetition of the past. Let us know for certain, and be able to tell our children and our children's children, as we look into their trustful eyes, that never again, in England at least, will it be possible for a Foreign Secretary to go down to the House of Commons on the eve of a declaration of hostilities, already resolved on by the Cabinet, and say, not verbally, but yet in effect :

" I have here an undertaking—please observe that it is not a treaty —which requires this country to go to war. I entered into it some years ago over your heads and over the heads of most of the other members of the Cabinet. Some inquisitive members of this House, suspecting its existence, once questioned me on the subject, when, evading a plain answer for reasons of State, I let it be understood that there was nothing in it, and that our hands were free. You are to understand to-day that there is very much in it, and that our hands are bound. In now divulging the facts for the first time I would warn honourable members that if they refuse to ratify my pledges the responsibility will rest on their consciences."

It would contribute to the breaking down of the secretive traditions of the Foreign Office if there existed a sessional Standing Committee of the two Houses of Parliament, which it would be the duty of the Foreign Secretary to keep thoroughly informed upon the current business of his office and to consult upon all important questions before decisions were taken. This Committee should be entitled to call for any information within the power of the Foreign Office and its head to supply. It will be remembered that so experienced and cautious a statesman as Lord Bryce advised the formation of a body of this kind, corresponding to the American Foreign Affairs Committee, and similar Committees exist in France and Germany. Such a Committee might be strengthened by the addition to its members of a representative of each of the Dominions (either the High Commissioner now resident in London or a special delegate, at the discretion of the Dominion concerned), and of India. Great Britain would rightly claim to have a preponderance of votes, and instead of securing this by making the Committee an unwieldy body the votes of the representatives of the home Parliament might count doubly. As the Committee would necessarily be small there is hardly greater force in the objection that it could lead to the indiscreet disclosure of inopportune information that exists in the case of the Cabinet or the Judicial Committee of the Privy Council.

CHAPTER XIII

COBDEN AND OUR DAY

I. His Doctrine Justified

> " Hail to the spirit which dared
> Trust its own thoughts, before yet
> Echoed her back by the crowd !
> Hail to the courage which gave
> Voice to its creed, ere the creed
> Won consecration from time ! "
>
> MATTHEW ARNOLD (" Haworth Churchyard ").

> " Servants of God !—or sons
> Shall I not call you ? . . .
> Yours is the praise, if mankind
> Hath not as yet in its march
> Fainted, and fallen, and died ! "
>
> MATTHEW ARNOLD (" Rugby Chapel ").

COBDEN'S principles of foreign policy and the arguments by which he substantiated them having been expounded, it remains to consider more particularly how far his teaching has been accepted, and what is its bearing upon the more urgent problems which confront us at the present time. Large as was the audience which hung upon his lips, and considerable though the influence which he exercised on national thought, no public man suffered more than Cobden from contemporary misunderstanding and undeserved disparagement. Now that the events of the period through which he lived can be seen and judged in a clearer atmosphere and a truer perspective, with light and shadow more equally diffused over the landscape, it is possible to be juster to his work and memory.

Any summing up of the influence of such a man must be more or less subjective, and perhaps suffer from the limitations which subjectivity imposes. History may be likened to statistics, in that it can be made to prove what it is wished to prove : it is simply a matter of choosing the convenient facts and giving to them your own interpretation. And yet, while admitting the ever-present danger of individual bias, it is broadly true, as Robert Louis Stevenson says, that " the worst historian has a clearer view of the period he studies than the best of us can hope to form of that in which we live. The obscurest epoch is to-day." [1]

Obviously much of Cobden's teaching has either lost in urgency or ceased altogether to have validity, not because it was not true and needful for his time, but because many of the conditions and problems of our age are altogether different from those of his. Thus, if it be asked, " Have later events supported his principles ? Would those principles work now ? " the rejoinder must be that any fair test of his claim to be a guide to the perplexing maze of foreign affairs which confronts us to-day cannot take that form. A more relevant question would be, " What in human probability would have been the effect of the operation of his principles had they been applied as and when he propounded them ? And, if their literal application be no longer possible, does the reason lie in any inherent defect and inadequacy in the principles themselves, or only in the fact that a new set of international conditions and relations has been created, having little or nothing in common with that which existed two generations ago ? "

As to the first of the alternatives here suggested, it is to be remembered that even when the letter of a principle, a truth, a law may be outgrown, its spirit may retain the power to influence, guide, and inspire, and this is unquestionably the case with much of Cobden's teaching. As to the other, it is only necessary to look around in order to see how part of that teaching has been invalidated by events which neither he nor anyone in his day could have anticipated.

At times critics of Cobden have spoken of him as a mere political theorist. How much more he was than that is proved by the accuracy of not a few of his judgments and

[1] Essay on " The day after to-morrow," in *Lay Morals and Other Papers*, p. 113.

predictions, though the clever world of contemporary diplomacy either ignored or pooh-poohed them as the fantastic speculations of an uninformed " outsider." Any man in the street can make wild guesses that this or that event will happen ; but guessing is no more prophecy than is fortune-telling. Cobden's great value as a thinker lay in his rare powers of discernment, which enabled him, as he studied the political problems of his day, to perceive before most other men the streams of tendency flowing not only in his own but in other countries, to interpret their significance, and within limits to foresee their issue. This faculty of clear, almost unerring insight, surely " the best gift " to be coveted by statesmen, was in part intuitive, but it owed much to laborious study and observation. He had unquestionably a great fondness for speculation, and he indulged it freely, yet he was no mere expert in the solution of political cross-word puzzles, but one of the shrewdest and most level-headed men of affairs that modern England has produced.

Viewing the events of recent years and the present state of Europe, it might appear that all his work for peace was wasted effort. Anyone who in July 1914 read his speeches, writings, and letters of the Crimean War period might have found it difficult to draw any other conclusion than that in foreign affairs the ruling statesmen of the Great Powers, and our own like the rest, had learned little and forgotten nothing during all the intervening sixty years. The personalities were different, the old parties were differently labelled, new parties had arrived, increasing the bewilderment of the public mind, hoary problems had developed fresh aspects and produced unanticipated situations. Yet, in spite of all changes, both those essential and those merely superficial, foreign policy continued to be governed by the traditions of a remote past, and most fundamentally by the superstitious doctrine of the balance of power ; phrases still took the place of real principles ; secret diplomacy had in the old way honeycombed Europe with intrigue ; all the great States, and some of the smaller ones in addition, had grouped themselves in military alliances and counter-alliances of the most incongruous kind ; the Continent was a vast armed camp ; and its peoples lived in constant dread of a convulsion which the temptation of

provocative combinations and the grinding burden of armaments were rapidly making inevitable.

Not for a hundred years had Europe presented so dismal
a spectacle of high political tension, pent-up animosities, and
lowering disaster as in the summer of 1914. Then came the
war, and now that the horror is over we are trying to console
ourselves with the thought that it came because it had to
come, since the powder train had been laid and lit, making
the explosion which followed a matter of course. President
Wilson put the matter in a nutshell when, brushing on one
side as an idle tale the idea that any one nation or Government had alone cut the leash which held back the hounds of
war, he said that "no single fact caused the war, but that in
the last analysis the whole European system is in a deeper
sense responsible for the war, with its complication of alliances and understandings, and a complicated texture of
intrigues and espionage that unfailingly caught the whole
family of nations in its meshes" (October 20, 1916). The
great catastrophe was, in truth, like the fall of an avalanche
which had been growing ever more menacing through years
and decades, until at last it crashed downward under its own
weight, strewing in its course wholesale ruin, devastation, and
death.

That events had long been making steadily for a crisis is
a fact which no serious student of affairs will now gainsay.
In proof of this statement it is only necessary to recall the
changes in the relations of the Great Powers which began at
the close of last century. The most important were Great
Britain's reconciliation first with France and then with Russia
and her simultaneous estrangement from Germany, owing to
the mutual feelings of distrust which first began to cloud the
relations of the two nations, like a creeping paralysis, soon
after Bismarck's dismissal in 1890.

To the end of his life Lord Palmerston maintained his old
suspicions both of France and Russia, and though he expended
little serious thought on the German question, rapidly matur-
ing under his eyes, and therefore failed to gain any clear perception of its full significance for Europe, he recognized the
importance of Prussia being strong enough to resist pressure
on both of her long-extended land frontiers. Writing to

Earl Russell only a month before his death, he said it was his wish to see Prussia strong so that " Germany in the aggregate " might be able to " control those two ambitious and aggressive Powers, France and Russia, that press upon her, west and east."

" As to France," he continued, " we know how restless and aggressive she is, and how ready to break loose for Belgium, for the Rhine, for anything she would be likely to get without too great an exertion. As to Russia, she will in due time become a Power almost as great as the old Roman Empire. She can become mistress of all Asia, except British India, whenever she chooses to take it. . . . Germany ought to be strong in order to resist Russian aggression, and a strong Prussia is essential to German strength." [1]

Palmerston died in 1865, and Russell, who succeeded him, ceased to hold office in the following year ; but the general lines of British foreign policy underwent no immediate change. In particular the doctrine of the balance of power continued to be a leading article of faith with both political parties. True to tradition, British sympathies were more on the side of Germany than of France during the war of 1870, though again, as during the Bohemian campaign against Austria in 1866, the old Conservative prejudice against Prussia as an upstart Power, and an obtrusive disturber of the long-established Continental status, made itself strongly felt. A Liberal Government was in office, however, and the political and social influences exerted from various sides in favour of intervention were held in check.

Four years later Disraeli came to office for the last time with promises of a " spirited foreign policy " and schemes of imperialism. Already in 1874 he wrote : " I believe since Palmerston we have never been so energetic, and in a year's time we shall be more." This eagerness to assert British influence in European affairs made almost inevitable inter-

---

[1] The passage occurs in one of Palmerston's last letters, dated September 13, 1865, written while he was Prime Minister, with Russell as Foreign Secretary. He died on October 18 following. The monumental work *Die Rheinpolitik Kaiser Napoleons III von 1863 bis 1870*, consisting of dispatches preserved in the archives of Prussia, Austria, and the South German secondary States, edited by Hermann Oncken, and published in 1926, throws extraordinary light upon the designs of France and more than confirms Palmerston's suspicions.

vention between Russia and Turkey in the dispute and war of 1877–8. The outburst of Russophobism which occurred at that time was fully comparable in violence with that of 1854–5, but there was the difference that the incitements to warlike passions came on the later occasion from the leading Minister of the day, who had gained the sympathetic ear of the occupant of the throne. When the danger had passed away, and it became necessary to allay the militant passions of the fire-eaters, now furious as wolves robbed of their prey, Lord Salisbury, the Foreign Secretary, wrote of his chief : " The Jingoes require to be calmed in their own language, and he is the only one among us who speaks it fluently " (June 23, 1878). By the Congress and Treaty of Berlin which followed the war the Great Powers supposed that they had satisfactorily regulated all rightful claims between the belligerent States on the one hand and between Turkey and her Christian races on the other, and had given stability to Eastern Europe. In the event hardly one of the stipulations of the Treaty of Berlin was faithfully observed, and within a few years the Eastern Question was in a more unsettled state than before.

In the meantime the friendly policy of successive British Governments in relation to Germany, which, on the establishment of the Empire in 1871, took the place of Prussia as a Great Power, continued without change. Writing seven years after that event Lord Salisbury drew satisfaction from the fact that " We are indeed the only nation north of the Alps which has been able to look with unmixed satisfaction at the position to which the German Empire has attained " (April 10, 1878) ; and it was he also who, at a later date, restored the cordial relations which had been temporarily interrupted by needless colonial bickerings. So well grounded was the understanding between the two Governments at that time that when in 1879, and again in 1887, Bismarck proposed a formal alliance Lord Salisbury received the idea sympathetically, though on neither occasion did the overtures go farther than a confidential exchange of views. In the earlier of these years, however, Germany formed an alliance with Austria-Hungary as a purely defensive measure against Russia, and in 1882 Bismarck achieved his ideal of a *coalition à trois* when Italy came in, so completing the historical Triple Alliance.[1]

The most important developments of the later years of the century were the drawing together of France and Russia and the more pronounced alienation of France and Great Britain owing to the British occupation of Egypt. France, which had made eyes at Russia as soon as the Crimean War was over, had been drawn closer to her in the time of depression which followed the *débâcle* of 1870, and still more when she failed to win Germany's support in her campaign of obstruction against British influence on the Nile. In 1891 the *rapprochement* became a formal *entente*, and from that time

---

[1] It may not be amiss to refer here to a curious misconception to which currency was given by Lord Grey of Falloden in the course of an address to a League of Nations meeting held in London on February 3, 1925. *The Times* reported him as follows :

" He had thought a great deal about the cause of the last war. After the Franco-Prussian War, what was the course pursued by the victor ? A triple alliance against the vanquished, and he believed that really was sowing the seeds of the war of 1914. He believed that if the victors of this war of 1914 were to pursue that policy of a triple alliance against the vanquished— for the moment they were perfectly safe, but the consequences in the long run would be the same."

What are the facts ? The origin of the Triple Alliance was the Dual Alliance of Germany with Austria-Hungary, which was concluded in October 1879, nine years after the Franco-German War, and when the combatants of 1870 were on tolerable terms. This Dual Alliance was aimed solely at Russia, which is expressly named in the Treaty, and Bismarck entered into it by way of answer to the menaces in which the Tsar had indulged because Germany had not, in his opinion, sufficiently supported Russian claims prior to and during the Berlin Congress ; it was not aimed, even indirectly, at France. By the terms of the Treaty the Allies undertook to support each other with their entire military resources in the event of attack on either by Russia, but they also pledged themselves " never to give to their purely defensive agreement an aggressive tendency in any direction." At that time Great Britain, too, was on strained terms with Russia, and for that reason Lord Salisbury welcomed the alliance as " good tidings of great joy," and as a guarantee of " the peace of Europe and the independence of the nations."

Italy joined the alliance in 1882, after France, then in a Chauvinistic mood, had appropriated Tunis against the warnings of the British Government; but the initiative came from Rome, and Germany—whose Chancellor congratulated the French Government on the Tunis exploit—insisted that Italy must first obtain Austria's consent. It is a well-known and documented fact that as late as 1901 Mr. Chamberlain, then Colonial Secretary, was willing that this country should join the enlarged alliance.

How far Lord Grey's misconceptions as to the origin and purpose of the Triple Alliance may have influenced him unconsciously against one rival Power and in favour of the other is a question on which he alone is competent to speak, but so curious a distortion of history makes an interesting addition to the perplexing jumble of fact and fiction, professions and pretexts, suspicions and prejudices which will have to be disentangled by the historian who finally solves the problem of responsibility for the Great War.

Russia was given no rest until she had agreed to convert this friendly but indefinite tie into the formal military alliance of 1893.

It was only at the beginning of the new century that any fundamental departure from the traditional Continental policy of Great Britain took place. For some time there had been a growing tendency to withdraw from European entanglements, and so far had the detachment gone that Lord Salisbury came to describe the position of this country as one of " splendid isolation." The Franco-Russian alliance, however, rained upon this country pin-pricks from all directions, and in 1898 Mr. Chamberlain, Colonial Secretary in the third Salisbury Cabinet, disturbed by the aggressive action of France in Egypt, Madagascar, West Africa, and elsewhere, and by Russian activity in China and Persia, revived the question of an Anglo-German alliance.

Now it was Germany which held back, her ruling statesmen counting on the expectation that Great Britain's position in Europe would before long become so intolerable that delay would make possible a harder bargain. Nevertheless, a step in the direction of closer friendship was made at the time by the conclusion of a secret treaty by which the two Powers divided the colonial possessions of Portugal into spheres of economic influence. The British alliance overtures were only suspended, however, and in 1901 they took more definite form. Lord Lansdowne, the Foreign Secretary, was now altogether of Mr. Chamberlain's mind, and while these Ministers were prepared to enter the Triple Alliance outright, Lord Salisbury's approval was won for " a defensive alliance, strictly defined." The German Government was given clearly to understand that for this country the choice had become one between a closer tie with Germany or reconciliation at all costs with France and Russia. Easy-going Prince Bülow regarded the warning as " a bogy invented to frighten us," and on German procrastination and irresolution the proposal finally foundered.

With the end of the alliance negotiations closed also a long and, on the whole, an amicable record of Anglo-German relations. Germany's faltering attitude and the suspicion to which it gave rise, that she was pursuing designs of naval supremacy from which she was not to be turned aside, led

British statesmen to look elsewhere. When a little later France, having failed to find allies against England, turned round and made friendly advances to her, these advances were accepted. The first result was the conclusion of Lord Lansdowne's convention of April 1904, embodying territorial agreements in regard to Egypt and Morocco, a transaction that created between the two countries an *entente* which, though one of convenience, opened a new era of confidence and good will on both sides.

Had she had her way France would have converted the *entente* at once into a second military alliance. She did, indeed, succeed in extracting from the Cabinet of Sir Henry Campbell-Bannerman—or so many of its members as were admitted into the secret—first a pledge of military support in the event of complications arising with Germany over Morocco, though the treaty of 1904 stipulated only for diplomatic support ; and later a wider pledge of naval and military co-operation against the same Power in certain eventualities. In effect these agreements, which were the result of a course of " conversations " between the Foreign Ministers, ambassadors, and naval and military experts of the two countries, continued from 1905 to 1914, gave to France—in return for no obligation or liability of any kind to this country—the cover of an alliance without the conclusion of a formal treaty, an arrangement which allowed of the two Legislatures and nations being kept in the dark until the time came for honouring the promises.

Nevertheless, in the meantime, when badgered by suspicious members of Parliament, the Foreign Secretary persisted in maintaining that the country in all its foreign relations retained full liberty of action. Technically this may have been true, but the actual fact was otherwise. Long before 1914 Great Britain, in effect, was as securely tied to France as Russia had been since 1893. How the cords had been fastened about her mattered little in comparison with the fact that her liberty was gone. To the last, however, Grey told the House of Commons (August 3, 1914) that " the Triple Entente was not an alliance—it was a diplomatic group." But so to speak was merely word play. What had a " diplomatic group " to do with military and naval agreements and plans of campaign to be carried out on Belgian soil?—for so far had the Entente Powers gone in their secret manœuvrings. The leading authority on the political history of our time has written: " The freedom of the British Government continued to be solemnly reiterated at intervals by the Prime Minister and the Foreign Secretary, but from 1911 onwards every Frenchman regarded Great Britain as bound in honour to come to the assistance of France if attacked by Germany "[1] So at last, when, too late for protest, the facts of his position were made known, thought every Englishman, resent though he might the deception which had been practised upon him.

One further step was needed in order that France might have the full sense of security upon which her mind was set and that was the reconciliation of her two allies. The way from the dual to the triple *entente* proved neither long nor difficult. Of the two great British parties which at the end of the century still monopolized the parliamentary arena, one had been traditionally friendly to Russia, though with varying degrees of cordiality, while the other had for some time been seriously considering how far its attachment to Turkey was a genuine article of political faith, how far a superstition. Increasing nervousness and irritation over the German naval preparations made a territorial agreement with Russia appear the natural complement of the Morocco-Egypt convention of 1904 which had " cleared the slate " with France. The result was a treaty of 1907 by which the two Powers divided Persia into special spheres of influence, just as Great Britain and Germany had similarly divided the colonies of Portugal nine years before. In this way two countries, whose Governments had been on bad or strained terms for the greater part of a century, made a new start, while France, the jubilant third, relieved of the last vestige of fear of isolation, was now prepared to meet her enemy across the Rhine whenever circumstances were propitious.

The student of human affairs has to admit, at times with despondent feelings, that in spite of all the oscillations of political life the broad principles and objects, the governing motives, even the miscalculations and follies of Governments continue the same from age to age. *Plus cela change, plus*

---

[1] G. P. Gooch, *Cambridge History of British Foreign Policy*, iii. 469.

c'est la même chose. After all, the transference of Great
Britain's influence, first diplomatic, as prescribed by the
Morocco treaty, and then military, as the Anglo-French
" conversations " provided, was only a readjustment of the
balance of power. And once again, as so often before, that
hoary doctrine was to prove a delusion, promising what it was
unable to perform. Directly the defensive alliance of Germany,
Austria-Hungary, and Italy was answered by the more challenging Dual Alliance of France and Russia the peace of
Europe was endangered. When the Dual Alliance developed
into the Triple Entente the outbreak of war became merely
a matter of time. Yet regard for facts requires the admission
that neither Lord Lansdowne, the inspirer of the *entente* in
its original and innocent form, nor yet his successor at the
Foreign Office, had any intention that friendly co-operation
with France should be used to isolate or " encircle " Germany
or become a menace to her. Nothing could better prove the
absence on the part of the British Government as a whole of
an anti-German bias than Lord Haldane's friendly mission
to Berlin in 1912 and the conclusion in 1914 of an important,
though unratified, colonial treaty greatly in Germany's favour.
Even the outburst of Mr. Lloyd George against Germany in
1911, when she was endeavouring to extract from France
a *quid pro quo* for her willingness to abandon her treaty
rights in Morocco in favour of that country, ceases to have
importance now that Grey has explained that he " acted on
his own initiative." [1] None the less, the fact remains unassailable that from the first it was the aim of Great Britain's
associates to pervert the *entente* into a " manifestation "
against their common enemy, and it will never cease to be a
mystery that the Minister who should best have known failed
to suspect where events were directly tending.

If it should be said, " Why go into questions which belong
to past history and are settled ? " the answer is that the
questions are raised because they are not settled, because

[1] Cf. *Twenty-five Years*, ii. 265. Speaking in the House of Commons on
August 3, 1914, Grey admitted that " in the Morocco question it was a dispute
which primarily concerned France," and recalled the fact, plainly affirmed in
the Morocco Declaration of 1904, that " No doubt we were pledged to give
nothing but diplomatic support." But both in 1905 and 1911 military
support was promised to France.

the wars of the past century have settled little permanently, and because no chapter of modern European history affords a more conclusive justification of Cobden's doctrine of foreign policy, or gives sharper point to his warnings, than that which covers the years from 1890 to 1914. The proof is to be seen in the fact that to-day, after the greatest war of all time, the world is no nearer to the reign of peace than when Cobden lived. Many if not most of the territorial readjustments made in 1919 will sooner or later—and some of them very soon—follow the way of similar forced transactions of the past : the only question that is uncertain is whether the readjustments shall be made peacefully or otherwise. This judgment proceeds not from sympathy with one country or antipathy against another, but merely from a cold and impartial recognition of inexorable facts rooted in history, ethnology, economics, and human nature. Although she came out of the war vanquished and has since been subjected to penalties more drastic than have ever in the history of civilization been inflicted upon a beaten enemy, Germany is to-day, by general agreement, the most important, and at the same time the most incalculable, factor in European politics.

Who, possessing even a glimmering of the historical sense, can believe that the Belgian and Polish annexations, the alienation of Memel, the severance from Prussia of Danzig, the isolation of East Prussia, or even the reappropriation of Alsace-Lorraine by France, at least in its complete form, will stand the test of time ? Cobden, like Palmerston, contended that Prussia should be regarded, in Europe's interest, as the natural bulwark against Russian and French aggression, and had he lived at the end of the century he would have urged that British diplomacy, while keeping clear of all alliances, should have been unchangingly directed towards that end. By her adherence to the peace treaties of 1919 Great Britain, her hands no longer free, cast to the winds a policy which had behind it the sanction of a century, and created in the East of Europe, in the interest of France, a brand-new Polish republic, containing some millions of discontented inhabitants of alien races, to serve as a buffer State between two resentful neighbours which in a few years will be again the strongest of Continental Powers.

With no more assurance can it be claimed that the Eastern Question has been permanently settled. European Turkey has been reduced to a fraction of its original area, but new complications have been created, and the most perplexing of these may prove to be the abandonment by Great Britain and France of their traditional opposition to the occupation by Russia of the Golden Horn. Will that Power, when rehabilitated, accept the present status, or brushing it aside, and with it the ambitions of Greece, claim the fulfilment of the promises made during the war ? For Russia, let it never be forgotten, is only temporarily disabled and out of the ring ; lamed and lacerated though she is, the strength and resiliency of youth are on her side, and wounds received in youth usually heal quickly and well. But, further, in order to endanger its handiwork still more the Paris Conference was at pains to leave in every one of the East European States created or enlarged by the treaties—Poland, Czecho-Slovakia, Jugo-Slavia, Roumania—a mass of highly combustible material in the form of large alien populations ; while Italy, forgetting how the rule of Austria outraged her spirit of nationality, has added many thousands of sullen Germans to her population, just as Belgium has had the hardihood to incorporate a large body of forced citizens of the same nationality.

In view of all these facts, how do Cobden's principles of foreign policy bear upon the record of the past half-century and the European situation as we see it to-day ? The unity of his political thought cannot be too strongly emphasized. Not one of his doctrines stood alone : all the principles and measures which he advocated, such as the freest possible international intercourse, commercial and personal, a resolute policy of non-intervention, the abandonment of alliances and political groupings in the interest of an illusory equilibrium, the reduction of armaments, and the adoption of universal arbitration, were designed to contribute, each in its way, to one supreme object, the abatement of international suspicion and rivalry, so creating not unity but harmony of interest, and removing the predisposing causes and occasions of strife and war. There may be difference of opinion as to how far the acceptance of his teaching would have had, in his time, the happy results which he expected of them, but there can be no disagreement that its rejection led directly to most of the antagonisms and convulsions which have made so large a part of later European history.

A short time before his death Lord Morley wrote of Cobden as the " representative of the sentiments and principles before which national rivalries disappear. It was the power and authority of the authors of diplomatic practice and tradition that confronted Cobden's sovereign principle of the inter-dependence of the nations of the world. This was his broad-guiding and far-reaching contribution to their progress." That is admirably said, and not less true is Morley's conclusion that " It was the antagonistic principle that landed us in the thankless war of 1914."

Is, then, his doctrine too idealistic, too simple, too naïve to afford a guide for international relations ? To think so is to ignore the fact that the supreme achievement of civilization in the life of every political community is the advance from the crude arbitrament of force and violence to that of reason and law. Cobden contended that what nations can do for themselves individually they can do for one another col-lectively if only they have the will. To deny that is to avow a pessimism which, in practice, would paralyse ethical effort and bar the way to human progress. The end of life left Cobden himself, though he failed to see the vision of a world " lapt in universal law," with his superb faith unshaken, still " nursing the unconquerable hope " that the future would be better than the past and that one day all would be well with the world. Speaking at the meeting which was called to decree the dissolution of the Anti-Corn Law League, he said, " Our body will, so to speak, perish, but our spirit is abroad and will pervade all the nations of the earth because it is the spirit of truth and justice, because it is the spirit of peace and good will amongst men." It was in the same sublime spirit of assurance that he viewed the peace move-ment ; its success was delayed and he was never to see the fruits of his efforts ; yet to the last, in spite of all discourage-ment, he clung to the conviction that so good a cause must triumph because it was good.

His claim to be regarded as a political seer has been mentioned. It would be easy to quote many utterances of his which, taken literally and divorced from their context, might seem to weaken this claim. Admittedly, his " yeas " and " nays " were often rashly positive, and he had an unfortunate habit of saying dogmatically that things " would " happen when less sanguine and less temperamental people might have been content with saying " might " ; though not seldom his avowals of exaggerated expectations and certitudes were strategic, and intended for the greater encouragement of himself and others. Nevertheless, there are few aspects or developments of European relations as they existed before the Great War, and have existed since, which Cobden failed to anticipate, and a volume might be made of anticipations and warnings contained in his speeches, writings, and correspondence which exactly describe the conditions and difficulties of our own time. Thus, while Peel had protested before him against the maintenance of armaments at a war strength in time of peace as causing a needless and oppressive burden, Cobden emphasized the actual danger to peace thereby caused, since " oft the sight of means to do ill deeds makes ill deeds done." In a long memorandum which he addressed to the Government early in 1862, he said :

" But the greatest evil connected with these rival armaments is that they destroy the strongest motives for peace. When two great neighbouring nations find themselves permanently subjected to a war expenditure, without the compensation of its usual excitements and honours, the danger to be apprehended is that, if an accident should occur to inflame their hostile passions—and we know how certain these accidents are at intervals to arise—their latent sense of suffering and injury may reconcile them to a rupture, as the only eventual escape from an otherwise perpetual war taxation in a time of peace."

Before 1914 how much talking and writing to this effect there was by statesmen fearful that the day might come when war would be welcomed in sheer relief ! Yet still the piling up of combustible material went on, until, like the dropping of a match, a single incident, occurring in an insignificant country far away in the south-east of Europe, set the world on fire.

With what fidelity also the following passage, taken from the fifth of his six pamphlets, *What Next—and Next ?* published just before the close of the Crimean War, fits the present relations of the several Powers concerned :

" England and France will find themselves with more powerful navies at the close of the war than were ever before possessed by two allied Powers, a state of things from which embarrassments may possibly arise in more than one direction. This naval armament has already roused the susceptibilities of the United States, and led to an augmentation of their navy. Hitherto that country has not entered into rivalry with the States of Europe in their military and naval establishments. But, impelled by feelings of insecurity or pride, the public sentiment appears to be undergoing a change as regards the navy. Should this spirit acquire strength in the mind of the nation, and reconcile it to the expense, there is no country in the world that in the course of a few years would be their equal at sea. . . . Is it wise on the part of the nations of the Old World, placed at such a disadvantage by their colossal debts, and the necessities they are under for keeping large standing armies, to fasten on themselves a hostile naval rivalry with this transatlantic people ? "

Perhaps the best modern comment upon this passage is contained in a recently published memorandum of Colonel House, the friend and confidant of President Wilson. He wrote, under date September 24, 1916 :

" The President came to my sitting-room in the morning and we spent several hours going over foreign affairs, principally our difference with Great Britain. . . . It was my opinion that the real difference with Great Britain now was that the United States had undertaken to build a great navy, that our commerce was expanding beyond all belief, and we were rapidly taking the position Germany occupied before the war. No one in England would probably admit that the things I mentioned were causing the growing irritation against us, but it was a fact, nevertheless. The President replied, ' Let us build a navy bigger than hers, and do what we please.' " [1]

Here, too, is a picture of 1849 in which present conditions are reflected as in a mirror. He is calling for national economy to be effected by less extravagant expenditure on warlike preparations :

" You have to make up your mind to one thing—you cannot afford all this waste. It is not a matter of choice with you. I tell you, you

---

[1] *The Intimate Papers of Colonel House,* ii. 317.

are spending too much money as a nation. It is not merely your general taxation—your local taxation likewise oppresses you. Mark me, the greater the cost of your armaments falling on general taxation, the more you will have to spend in poor rates and other taxes. The more you waste the capital of the country, the more people will be wanting employment; and when they want employment, it is the law of England that the poorest, who are the first to suffer under a course of national extravagance or decay, have the right to come to those above them and demand subsistence, under the name of poor rate."

On this question of the finance of war how pregnant with significance is the truth, which he was never tired of uttering both in Parliament and on the platform, that "Our Budget is framed with reference to our foreign policy." In other words, foreign interventions and entanglements necessitate ever larger armaments, with taxation increasing in proportion, and sooner or later the inevitable outcome is war, shattering at one stroke the national prosperity. To-day about two-thirds of our national expenditure, including the interest on the public debt, is due directly or indirectly to warlike measures of various kinds, and practically the whole of that debt, in amount over six thousand millions sterling net, is attributable to the same cause.

Take, too, his warning that no assurance of peace could be drawn from the discoveries and inventions of science, and that war, horrible as it was already, would one day be a hundred times more malefic, since human ingenuity was busy perfecting the instruments of slaughter. In a speech on this subject made in the House of Commons as early as June 1849, anticipating much that has happened since, he contended that the human race was actually going backwards; for "instead of making the progress of civilization subservient to the welfare of mankind—instead of making the arts of civilization available for increasing the enjoyments of life—you are constantly bringing these improvements in science to bear upon the deadly contrivances of war, and thus are making the arts of peace and the discoveries of science contribute to the barbarism of the age." Since then new and greater terrors have been added to warfare, until the late struggle saw civilized nations fighting one another by the use of submarines, aerial bombs, flame-throwers, poison gases, and other horrible devices of chemical warfare, designed less to destroy than to maim, wound, and torture their victims.

Not content with these achievements, science, degrading itself still further in the service of war, has since been engaged all over the world in the invention of still more hideous methods of murder. Speaking in September 1923, Sir Richard Gregory said :

" The time is rapidly approaching when the civilized world will be in the possession of forces sufficiently strong to destroy itself if these forces are used for the destruction instead of the preservation and development of human life. We are now facing the supreme test as to whether the discoveries of science are to be exploited in mutually destructive warfare born of suspicion, ignorance and hatred, or to be used for the promotion of human welfare."

All present indications point to the worse choice being made. Not only so, but experts now tell us that war on civil populations, non-combatants, women and children, already waged in the form of a hunger blockade during the late struggle, is to be developed in still more terrible ways. What a chivalrous business war has become when a military expert confesses that, while he did not believe that " cities would be blotted out in a night or in many nights "—though their destruction is to be merely a question of time—" the civilian population must be prepared to suffer as they had never before suffered in warfare." [1]

Two other matters in which Cobden showed himself to be far ahead of the imagination of his age deserve to be mentioned. First, he clearly anticipated the doctrine of self-determination which was proclaimed as a new discovery during the war. " Conquest of territory," he wrote to Sumner as early as November 7, 1849, " offers no prospect of increased power to any Government. On the contrary, half the Powers of Europe are at this moment suffering internal throes from the acquisition of fresh territory, with disaffected races, at the great settlement of 1815. For one of the peculiar features of the day is the assumption on the part of the peoples of a right to a choice of their rulers and of their

[1] Lecture by Colonel W. L. Marsh, reported in *The Times* of January 29, 1926.

countrymen. Race, religion, language, traditions, etc., are becoming bonds of union, and not the parchment titles of Sovereigns." He also foresaw the end of the great Muscovite despotism, that imposing image with head and breast of gold and silver but limbs of iron and clay, and predicted that when the time came for Russia's emancipation it would be heralded not by the still, small voice of reason but the thunder and tempest of passion and revolution.

If to-day Cobden were to return to the scenes of his life's work, would he turn aside, saddened and disgusted, from the spectacle of a world still war-ridden and chaotic, which would greet him, leaving it to work out its own salvation or perish, as it might choose ? Or would he at once engage again that strong will, unbounded energy, and indomitable faith of his in the task of retrieving the lost ground and wresting good out of evil ? It cannot be doubted that he would have followed the latter alternative, though not without renewed rebuke of the nations which had continued blind to reason and their own interests. Recalling the European political situation in the summer of 1914, the pledges and assurances by which the war was justified, and the enthusiasm with which the people of this and other countries threw themselves into the struggle, he might have used again some words which he uttered early in 1855 in relation to the Crimean War.

" My first and greatest objection to the war," he said at that time, " has been the delusive, I had almost said fraudulent, pretences under which it has been made popular in this country. I mean that the feelings of the people have been aroused into enthusiasm in favour of the war by being led to entertain the belief that it was to effect objects which I knew and felt, at all events, it was never intended to effect.

" There is a moral in this, for it is an illustration of the lamentable fact that when once involved in war we forget the very motives and circumstances which led us into it, and transfer all our enthusiasm to the war itself."

It will be remembered how, a short time before his death, Lord Morley wrote in the same sense. " The contrast," he said, " between the promises and confident expectations on the lips of the rulers of the world—even some of them then quartered in Whitehall—when they opened the war of 1914, and the results in which they have been overwhelmed, looks like the most savage irony in the history of civilization."

Not only in its outcome but in its origin the Great War has been like so many wars in the past, for it did not come without warning. How many people in this and other countries, who twelve years ago accepted in good faith the assurances of the statesmen in power on both sides that the war found them unprepared, suspected that workers of mischief had for years been secretly conspiring in several Continental capitals to bring about the disaster at such a time and in such circumstances as might appear favourable to their designs ? What the plotters failed to foresee as they were sowing their dragons' teeth, was the abundant harvest of loss and misery which would one day have to be reaped by their own countries as well as by others.

While Cobden would have regarded the war as amongst the ghastliest events of history, there can be no doubt as to the only kind of peace which would have satisfied him. " Do not let us," he said at the close of the Italian war of 1859, " have any more Congresses of Vienna where we are parties to treaties that partition off Europe and apportion the people to different rulers, with the same indifference to their wishes and their instincts as though they were mere flocks of sheep." The Congress of Vienna did a good deal of bartering of that kind, though with incomparably less disturbance to traditional political associations and historical frontiers than the treaties of 1919, for most of the territorial changes of 1815 were merely changes back to a status violated by revolutionary France only a few years before. How ready is one nation to condemn the follies of another—to see the mote in its neighbour's eye, while ignoring the beam in its own ! Guizot, smarting under the Treaty of Frankfort of 1871, said of the Germans, " Their present policy is one more example, after so many others, of the insolent and blind folly of victors who sow the seeds of war at the moment they are making peace."

Could any words better describe the peace treaties of Versailles, St. Germain, and Neuilly, which owe their inspiration and their vindictive provisions more to the influence of France than of any other country ? Not content with carving large slices out of Germany, Austria, Hungary, and Bulgaria, in the interest of neighbouring States and new States of uncertain life, the authors of these treaties committed the crowning folly of annexing Germany's colonies. When the Congress of Vienna decided to return to France most of the colonial territories which had been taken from her during the Napoleonic wars, Lord Castlereagh gave as a reason for supporting this decision that it was " not to England's interest that the French should become a military rather than a commercial nation." Bismarck followed the same policy in the treatment of France in 1871, refusing to take from her a single yard of her colonial empire, and only insisting upon the restitution of a piece of old German territory which had been seized in the time of national impotence. Who will dare to maintain that the treaty-makers of Versailles in 1919 were wiser in their decisions ? [1]

Further, did it never occur to the representatives of the British Empire in particular when, at the bidding of republican France, they struck at monarchy in the principal countries which had been at war with the Allies, that in so doing they were destroying a centrifugal force which everywhere, and not least in our own land and Dominion, has proved one of the most important safeguards of political stability ? Is not France herself, in view of her record of six revolutions in the course of last century, of the proverbial instability of her Governments—" a change of Ministry every Thursday," Bismarck used to say—and her incalculable future, a witness to the need of a steadying constitutional influence above parties and controversial politics ?

Assuming the ultimate disappearance of most of the territorial changes which have made the new map of Europe the scorn of the historian and the ethnologist, there will nevertheless remain the evil precedent which they have affirmed—the fact that these forced treaties have invoked the sanction of international law to the principle of vindictive punishment. Future nations victorious in war will only need to point to the example set in 1919 as a justification for equally or more relentless measures of oppression. If the

[1] Yet, speaking at Westminster on January 5, 1918, Mr. Lloyd George said of the demand of Germany for the return of Alsace-Lorraine in 1871, " There can be no better illustration of the folly and wickedness of using a transient military success to violate national right."

statesmen of Versailles had not taken so pathetically a serious view of their influence upon human affairs, and, as Cobden would have said, had left a little more for Providence to do, the world would have been spared the odd spectacle of their strenuous endeavours to repair some of the worst effects of their own violence. For no sooner had they done their best to strangle half a dozen nations than they began to try, through the League of Nations, to restore them again to vigour.

And how is it with the balance of power in Europe to-day ? Are we better off or worse ? If ever in the history of the past two centuries there was a time when the invocation of that doctrine was called for it was in 1919, when an old epoch closed and a new one opened. Yet while the war put an end to domination by one Power, the peace might have been deliberately designed to make another more supreme in Europe than ever since the time of the first Napoleon. For just as the political hegemony which Germany exercised on the Continent has been gained by France, so the German naval rivalry, which led Great Britain to abandon her strong position of isolation, has been taken over by the same Power. Simultaneously, France has strengthened her military force to an extent hitherto unexampled in time of peace, though Great Britain has reduced hers below the pre-war level, and now the same Power is busily engaged in creating an air force which shall have no rival in the world, and boasts of a coming army of a million blacks.

Happily at the present time France is more settled, and probably far more peaceably inclined, than since the war ; but it remains to be seen whether the policy of moderation which has been pursued of late will prove lasting. That she will be able for any long time to maintain the dominating *rôle* which she has assumed is doubtful, and no more hopeful omen exists than the financial difficulty into which her military expenditure and the loans which she has made to her allies for the same purpose have in part brought her. Nevertheless, so long as France cherishes the ambition to succeed where the late German Emperor failed, and be herself the " balance of power " in Europe, there can be no security for any single country, and hence no hope of disarmament on any large and general scale.

For the present a condition of apparent stability exists, but it is due far more to the restraint consequent upon exhaustion than to the deliberate acceptance of the new status. Only when in process of time the impaired forces of the nations have revived and their wasted wealth has been replaced, when in the late enemy countries a generation born in sorrow and humiliation, and trained to regard the work of national renewal and revindication as a sacred duty, has come to maturity, and when the material penalties imposed by the treaties of settlement have been paid and the treaties themselves torn up—if, indeed, the peace can last so long—will it be seen upon what insecure and treacherous political foundations the edifice of a New Europe has been built.

To admit the dismal story of the past and the still depressing outlook, however, is not to say that Cobden's work for peace was a failure, still less that his political teaching affords us no help or encouragement in our present perplexities. Let us criticize his doctrine in details as we will, and confess, as we must, that in part its application presumes in human nature far greater wisdom and a far higher standard of morality than it has yet achieved ; yet the fact remains that it points the nations to the way which they must needs travel if their desired goal is the outlawry of force and war as arguments between nations and the establishment of law and peace. His admirers need not stop at the demonstration of his clear perception of what was wrong with the political doctrines and diplomatic methods of his generation, the foresight which enabled him to see so plainly the disastrous course along which British and European statesmanship was drifting, and the pertinency of his repeated warnings. The strongest testimony to the soundness of his principles of foreign policy is the fact that, though the treaties which followed the late war are so full of causes of present discontent and future strife, the simultaneous formation of the League of Nations was a confession by their authors that the world must look to Cobden's way and not theirs for hope and safety. The fact that the League owed its inspiration to President Wilson also gives point to his prediction that the impetus which would lead to Europe's final emancipation from the order of ideas to which war belongs would come from America.

It has been shown that Cobden did not favour the formation of any organization corresponding to the League, and that though he occasionally spoke of the idea it was only in order to disclaim it, out of consideration for the fears of critics who hesitated to go one step with him because of uncertainty as to where it might lead. Nevertheless, no man of his time did more to prepare the way for the work which is now being done at Geneva ; and, in fact, the faithful acceptance and courageous application of the principles and pledges stipulated in the Covenant of the League would mean the complete victory of his peace programme. The various reciprocal obligations which the Governments associated in the League undertake in subscribing to that document—" open, just, and honourable relations," the abolition of secret treaties, the acceptance of arbitration in place of war, respect for treaty obligations, the reduction of armaments, the discouragement of alliances, the avoidance of external aggression, safeguards for the good government of undeveloped races, and the like—are little more than restatements of principles of international policy which he propounded with greater definiteness and a more confident conviction. Not only so, but all that the League and its Council have so far achieved for the reconciliation of disputing nations has followed the lines which he laid down.

Already the League, by providing a forum and council board for the exchange of opinions, has created on some questions a *communis consensus* of Europe and on others has relieved tension between rival States which, without its friendly mediation, might have gone their own way and eventually drifted into the current of suspicion and ill-will which so often in the past has led to war. Similarly the old conception of an equilibrium, taking the form of diplomatic groups and military alliances, is by implication condemned by the very existence of the League, for unless that body is itself to be accepted as an effective balance of power its most important function will be ignored. The policy of intervention is no less discredited, since the recognition of the League as the legitimate mouthpiece of the associated nations, and the instrument of their collective influence, has undermined the claim of powerful States to interfere in the affairs of weak ones and in the event of disputes to take the law into their own hands. It may even be expected that intervention by the League itself will seldom need to take any stronger form than that of friendly advice or expostulation.

It is also a distinct advance in Cobden's footsteps that the League carries farther the work already done at the Hague by rallying its members to the support of the arbitral method of settling their differences, though for the present the provisions of the Covenant on the subject are too permissive, at best minimizing the risk of war by offering facilities for arbitration and stipulating a period of delay during which pacific counsels may have a fair chance of asserting themselves. Yet the key position to the attack on militarism and war remains, now as before, the universal acceptance of arbitration in international disputes of every kind. The halting attitude of Great Britain on this crucial point, laudable as has been her example in other respects, has been mentioned in an earlier chapter. At the same time, Cobden would have opposed the idea of keeping defaulting States to their pledges by military " sanctions "—aforetime an honourable word, the degradation of which is one of the smaller penalties of a vindictive peace—though he might have countenanced some mild form of ostracism in extreme cases. " If you need military coercion," he would have said, " you are not ready for a League of Nations ; to provide for it is to introduce the spirit of strife into a partnership which, unless it be one of harmony and peace, can have no meaning."

Further, serious measures for the reduction of armaments are no longer sneered at and frowned upon as they were in Cobden's day. The Hague Peace Conferences of 1899 and 1907 explored the ground, even if they did little more, but before the Great War several minor inter-State agreements for the restriction of armaments had been concluded and others attempted. The Washington Naval Conference of 1920, though it confined attention to capital vessels, finally carried the question out of the realm of abstractions into that of realities, and the movement so begun will inevitably be continued and extended to every branch of national defence. To her credit Great Britain has not only complied already with the provisions of the Washington naval convention, but has set an example to the Continental States in reducing her military force likewise, even below the level of 1914, so endorsing the pleas of Cobden and before him of Peel, who urged as long ago as 1849 that war could never be prevented by great armaments, and that it was the duty of this country to " take risks " in time of peace rather than continue to bear an oppressive burden of taxation for military purposes which only the existence of imminent danger would justify.

Here, however, it is the League of Nations which has hung back, for the provisions of the Covenant on the subject are weak and go little beyond the utterance of pious phrases. All that Article 8 does is to pledge members to " recognize that the maintenance of peace requires the reduction of national armaments to the lowest point consistent with national safety." But that platitude had been universally accepted long before the League was formed ; for not a single State can be named which in the past was not honestly convinced that its armaments were barely " consistent with national safety." In effect, the article leaves every Government free to maintain just such armaments as it wishes. For though a further stipulation requires the Council of the League to formulate plans for curtailing these preparations for war, these plans cannot be forced upon the Governments concerned, but action will follow or not follow at their unqualified discretion.

Moreover, while the members of the League affirm that the manufacture by private firms of munitions and implements of war " is open to grave objections," all the League Council is authorized to do in the matter is to " advise " upon how " the evil effects attendant upon such manufacture can be prevented." There is here no suggestion of prohibition ; yet if the pernicious practice which makes war-mongering profitable is to be abated, either a clean sweep will have to be made of the armament companies, which in the past have had their agents in every capital, pushing their murderous wares by every device known to the practised tout, often with the help of their countries' embassies, or these undertakings must be licensed, their output rationed, and their entire activities drastically controlled. Meanwhile, it is not an inspiring reflexion that so recently the British Government was in some way concerned—to what extent the House of Commons has not yet been told, for the answers given to questions on the subject (August 2, 1926) were of the usual evasive kind—in negotiations over the sale to Turkey of rifles and ammunition sufficient to equip a large army. That is not the best way of convincing other nations of our own profound concern for international peace.

Where, in spite of the League and the practical start on the way to peace which it has made, there is special reason for misgiving is in the fact that amongst some of the late belligerent nations of the Continent the old confidence in the broken reed of alliances continues. The combinations which existed at the outbreak of the Great War were allowed to lapse when their purpose had been served, but a whole series of new ones has been formed. The tragi-comedy which was enacted at Geneva in April last over the proposed admission of Germany to the Council of the League, when disagreement as to the method of procedure at once divided the members of the League into rival and irreconcilable groups, made it clear that the spirit of jealousy and distrust which has been at the root of all past attempts to create in Europe a balance not of power but of good will still lingers, and that time will be needed before this spirit can be effectively exorcised.

CHAPTER XIV

COBDEN AND OUR DAY—*Continued*

II. EUROPE OR THE EMPIRE—WHICH?

" We should show in our foreign policy that we have learnt something from the past. I want both sides of the House to consider whether it would not be a wise thing for us now to come to the conclusion that in future we shall hold ourselves strictly aloof from Continental wars in which we can have no interest, or at least our interest in which can only be such as we must always feel whenever any people in any part of the world is suffering. If we do so, we shall set an example which must have a great and beneficial effect ; and if at any time two foreign nations should, through unhappy circumstances, become involved in war, as it would be known that it was the solemn principle of England never to shed its blood in European conflicts, we should be a tribunal altogether impartial to which our Continental neighbours could appeal with the belief that if our counsels or our good offices were asked they would be given in that spirit of generosity and confidence in which they were solicited."—MR. BRIGHT in the House of Commons, June 9, 1859.

A FINAL question remains to be considered. It is the special moral which Cobden's teaching on foreign policy conveys to our own country and Empire in the position in which they stand to-day. It is true that it is impossible, in any literal sense of the words, to " go back " to Cobden or anyone else. Nations never do and never can go back : always their course must be forward, whether on straight paths or crooked. None the less, his doctrines may still way as beacons, marking here and there the way of safety. Of these doctrines perhaps none is so important for the British peoples at this time as that of non-intervention. I do not hesitate to say that the interest and the very security of Great Britain and of her world-wide dominion lie in the practical application of that doctrine to the utmost limit of possibility.

It is not the least unhappy of the war's ironies and unanticipated results that the present position of this country in relation to Europe is in some ways far less favourable than ever before in living memory. Before the war Great Britain was at least the mistress of her own fate, except to the extent that undetermined responsibilities and commitments, undertaken without the nation's knowledge, represented potential causes of difficulty and danger. To-day she is in the grip of forces beyond her control, having for the present forfeited the power to devise and follow any independent foreign policy of her own. At the end of a war which has proved so terrible a drain upon her manhood, and has heaped upon her shoulders stupendous debts, which it will take generations to liquidate, she finds herself bound by treaties of all kinds to a still disturbed and contentious Continent, and facing a future obscured by many uncertainties and possibilities of disaster. Little as the fact seems to be recognized, the most momentous of all our commitments may be found to be those incurred under the well-meant Locarno Pact, for unless the so-called peace settlements of 1919 are subjected to radical revision this far-going treaty will inevitably become operative within a period which can be definitely limited. For, after all, when we look behind the euphemistic phrases by which they have lately been commended, security pacts like that of Locarno, however useful their purpose in moderating present frictions, are only alliances *in esse* or *in posse*, and to that extent they simply perpetuate the old system of political groupings under pleasanter names and less obtrusive sanctions.

It is obvious that the duties and liabilities which the war and the peace have imposed on us make any immediate withdrawal from Continental entanglements impracticable. Yet the validity of treaties depends upon the ability of the contracting States to fulfil them, in accordance with the maxim *Ultra posse obligatur nemo*, and, further, permanence can be claimed for no treaty which ceases to be in accordance with the conditions which called it into existence. The treaties concluded in Paris in 1919 and the later Locarno Pact have been designed to give peace and stability to the contracting States and to Europe generally. If, after fair trial, events show that they are unable to achieve this object, no legal or moral consideration could be advanced against our right to obtain release from any one or all of them.

Are we not nearing the time when it will be legitimate, nay, necessary, to claim back our full independence ? What is the position of Europe eight years after the war ended ? Pessimism is one of the most paralysing of vices, yet an optimism which ignores facts because they are unpalatable is equally mischievous. It is a deplorable fact that the greater part of the Continent has fallen back into the prodigal's ways —back to the husks that the swine do eat, wallowing in the old diplomatic mire, as it has wallowed for so many generations, in intrigues, secret conspiracies, and faithless dealings. Perhaps never before was the peace spirit amongst our own people in general so conscious, strong, and sincere as now, and the successive Governments in power since the end of the war have on the whole played up to this spirit consistently and loyally. It is hardly too much to say that it is the ardent longing for an enduring peace which prevails in this country, a longing rooted in the main in genuine moral impulse, and only unconsciously in self-interest—though that, too, may be a perfectly legitimate motive of conduct—that alone keeps the League of Nations alive and on its feet. Without British sympathy and support the League would speedily be undermined and ruined by open enemies and secret plotters in some of the Continental countries, of which Soviet Russia is not the worst offender.

Perhaps few responsible people would like to see this country suddenly leave Europe in the lurch in the midst of its appalling disorder and muddlement, but at least we are justified in imposing as a condition of our co-operation with it that the peoples for or against whom we fought from 1914 to 1918 shall show a wish for peace and a determination to secure and maintain it equal to our own—in other words, shall return to orderly ways, abandon their military ambitions, husband their resources, and let it be understood that they will be ready to face at the proper time all such readjustments of existing political and territorial conditions as may be necessary to a real and enduring all-round settlement. If they refuse to do these things, and persist in perpetuating the feuds and rancours which are everywhere holding back recovery, we should formally denounce every treaty and liability which is opposed to peace and to our own interest, and go our own way, allowing other nations to do the same.

Whatever the blunders committed by their spokesmen in Paris in 1919, Great Britain and the Empire did not go to war in order to give to war a further lease of life. The ruling principle of our foreign policy in future should be resolute abstention from war over purely Continental disputes. While cultivating friendship with all European States, as far as they will allow us to do, we should reduce our political relations with them within the narrowest possible limits and refuse to incur further commitments of any kind which might be capable of involving participation in military action. It should be a fixed principle of our public policy not to take sides with any Continental Powers : our relation to those Powers should be that of friendly association with all of them ; and the only interests which should be allowed to draw us into political action of any kind should be the purely pacific interests which all, including ourselves, might have in common. If our neighbours do not want peace, that is no reason why we should deny to ourselves that supreme blessing if it can be had, as it can, on conditions of safety and honour.

It is high time that Great Britain adopted a foreign policy of her own and kept to it, thinking less of other countries and more of her own people and the Empire. An uneasy feeling is prevalent amongst all classes and parties that the subordination of this country, its external relations and interests to the wishes and convenience of a single Power has been carried much too far, and that it has now reached a point inconsistent with either national dignity or national security. Every sane-minded man must wish that the British attitude to France shall be as cordial as possible, always without prejustice to a similar relation to any and all of the other Powers ; yet the fact has to be faced that no country in Europe, with one abnormal present exception, is, from the standpoint of prudence and interest, so undesirable, and indeed so dangerous, as a political ally as France, whose statesmen in 1919, with an amazing lack of sagacity, staked her future on a series of measures of punition and restraint, embodied in treaties which in a few years will have no more meaning and value than a judge's sentence when the prisoner has regained his liberty. Implicated as she is directly in all European territorial changes, most of which were made in her interest and at her instigation, she and the satellite States which she has attached to her will stand or fall together when these changes are challenged, as one day they will be. Shall Great Britain pour out her blood and treasure in the next Continental struggle? If not, no time should be lost in making her position clearly known.

Lord Palmerston's vigorous foreign policy would not do for the present day, but a warning uttered by him in the House of Commons over half a century ago has even more force now than then. " I hold," he said, " with respect to alliances that England is a Power sufficiently strong to steer her own course, and not to tie herself as an unnecessary appendage to the policy of any other Government." At present we are not even the ally of France on any terms of reciprocity, but her most obedient servant ; for while in given circumstances France can call up our assistance to the last ship, man, and penny, we have no corresponding claim upon her in any circumstances whatever. We have put ourselves at her disposal for the maintenance of a territorial status which is opposed to good policy, since it keeps Europe disturbed, rancorous, impoverished, and armed to the teeth. The spectacle of this great country limping in the rear of Continental States inflated with egoism, vanity, and mad ambitions is to hundreds of thousands—perhaps millions—of people throughout the Empire humiliating in the extreme. It should be our business to extricate ourselves from the European imbroglio as soon as possible. We have other and better work to do in the world than to be for ever fighting at the call of the Continent, in order to compose disputes over matters which do not seriously concern us, to establish order which never lasts, and to maintain a balance of power which always has proved illusory and always will so prove.

Many years ago so far-seeing and imperialistic a statesman as Sir M. E. Grant Duff advocated the abandonment from time to time of such portions of the Empire as could properly be regarded as *damnosa hæreditas*. Let us, at least, regard

Europe as such a bad speculation, and for the future, cutting our liabilities as far as may be, let us have as little as possible to do with it politically. If the Balkan States wish to fight each other, let them do it ; the sooner each of them finds its level, the sooner they will learn that fighting does not pay. If Russia and Poland, France and Germany, Hungary and Roumania refuse to come together and find ways of adjusting the *impasses* created by the peace settlements, or to allow the League of Nations to do it for them, let us wash our hands of them all, and, following Cobden's advice, await " the natural course of events " : it might bring drastic solutions of their difficulties, but nations which will not be ruled by the rudder must be ruled by the rock.

To such sombre possibilities, however, there is an alternative. For it is not too much to expect that the known determination of this country to abstain from future Continental quarrels, except in the capacity of a conciliator and pacifier, would have a great and immediate influence upon other European nations, and do much to discredit the war mentality which now spreads like a pall of poison-gas from the Atlantic to the Ural Mountains. Continental nations must no longer be allowed to assume that Great Britain will always be at their beck and call when required. To have the " international mind " and be " good Europeans " does not mean readiness to go to war whenever called upon by other nations, nor yet entering into alliances with any of them, but persistent well-doing in the common cause of good will and peace. That is the truest and highest mission for any people, and if we fulfil it faithfully we shall have performed the only service which Europe has a right to expect of us. Englishmen proud of their heritage should be weary of the undignified position into which their country has fallen as a mere hanger-on of Continental Europe—its handyman, its fetcher and carrier, its policeman and pawnbroker.

If such doctrine sounds like going back to Cobden, it is at least reverting to Canning also.

" What," asked that statesman, when challenging the interventionists of his day, " is it to become a maxim with this country that she is ever to be a belligerent ? Is she never under any circumstances to remain neutral ? If this proposition be good for anything it must run to this extent—that our position, insulated as it is from all the rest of the world, moves us so far from the scene of Continental warfare that we ought always to be belligerent—that we are bound to counteract the designs of Providence, to reject the advantages of nature, and to render futile and erroneous the description of the poet,[1] who has said to our honour that we were less prone to war and tumult, on account of our happy situation, than the neighbouring nations that lie coterminous with one another."

In a recent address (April 30, 1926) the present Foreign Secretary, surveying the European distractions, warned his hearers against discouragement, and bade them "take comfort in the troubles of to-day by reflecting on the way in which their ancestors had faced and overcome what seemed to them equal difficulties." "Might they not," he asked, "amidst the disappointments and discouragements which crossed their path, renew their faith as they read their history and saw how ever in this country public spirit and public resolution had risen to meet the needs of the occasion?" That may all be very true and inspiring; yet instead of having, every time we find ourselves as a nation in difficulties, to fortify our hearts by remembrance of the courage and endurance with which our forefathers came through like troubles, would it not be more to the point to consider whether there be not a national policy which would avert the perplexities and disasters which intermittently threaten to overwhelm us, so reserving our moral and material resources for other and wiser employments than quarrelling, and fighting for other people? The idea of Great Britain accepting the historical *rôle* of a sort of strong man of the fair, who is able to lift incredibly heavy weights, for the admiration of the on-looking world, does not suggest a high or even an intelligent conception of national destiny. There is a better policy, and its broad basic principle is Cobden's doctrine of nonintervention, carried to the extremest practicable limit.

Sooner or later we must be prepared for modifications of our status in the Far East likewise. Sixty years ago Disraeli startled England with the declaration that she was not a European but an Asiatic Power, and for a time he gave to British foreign policy a distinctly exotic tendency. It was a

[1] Shakespeare, *Richard II*, ii. 1.

divagation, however, unnatural and impermanent, as we can see to-day, and shall see with increasing clearness the more the blessed doctrine of self-determination rouses the spirit of racialism in the still but half-awakened East. Those who have not hitherto shared this view will do well to follow the developments of the new Pan-Asiatic movement, whose principal leaders represent India, Japan, China, Siam, and Korea, and whose ambitious programme includes, among other objects, the creation of a strong Asiatic self-consciousness and sense of solidarity, co-operation by Asiatic peoples in all Asiatic affairs, the demand for the recognition by the League of Nations of the full equality of those peoples with other races, the formation of a Pan-Asiatic university in China, and the building of Pan-Asiatic conference halls in Tokyo and Pekin.

For the future British policy in external affairs should follow the lines of a progressive detachment from purely European and Asiatic affairs and an increasing concentration upon the development of our great Dominions, together with the simultaneous fostering of a cordial understanding and close co-operation with America. In the creation of a strong and enduring comradeship with the great transatlantic branch of the Anglo-Saxon family in particular lie the true interest and welfare not only of the British Empire but of the world at large.

Our heavy and increasing imperial responsibilities alone point to the urgency of an entirely new orientation of our foreign relations. Great Britain cannot do justice to the tasks of Empire so long as she is harassed, hampered, and exploited by a cantankerous Continent which has never lived in peace for a longer time than was necessary in order to be prepared for new wars, and which, though for the moment vaguely conscious of the need for settlement, refuses to have it on the only possible terms and conditions. The choice which has to be made is the most momentous in national history. It is the choice between the Empire and Europe ; for the time has come when Great Britain must face the fact that she cannot at the same time do her full duty as the head of the great Commonwealth of English-speaking nations and as the burden-bearer of the Continent.

The truth needs to be taken to heart that the Empire has become too big an undertaking to be any longer regarded as a part-time job. It deserves and demands the best thought and capacity which the British peoples have at command ; more, if its future is to be assured, it will have to be established in the confidence and attachment of our nation in a way it never has been in the past. Already a large and increasing section of the electorate at home has begun to regard the Empire with declining sympathy, and if we would be candid and honest with facts and with ourselves we shall admit that the cause lies to a large extent with the policy of indiscriminate aggrandizement which followed a war undertaken with the solemn repudiation of any idea of annexations. Because imperialism has been allowed to convey to the minds of the working classes the idea of subjecting native populations to alien domination against their will, they are yielding to the temptation to regard the Empire as necessarily aggressive and predatory. Unless every appearance of justification for suspicions of that kind can be removed, the time may come when the very stability of the Empire may be threatened. Those who are so ready to criticize the attitude of the organized workers in this matter might in simple fairness remember that their stake in the common country and the Empire is larger, in virtue of their numbers, than that of any other class, and that these men bore the greatest part in the struggle which left our land and Empire scatheless eight years ago. There are different kinds of patriotism, and the kind which chiefly finds expression in boisterous boasting and flag-waving is not the best, or necessarily genuine at all.

The most important task to which British statesmanship can apply itself to-day is to take stock afresh of our country's position and responsibilities in the world, and to do it in that spirit of complete open-mindedness which, while paying due regard to living as distinct from dead traditions, refuses to distrust and taboo new ideas, new ways, new departures simply because they are new. Still, as in Cobden's day, British statesmen are largely living on the intellectual capital left them by their Tory and Whig predecessors. They are following inherited ideas, some of which have never been thoroughly thought out, or they would not be adhered to for twenty-four hours longer. Neither foreign policy nor imperial policy can be said to proceed from rational, self-explanatory principles capable of affording either adequate justifications for the past or helpful positive guidance for the future. We have stumbled into our present foreign difficulties for the very reason that we have seldom known clearly what was our objective or why we did one thing rather than another. So, too, in relation to the Empire : that vast realm, spread over every continent and sea, has grown as it would, following no principle and no design. We may be grateful that it has grown so well ; yet the fact that our haphazard ways of Empire-building are faulty is being shown before our eyes to-day by two facts. One is the embarrassing problems which have been created by the thoughtless policy of land-snatching which was followed after the war, and the other is the fact that now that a critical stage has been reached in the relations of the Dominions to the Mother Country, and these autonomous communities are clamouring for a definite place in the councils of the Empire, we have not only no plan ready but have hardly begun to think of one, and are about to invite spokesmen of the Dominions to come and tell us what to do.

Need it surprise us that it is from the Dominions that there comes to-day the loudest and most insistent call that the Empire shall cut itself adrift from Europe and the European policies which make so conspicuously and unchangingly for complications, mischief, and war ? The Geneva episode of last April led to much plain speaking on this subject. Thus the *Cape Argus*, asking in a leading article the question, " Why, ever since the Armistice, has Great Britain been dragged in the train of some European nation ? " answered :

" Because she has forgotten that she represents an Empire and has been fascinated by her difficulties and dangers as a European Power. The failure of the Dominions to show an active interest in international affairs, or to give material backing to their new status, is no excuse for the ' looking-to-Europe ' attitude of British statesmen.

" Great Britain should take her stand before the European nations, not as a European Power, but as the delegated spokesman of the Empire —a world Power. Whenever she goes into an international conference,

she should insist that Dominion representatives be there to criticize the
perspective and temper the sentimentalism of her representatives.
Further, the Dominion instinct in foreign affairs is the true instinct of
the British "people, as opposed to the clique of European-trained
diplomatists and civil servants who rule the roost in Whitehall.   This
instinct, suppressed since the Armistice, distrusts European entanglements.   It is much more vocal and dominant in the Dominions, which
represent thus the soundest tradition of British diplomacy."

That utterance is a fair conspectus of well-informed
Dominion opinion generally, though in South Africa Dutch
utterances on this subject are naturally more emphatic
than British.   Even more clearly than we at home do our
kinsmen across the seas recognize that Great Britain has
already laboured too long under the double strain, imposed
on the one hand by a European policy of indefinite liabilities,
and on the other hand by the multitudinous and ever-growing
claims of Empire, and that in trying to perform two such
huge tasks at once she is vainly attempting the impossible.
The drastic limitation of the former is absolutely necessary ;
the restriction of the latter is also desirable in so far as it may
be found prudent and practicable.

Nothing has contributed more to create the feeling of discomfort and anxiety regarding the imperial outlook which
exists to-day in wide circles than the enormous addition
made during the present generation to the national responsibilities—financial, administrative, and military—by the needless, and in part purposeless, acquisition of territories of vast
extent in all parts of the world.   Much of this imperial
expansion has been no more rational or moral than the craze
of the millionaire of a certain type who accumulates wealth
merely for the satisfaction which the knowledge of possession
affords.

The mandated territories are the most notable illustrations of unintelligent imperialism of that sort.   How many
people in this country know that by the peace treaties and
supplementary conventions they have taken upon themselves
responsibility for the good government and welfare of territories aggregating nearly a million square miles—so adding in
area another quarter of a Europe to the four Europes of
which the Empire already consisted—and with a population

exceeding nine millions ? [1] And of those who are aware of this stupendous fact how many have given a thought to all that it means ?   No time could be less propitious than the present for so gratuitous a challenge to fate.   A large part of the Indian Dependency is in a ferment of disaffection, assiduously fostered by clever native leaders bent on freeing their country from alien rule.   We have had to capitulate to similar agitation in Ireland and Egypt, and the fact should have sobered even in the most intemperate of expansionists.   Every thoughtful mind admits to secret fears that, owing to the decimation of the best of our youth in the war, the efficient manhood necessary to the full discharge of our imperial tasks may prove inadequate.   Added to these warnings, the war left us from the first a deplorable aftermath of domestic discontent and unrest, further deepened by prolonged unemployment, insomuch that an ex-Prime Minister lately told the House of Commons that violent developments had only been prevented by the grant of public doles, subsidies, and benefits of all kinds, which have already cost the taxpayers in the short space of eight years the huge sum of £340,000,000.[2]

A time like the present was surely one for limiting and diminishing our foreign commitments rather than for increasing them.   There is a great fear—and they are the truest patriots who recognize the fact—that this insatiable craving for territory and the burden of taxation which it imposes

---

[1] The approximate areas and populations of the mandated territories falling to the British Empire are as follows :

	Square miles.	Population.
Palestine	9,000	757,000
Iraq	143,300	2,849,000
The German Colonies—		
Cameroons	31,000	550,000
Togoland	12,600	188,000
East Africa	365,000	4,122,000
South-West Africa	332,400	230,000
New Guinea, etc.	90,500	440,000
Totals	983,800	9,136,000

[2] Mr. Lloyd George stated in the House of Commons on March 18, 1926 : " What would have happened during six years of unemployment, running from a million up to two and a half millions, if you had not made these efforts to prevent hunger and famine ?   We have had from a million to two and a half millions walking the streets for six years, and not a drop of blood has been shed, there has been no riot ! "   The facts are happily as stated, but the argument carries a somewhat dangerous implication.

may provoke the same reaction against Empire which, in the middle of last century, spread to all classes and parties, and made even Disraeli willing to cut adrift Canada and other " wretched colonies," in the hope of so reducing the naval estimates as to enable better budgets to be produced. While expenditure upon some of the most pressing needs of the home country—education, health, housing—is being reduced at every turn, and Ministers are continually warning the nation of the " stern duty of economy," fabulous sums have been squandered on the mandated territories, and millions are still going the same way every year. When a short time ago an American statesman, taking us at our word, talked of England as a " poor country," the Government cheerfully decided to spend several additional millions in naval defence at Singapore, just to prove that there was plenty more money where that came from, and that in love of Japan and a desire not to excite her susceptibilities in the least degree the American Senate itself could not excel us.

The last of the imperialistic extravagances is the prolongation of the mandate for Iraq, which promises to impose indefinite liabilities upon British taxpayers for twenty-five years, to begin with. And what afterwards ? What is behind this fresh exploit ? Is there to be a repetition of the Egyptian episode—first temporary occupation, with pledges to withdraw repeated at intervals, then the discovery that new imperial interests and the work done and still to do justify our remaining indefinitely, until finally, after forty years of effort and sacrifice, circumstances force an abrupt and sullen departure, as we are told in imperious tones that we are no longer needed and our presence has become inconvenient ? It is true that in the interval a great work for civilization was achieved. But does anyone pretend that we should ever have dreamt of undertaking that work for Egypt if we had known that evacuation would be the end of the story ?

Granting that the success of British administration in Egypt deserves, as it does, far more gratitude from those whom it has benefited and from the world at large than it will ever receive, is it just or right to spend and be spent so freely for other lands while at home and in the Dominions so much work that is necessary and urgent remains either half done or not begun at all ? Are the German colonies in East and West Africa, are Palestine and Iraq in Asia, similarly to point the way to long years of expensive and unrequited philanthropy of the same kind—money, solicitude, and sympathy poured out in streams for the good of alien countries and races thousands of miles away, instead of being employed for the benefit of our own land and the elevation of its people ? Not one of these territories will ever offer homes to any large number of British settlers, nor would their possession be justified if they did, so long as the vast empty spaces of our Dominions are still calling for population. If we have so much money available for settlement and schemes of development abroad, why not, in the name of reason, employ it there ? A fraction of the immense sums which have been thrown away since the war in Asia Minor and Africa would have settled hundreds of thousands of unemployed British families in comfort in the Dominions, and given them a good start in a new life.

That we shall before long abandon the German colonies, or some of them, and be glad so to do, is certain ; but that those who obtained the mandates for the government of Palestine and Iraq meant and mean that we shall stay there permanently, if we can, is just as certain. Every year the wish and with it the claim to remain will become stronger, as vested interests of all kinds multiply and take root—as British money, capacity, and blood are transfused into the sluggish veins of these hitherto backward communities, as British ties and traditions are established which there will be a natural desire to conserve, as the British *cachet* is more and more firmly impressed upon native life, thought, and institutions, until at last justifications, or at least excuses, for remaining will be pleaded which it will be difficult to override. So the day will eventually come, as in the case of Egypt, when, abandoning all pretence, a Government will go to the House of Commons and say, " See how much we have done and spent in Palestine and Iraq ! They cannot repay us in money, so we will take payment in kind by remaining. These great provinces are henceforth integral parts of the Empire. Withdrawal is unthinkable ! "

But we are told that the mandates have been undertaken

as " sacred trusts " in the interest of civilization and humanity. The less said about this pretence the better, for the facts utterly discredit it. The Allies early in the war divided the German colonies amongst them as the prize of expected victory, and it was only when President Wilson objected to any such barefaced annexation that the mandate idea was accepted as a *pis-aller*. In the case of Palestine and Iraq there was never a thought of supplanting Turkey in these territories until she decided to throw in her lot with the Central Powers. The justification given by Lord Curzon (August 4, 1920) when our Government obtained the mandate for Palestine was that Turkish rule in that country " for the last 500 years had been one of the great scandals of history." Yet, in spite of this, when the war broke out our Government offered to guarantee to Turkey " the absolute integrity of her territories " (including Palestine) provided she remained neutral !

It was well said at the Oxford meeting of the British Association that " the real man of science could not be charged with the childish love of mere bigness." That is no less true of the real imperialist, as distinguished from the pseudo-imperialist who has not yet advanced beyond the crude materialistic and geographical conception of Empire. Is it not time to make an end of imperial expansion of that sort ? Is it worth while to engage in sheer gambles in unneeded territory when the result is that the illusory gains reaped abroad are counterbalanced by such tangible losses at home ? For are not these dubious transactions sapping the imperial attachment and feeding the discontent of the masses of the workers ; swelling the ranks of the disruptionists both within our own shores and abroad who, foolish in so many things, are wise enough to know that the British Empire in its rightful limits is one of the few stable structures in a shaken and chaotic world, since otherwise they would leave it alone ; and giving point to the bitter reproach of " the armies of the homeless and unfed,"—" Our Governments can save others, but their own people they will not save ? "

There is, indeed, something radically inconsistent and wrong in our ideas of democratic government when Ministers can get up in the House of Commons and talk in

X

glowing terms of self-satisfaction about the beneficent work of civilization in which their Departments are engaged in distant parts of the globe, while at home, at their very doors, within sight and sound of the Clock Tower, tens of thousands of their own countrymen, all in one way or another taxpayers, and therefore contributors in some degree to the bounty so freely bestowed on far-away alien lands and races, are herded together in conditions of poverty, squalor, and degradation.[1]

Where is the merit or even the justification of a world-wide imperial realm unless we can be sure that it will continue to be supported, not merely at the circumference, but even more at the centre, by a race itself worthy to be called imperial—a race sound in body and mind, intelligently educated, capable of large and generous ideas, consciously inspired by high ethical motives in the civilizing mission which Empire, on any rational principle, imposes upon a governing people? Yet are we British at the centre even now, on the whole, such a race, and can we be satisfied with ourselves? What of our C3 grades of manhood and womanhood, our record of crime, insanity, and illiteracy, our drink bill of over three hundred millions a year, our urban and rural housing conditions? What of the national riot of gambling, the morbid devotion to sport characteristic of all classes, the lives of empty, useless, criminal indolence lived in every rank of society, from the lowest to the highest, the pornographic literature and picture palaces licensed to degrade and demoralize the nation's youth, the hideous pictures of social life unfolded daily in the divorce and police courts? What of the grinding weight of a poverty which dooms its countless victims to inhuman conditions of life, and by contrast the prodigal luxury and extravagance of a wealth uncontrolled by any ideas of responsibility? Can a nation whose life is besmirched by blots like these still claim to be a truly imperial breed; is it morally fit to be entrusted with the responsibilities of Empire; and if the forces which now are pulling it downward be not checked, how long will it be able to bear the ever-increasing burden?

It is no boast but the simple truth to say that in capacity,

[1] As this chapter is being revised the Thames magistrate is reported as saying, " I think the housing conditions of East London would be a disgrace to a savage community."—*The Times*, April 29, 1926.

fidelity, and probity British administrators, wherever the call of duty takes them, are second to none in the whole world, and superior to those of most other races. But no Empire can be saved by its administrators alone. The governance of Empire is a whole nation's business and responsibility, and when once subject peoples begin to doubt that behind the emissaries of the Crown, however upright, capable, and devoted they may be, there is a race so much higher in intellectual and moral qualities than themselves as to justify their claim to ascendancy, the days of that ascendancy will be numbered.

It is no pleasant duty so to turn the searchlight upon the darker places of our national life, yet to ignore ugly facts in pharisaic self-satisfaction is to sin against the light and to court ultimate disaster. In these days the normal Englishman's prompt answer to any criticism of national failings is, " What does Mr. Page say ? " Walter Page was a fine character, and he did splendid service to this country and to the cause of British-American friendship for which no living Englishman will cease to be grateful ; but it is doubtful whether he would have been half as popular amongst us, and his name might not have adorned a public memorial, had he not confirmed estimates of the national virtues of whose existence most of us were already well aware.[1] Not a few discriminating people, to be ranked amongst the warmest of his admirers, find his criticism far more helpful than his praise ; for while praise, if sincere and administered in due measure, may be excellent as a tonic, as a food it is lacking in vitamins. Wise men and women wish to know the worst as well as the best about themselves. Is it ungracious to suggest that a great nation, burdened with world-wide responsibilities, which every day put to the test in a thousand places the quality of its manhood and character, in statesmanship and diplomacy, in administration and commerce, and in all

---

[1] Colonel House's *Papers* show that Page became too English for Washington. We are told, under date May 17, 1916, that " Wilson . . . wrote House that the Secretary of State was so disappointed with Page's whole conduct of American dealings with the Foreign Office that he wanted to bring him back for a vacation ' to get some American atmosphere into him again.' " House replied to the President, " No one who has not lived in the atmosphere that has surrounded Page for three years can have any idea of the subtle influence ; therefore he is not to be blamed so much as one would think."—*The Intimate Papers of Colonel House*, ii. 267-70.

the other multifarious services of civilization, needs, far more than laudation and compliment, the homely but nourishing fare of honest criticism ? That, too, was Cobden's belief, and it explains why, as we have seen, he uttered his opinions of his countrymen's shortcomings so freely in speech, writing, and correspondence.

The immediate duties of our nation, unfulfilled and waiting, are that it shall make itself fitter and worthier to hold the trusteeship of Empire, and shall consider how far the discriminating contraction of needless responsibilities would minister to the greater unity and concentration of our rule wherever the British race and British influence are so strong and well rooted as to give promise of becoming indigenous, of progressive growth, and of permanence. We need to think more about the development of the true and abiding centres of Britishry—the Dominions already formed and those still in embryo. In comparison with that high and inspiring task what are Europe and Asia to us or we to them ?

For years our Empire-augmenters have been loading Atlas more and more heavily until at last the weary Titan really seems to be bending beneath " the too great orb of his fate." Will they not see in time that the stability and security of the Empire cannot be promoted, but must be diminished, by increasing our responsibilities abroad and neglecting our far more pressing duties at home, and that the continual grasping after territory wherever and by whatever means it can be had, for no other purpose except to make the Empire larger, must weaken and discourage the true and sober imperial spirit even amongst patriotic citizens whose pride in the Empire has hitherto been one of the most precious parts of their lives ? For them the things that matter supremely are that their country's honour shall be unsullied, its faith be proof against egoism, and its titles and claims in every part of the world be clearly established upon the only safe foundations of either national or international life, which are legality, justice, and right. Never will they be willing to barter for apparent temporary advantage the Empire's real and permanent interests.

Let no one raise the foolish cry that those who call for the limitation of our appalling imperial responsibilities are craven-hearted and doubt the Empire's future, or imagine that their scruples and misgivings can be silenced by hurling at them chunks of crude imperialistic verse taken from Tennyson, Kipling, and lesser " poets of Empire." It is no sign of either cowardice or lack of faith to raise the warning that ageing nations need to adjust their exertion to their strength, and that only by so doing can they hope to work on with unflagging efficiency and success. The critic may object that nations renew their youth every hour and every moment of time. Yes, but let it not be forgotten that our nation is now being renewed in part from a slowly deteriorating stock, since the multitudes who leave our shores every year to seek fortune in other parts of the world are the young and vigorous, and not the mature and exhausted, with the inevitable result that we are becoming an older and, both physically and mentally, a less virile people.

Taking a long look forward—and it is wise to take very long views in these days, since history henceforth is going to be made far more rapidly than ever before in the life of mankind—there is a special rock ahead which, though as yet it appears to give rise to little anxiety, should occasion much. One quarter of the land surface of the entire earth falls within the British Empire (and yet in 1919 we wanted still more and took it !). The empires of the remaining six colonizing States of Europe have together an area half as large as that under British rule. Nearly all the other independent sovereign States of the globe, about sixty in number, in so far as they need outlets for surplus population, or will need them in future, are dependent upon the good will of their neighbours and particularly of the seven European States which between them own three-eighths of the globe. Is this a condition of things that can count on permanency ? On the contrary, is it not bound within a very short time to provoke keen controversy, now that the League of Nations has become a platform for the ventilation of the world's inequalities and grievances ?

Imperial nations may be perfectly, and in good faith, convinced that the colonizing and civilizing work which they are doing will establish their title to retain their possessions and privileges undiminished for all time. The important question is, does the rest of the world agree with them ? Can it be said that the British, French, Belgian, and Portuguese nations hold their vast domains by that sanction ? We are in the habit of talking of our imperial destiny and of how we are fulfilling it, and we are sincere in so doing. But other nations are also eager to fulfil destinies of which they are no less conscious than we, and they are unable to do it ; since they find their legitimate desire and ambition to grow, and widen their political and cultural influence in the world, blocked at every turn by the fact that the only possible spheres for such expansion have already been appropriated by older nations, whose earlier progress gave them a great start in the race for Empire.

It is the disproportionate partition of Africa in particular —for the most part unappropriated half a century ago— which most impresses the landless countries. Here are some illuminating figures, which deserve to be thoughtfully pondered. The African continent has an area of eleven and a half million square miles, and nine out of every ten of these miles are in the hands of six of the seven colonizing Powers of Europe. The shares of these Powers are as follows : Great Britain 3,820,000 square miles, France 3,649,000, Portugal 917,000, Belgium 910,000, Italy 780,000, and Spain 129,000 square miles. To put the matter in a more tangible way : the ratios of African territory to their home populations are one square mile to every seven inhabitants of Portugal, one to every nine inhabitants of Belgium, one to eleven in the cases of Great Britain and France, one to fifty in the case of Italy, and one to every 168 in the case of Spain.

At the present moment two of the most prolific nations of Europe are clamouring, the one for more colonies, the other for the return of the colonies wrested from her in the hour of defeat in war. On behalf of Italy Signor Mussolini complains with justification that the outlets which before the war were open to her surplus population are now to a large extent closed. Then the Italian emigration overseas alone exceeded one-third of the yearly increase of population, but now for the reason stated it is only half this figure, and he has unkindly suggested that the share of Africa which has fallen to his country is inadequate, particularly when comparison is made with countries of far less population and importance. His recent visit to Tripolitania, his spectacular reception in Rome on his return home, and the " Colonial day " which has been inaugurated in Italy must all be regarded as part of a systematic piece of Fascist propagandism, and it would be a mistake to ignore the purpose in view. Germany, on the other hand, has urgent need of independent sources of certain raw materials for her industries, to which end she claims back as a minimum the tropical colonies in Africa which her explorers and pioneers, her administrators and doctors, her missionaries and traders had brought to so high a state of development. Anticipating also the time when her population will again begin to overflow, she wishes to know where it shall go.

In time other nations will inevitably join their voices to those of Italy and Germany, Poland, and other of the new East European States. How shall their plaints be answered, since ignored they cannot be ? For it is inconceivable that a few favoured States can permanently claim the right to control vast areas of the earth's surface which they do not and cannot fill ; while other countries, though crowded to overflowing, seek in vain for territories in which their surplus populations may settle, without being exposed to the galling humiliation of forfeiting their nationalities and forswearing allegiance to their natural rulers.

It is the question of nationality that is the obstacle in this as in so many other of the problems that perplex the modern world. The difficulty is not that the suzerain Powers which now own or control these great regions necessarily object to the admission of any but their own nationals— though there are British Dominions which are just as unwilling to allow even British subjects without ample means to enter their gates as to admit people of Asiatic race—but that permanent settlement under an alien flag means a violent rupture of traditional, personal, and sentimental ties which, as people of British birth know so well, mean so much in the life of highly organized communities. The European nations which now send their surplus populations overseas naturally want to have the satisfaction of knowing that they are making their own independent contributions to civilization, by planting in other parts of the earth their distinctive ways of life, their institutions, customs, and modes of thought, just as the nations of antiquity and the great colonizing nations of modern times have done. How to meet that reasonable expectation is one of the most difficult aspects of the problem of Empire, and it cannot long be evaded.

But there is another aspect akin to it. What of the future of the native races, now struggling upward, in some parts of the world rapidly, to a higher civilized status ? What provision is being made for their needs as they will be apparent thirty, fifty, and still more a hundred years hence, for it is not too soon to be thinking so far ahead ? Take Africa again, though Spanish America and the islands of the Pacific and Indian Oceans in which the white races have asserted sway should not be forgotten. Will the native races, as they advance in civilization, be given parity of political and civic status, and eventually be allowed to develop side by side with the Europeans, on the same plane, in common spheres of activity ; or will they always be required to live apart, and permitted only to look at their white neighbours from the other side of the fence ? If the former alternative is contemplated the transition, remote or near, need not create insuperable difficulties ; if the latter, where, and on what conditions, are the segregated native races to live their own self-centred lives ?

Does it never occur to British, French, Belgian, and Portuguese statesmen, if not to the land companies which have appropriated so large a part of the habitable yet still undeveloped regions of Africa, to ask what will happen when the indigenous populations, arrived at puberty, begin seriously to question the titles by which the vast tropical regions of that continent have passed under the control of the white races, not for settlement, but only for commercial exploitation ? Every colonizing Power has claimed the right to dispose of the native territories under its self-imposed dominion according to its own laws, enacted for the purpose, usually paying but scant regard to prior native rights, and often repartitioning the land on the principle that natives possess no rights at all except those which their new masters may be pleased to confer upon them. This highly disputable claim is supposed to be justified by the plea that the native races which have been supplanted were living in a more or less savage state. But so lived the ancestors of the white conquerors not so very long ago ; yet that fact did not prevent them from evolving their own civilizations in the environments natural to them. Is it certain that coming generations, even the next one, will recognize the equity of the wholesale expropriations which have been applied to the native races of Africa in the past, based as they have been on alien legal systems, arbitrarily enforced ? Could the League of Nations be expected to approve of what has been done if the question were referred to it for decision, and should we wish it to approve ?

A " colour bar " policy which closes some of the best parts of the earth to the immigration of the coloured races, yet at the same time appropriates the territories in which those races have immemorially had their home, cannot stand the test either of time or reason. Every argument which can fairly be advanced in favour of reserving great countries for an exclusively white population strengthens the claim of the dark races of Africa for a radical redistribution in their favour of the habitable regions of their own continent.

When the institution of international law has been carried to a higher stage of justice and morality, it will be recognized that there was something radically amiss with the social conscience which allowed European nations, under the comforting pretext of a duty to the sacred cause of progress, to supplant these indigenous African peoples at will, simply because their primitive tribal life failed to commend itself to Western ideas of civilization. The day will assuredly come, and it will not be far distant, when the threatened conflict between the weakening white communities and the virile and progressive native races of the African continent will only be averted by a great and magnanimous policy of restitution. It may be too soon to discuss the form which this policy will take or the process by which it will come about, but it is not too soon to recognize this to be a practical question which calls for a very practical solution.

If the Armageddon which the world talks of and fears to-day comes at all, it will rage over the unequal distribution of the empty spaces of the world. For the earth and its bountiful resources exist not for men but for man, and the problem of how to put them to the best possible use is an international and a world problem, in the settlement of which not only the colonial nations which have at disposal territories sufficient to meet their needs for untold centuries, but all nations, will claim a voice. The problem comes home to us and to the Empire in a special way, because we have so much at stake, controlling as we do so large a portion of the earth's surface, containing most of the still unoccupied territories suitable for habitation by Europeans.

For these problems I have no cut-and-dried solutions to offer, nor is the time ripe for such. All I am concerned to do here is to state the facts in the hope that they will provoke the thought which they deserve. So far as European nations are concerned it is possible that relief might be found in schemes of territorial repartition on some sensible principle of rationing according to needs, or in the internationalizing of large areas suitable for settlement yet at present but little populated. The needs of the native races should be easier to meet, for in their case it is a matter of reserving for their use territories normally but little suitable for European settlement. What is certain is that unless amicable solutions, giving weight to all rightful claims, can be devised in time, the " haves " and the " have-nots," white or coloured, will inevitably settle their difficulties by conflicts of the old violent kind. How the choice shall fall is a question which will tax to the utmost the wisdom and resource of modern statesmanship.

As to this I would add, at the risk of stating a platitude, that those nations can best serve at once mankind and their own permanent interests who view the world as an interdependent unity and their position in it in the right perspective. Has the maxim, " Every man for himself and the devil take the hindmost," or, to put it more colloquially, " First come, first served," to continue always, for nations as well as individuals, a rule of conduct and life—always ? Is not " Live and let live " a better, worthier, even a safer principle of international relations ? And if that principle is to be more actively followed in the future, what nation is so able as our own to set the world an example ? Perhaps by doing it

Emerson's prediction would be fulfilled, and the result would be " to give to England a new millennium of beneficent power."

To return to first principles, I come to the conclusion that the great moral which the war and the peace are going to bring home to this country and the Empire is that Cobden's doctrine of non-intervention—which means for us keeping ourselves as far as possible to ourselves, and renouncing once for all the idea that we have a mission to civilize, moralize, and Anglicize mankind—is not, after all, unreasonable. The application of this principle may be more difficult in our day than it would have been half a century ago, yet national and imperial security will only be safeguarded in proportion as we are able to detach ourselves politically from countries which do not vitally affect us, and concentrate attention upon our own rightful affairs. We shall have to come back to the dictum of Lord Salisbury—and the sooner the better—" *We are strong enough to take care of ourselves without alliances, if only we do not waste our force on matters which do not concern us.*" [1]

The case for a policy of severe restraint, alike in foreign and imperial affairs, was forcibly put by Mr. Gladstone in the course of a speech made at West Calder in November 1879, when he laid down the following principles : That the strength of the Empire should be fostered by just legislation and by economy at home, thereby producing those great elements of national power, the physical element of wealth, and the moral elements of union and contentment ; that the imperial strength should be reserved for " great and worthy occasions " ; that Great Britain should do her utmost to preserve the concert of Europe and the world's peace, yet should avoid needless and entangling engagements ; and that she should acknowledge the equal rights of all nations.

A policy based on these principles, and scrupulously followed, would have preserved us from much recent mischief and present difficulty, and such a policy is our only hope for the future. Any suggestion of associating ourselves either in Europe or elsewhere with projects of equilibrium and intervention, however remote may appear to be the situations

[1] Letter to Lord Lytton, September 4, 1877.

which they contemplate, should be resolutely eschewed. If harmony with other nations cannot be promoted by good will, friendly intercourse, and the nexus created by common interests, it will never be obtained by alliances, pacts, or protocols of any kind. Nations which honestly wish each other well do not need to put it down in treaties ; still less do they make provision for " diplomatic groups " and military alliances, and formally stipulate the circumstances in which peaceful co-operation shall give place to armed action. All the recent attempts to give Europe security by such means proceed from the presupposition that the contracting nations do not trust but distrust each other.

Is the Pact of Locarno fundamentally different ? For in spite of all the fair phrases and mutual compliments with which it was promulgated, what it does in effect is to create a new system of conditional alliances based on the old doctrine of the balance of power, with the difference that Great Britain has now pledged herself to guarantee, in certain contingencies, the independence and integrity of several States, not one of which is under any sort of liability to raise a finger if her own territory should be assailed. Worst of all, so long as this pact continues neither France nor Italy, neither Belgium nor Poland will have the slightest inducement to do anything that might mitigate the harsher and more intolerable provisions of the treaties of peace, which yet are the real hindrance to security and therefore to settled peace.

One of the signatories, and the chief British inspirer, of the Treaty of Versailles spoke not long ago of the " commotion " which would be created if our Government were to speak of revision. It is a point of no consequence what Government has the courage to take the first step : the important fact is that there will be infinitely greater commotions if some of the provisions of the treaties are not revised, and that speedily. For time passes quickly. Already one half of the period of Germany's sentence to Coventry is over. What will happen when the other half has expired ? What Power will then be able, or have the right, to prevent her from arming at her discretion, and why will she arm but in order to be a strong military Power again and to regain her position of parity in the councils of Europe ?

Nothing would contribute more to the restoration of normal conditions at home—the abatement of the prevalent discontent and the creation of a new spirit of hopefulness and confidence, than such a reorientation of our relations to the world outside the Empire as has been suggested. For the maladies from which the nation is suffering are moral as well as economic and material, and the former go deeper than the latter. The most cruel wrong ever done to the soul of a nation was that committed in Paris in 1919 when, after a war into which the British peoples had thrown themselves in an unexampled spirit of idealism, the great moral gesture which would have saved the world, giving back to it a precious recompense for all it had endured and suffered, setting it on a new and broad highway of civilization, was withheld, and the birthright of a new era was bartered for the unholy spoils of conquest.

Most statesmen and politicians, whose special business it should be to interpret the mind and temper of the people for whose government they are responsible, have failed as yet to understand the social unrest which has followed the war and the peace. They profess to see in it merely the inevitable effects of reaction. They tell us that people are tired, their nerves are unstrung ; and then there is the protracted trade depression, resulting in so much worklessness. What is wanted is longer rest, with more unemployment doles, and all will come right in due time. Yet, after eight years of peace nothing has come right as yet, and there is little sign of a brighter outlook. The prevailing *malaise* is neither to be explained nor cured in any such conventional way, for it is due far less to physical and material than to moral causes— the disenchantment, disappointment, and resentment caused by the non-fulfilment of the bright hopes and prodigal promises which were held before the nation at a time when the greatest sacrifices of which men and women are capable were asked of them.

In some stern words uttered in the course of his last public speech Cobden anticipated the real malady from which this country, and not it alone, suffers to-day. " There is nothing," he said, " that breeds such a resentment in the great mass of the people—all history shows it—as *a sense of having been betrayed.* You will find in all history that the mass of the people are magnanimous for everything else but the conviction—sometimes erroneous—of having been betrayed." That a consciousness of deception, in this case only too justified, lies behind very much of the prevailing social discontent, and of the efforts of unpractical enthusiasts to persuade their fellows that their only hope lies in fundamental social changes, will not be denied by anyone who has made a serious attempt to understand the present mind of the working classes. That the same popular consciousness of betrayal exists in other Allied countries is shown by an article in *Foreign Affairs* (America) for January 1926, in which Signor G. Salvemini writes :

> Take a people peacefully inclined, force it into a gruelling war, and then send it home with the conviction that all its effort has been in vain, that all its sacrifices have been wasted, that its objectives have not been attained, that it has been cheated by everybody—and can one be surprised if it kicks over the traces and begins to rear around ? In very truth Italians have shown themselves possessed of the kindest of hearts, in that they have not massacred every one of us who dragged them into the war, and who then—as the author of our war, our Minister of Foreign Affairs, assured them—failed to press from the victory the peace for which they had fought."

There is good reason to believe that an impetus, forcing us into the direction indicated in the foregoing pages, will come from two quarters—from the Dominions and from the new estate of organized Labour. The moderation and restraint which the influence of both of these factors is bound to exert upon foreign and imperial policy will also make possible, for the first time, that stability and continuity which are supremely necessary if the Empire is to hold together. To this end foreign and imperial questions will need to be removed from the sphere of party contention in virtue of complementary *concordats*, one between political parties at home and the other between the Imperial and Dominion Governments and Parliaments, based upon such a common understanding upon broad principles as will satisfy all reasonable opinions.

In the absence of such agreements it is inevitable that at

home we shall have three parties all pulling different ways, and rare indeed will be the occasions when Great Britain will be able to speak with single voice on any capital question either of foreign or imperial policy.

Those whose political memories go back forty years will recall the time when there still survived in parliamentary life the healthy tradition which was supposed to exclude the display of party spirit from discussions of foreign affairs. However old the tradition was, and whatever were the circumstances which led to its decline, all visible traces of it had disappeared before the end of the century.[1] Even upon questions of imperial policy, and particularly those relating to the Dominions and India, there exists no longer the general accord which began to prevail after the statesmanlike winding-up of the Boer War and the end of the irritating sequence of Indian frontier wars which fell to the vice-royalties of Lords Elgin and Curzon.

Division has been accentuated, however, by the appearance of the Labour Party in parliamentary life, giving prominence to views on both foreign and imperial questions differing radically from those hitherto held in the older parties, and carrying us back, in some respects, to the undiluted doctrine of Cobden, particularly in the strong emphasis given to the policy of non-intervention, to what may be called the humanitarian aspect of imperialism, and to the conception of Empire as a trusteeship in the name of civilization, whose success in undeveloped territories is held to be best proved in proportion as, by the training of the native populations in self-government, it can make itself superfluous. It is probable that the action of the Trade Union Congress of 1925, in adopting with practical unanimity a strong resolution against colonization in general as at present practised by Western nations, fairly represents what may be called the political mind of the working classes, and it is a sign of the times which it would be unwise to ridicule or ignore.

Is it too late, or still possible, to revive the earlier parliamentary tradition, remembering the dangers inseparable

[1] As late as 1880 Sir M. E. Grant Duff wrote : " The broad outlines of British foreign policy are commanded by circumstances, and there is no dispute about them among reasonable men." That can be said no longer.

from the unbridled party spirit which to-day prevails in political life ? It can be done, but only by a compromise calling for concessions on every side favourable to moderation. Probably the reactionary wing of the Conservative party and the extremer section of the Labour party would find it most difficult, or least easy, to feel comfortable at first in a common tabernacle, which for the one might be too plain and for the other too gorgeous ; but if the need for such an arrangement were recognized, it is not too much to expect even die-hard politicians to adapt themselves to a change which would be so palpably for the public good. The mere existence of an agreement of this kind would impose upon the most imperialistic of Governments a restraint which often has been sadly needed in the past.

Equally important and urgent is a similar *concordat* between the centre of the Empire and the Dominions in regard both to foreign relations and imperial policy. The attitude of the Dominions to foreign affairs is no longer as indifferent as it was before the war. In that sphere many things now matter greatly to them which never troubled them in the past. For our fellow-subjects in the Dominions have likewise been sobered and disenchanted by the European tragedy and all that has followed it. They know the Continent better than ever before, and having seen the hopeless muddle into which the greater part of it has been brought by short-sighted statesmanship, and how both old States and new seem equally resolved to flounder on in the old evil way, they view with suspicion every step taken by the home Government which might have the effect of landing them anew in the morass of European strife.

It is questionable whether they would ever again rally to the side of the mother country in any dispute which could not be clearly shown to involve interests directly vital to themselves, and it is certain that they would not take part in another war for the defence of France, Poland, or any other part of Europe. It is not without significance that the Canadian House of Commons recently adopted unanimously a resolution, proposed by the Premier, laying down the principle that the formal approval of Parliament must be obtained before the Government advised the ratification or acceptance of military or economic treaties entered into by Great Britain.

In regard to Empire questions the Dominions are specially conscious of the need for continuity of policy. At the present time no guarantee of such continuity exists, so that they have no assurance that what one British Parliament does will not be promptly undone by its successor. The mere possibility of such a conflict of purpose arising should be sufficient to convince us of its danger, but quite recently it has actually happened. In 1923, while a Conservative Government was in power on sufferance, the third Imperial Economic Conference met in London for the purpose of discussing the question of inter-Empire trade. As a result of the discussions, facilitated by previous negotiations, an elaborate system of preferential duties was adopted in favour of the Dominions, India, and some of the Crown colonies, and it was to have come into operation in April 1924. Before the Government had obtained a vote of the House of Commons on the subject, a Labour Ministry, hostile to the preferences, came into power by the help of Liberal votes, and when the question came up for decision the entire preference system was negatived, to the natural disgust of the Dominions, several of which angrily threatened reprisals. In October 1924 a general election placed the Conservatives in power with a large majority over both of the other parties, and the preferences were duly approved by an overwhelming vote of the House of Commons.

On this occasion, therefore, only a little delay, without irremediable mischief, occurred as a result of the contradictory attitude of successive Governments ; but it is easy to imagine cases in which similar conflict between the British Parliament and the Dominions might lead to serious friction. The action taken by the Labour Government, whether one agreed with it or not, was strictly regular, and the censures passed upon it by several Dominion politicians, insufficiently acquainted with our constitutional system, were altogether unjustified. The preferences had not received parliamentary sanction, and had behind them only the promise of a Ministry which was kept in power by the accident of a divided Opposition. What was irregular and impolitic was the holding of an Imperial Conference for the purpose of adopting a practically prearranged

Y

tariff of duties, which marked a departure from the traditional British fiscal system, without taking into consideration the probable attitude of either of the two parties in the House of Commons with which the final decision of the question lay.

The episode carries its own moral, which is that imperial, like foreign, questions should be altogether removed from the sphere of party contention. For any Government, whatever its complexion, and whatever the voting power for the moment behind it, to use what, after all, is a position of temporary advantage in order to force through Parliament highly controversial measures is to trifle both with the nation and the Empire. The only safeguard against danger of the kind is a *concordat* of the character suggested.

How far the system of Imperial Preference is in itself wise and prudent is an independent question, to be discussed and decided on its merits. The modern system is, of course, only a reversion to the custom of the " old colonial days," when legislation regulating the foreign trade of the colonies, as passed in the English Parliament, generally contained the stipulation that colonial products should be admitted into the homeland subject to lower duties than were imposed on the same products imported from foreign countries. The earliest practice was to prohibit altogether trade between the colonies and foreign countries, so giving to the Mother Country a complete monopoly. If preference on the modern lines is to become a feature of imperial policy it is necessary that it shall have behind it the substantial acquiescence of all parliamentary parties and the nation at large, and to that end it must be a fair and square business " deal "—the exchange of advantages for equivalent advantages, with no sentimental nonsense about it.

There can be little doubt as to what would have been Cobden's attitude on the question. On principle he would have condemned any fiscal arrangements with the Dominions which failed to give to the Mother Country a full measure of reciprocity. Free Trade throughout the Empire he would have understood and applauded, though Free Trade throughout the world he would have liked far better ; but an inter-Empire policy which consisted of Free Trade on one side and a more or less modified Protection on the other he would have opposed as contrary to fair-play. He would also have warned us that any policy which aimed at converting modern empires into *terræ clausæ*, with which other nations were allowed to trade only on sufferance, must in the end be defeated by the economic laws of exchange, since a country which will not buy from other countries *pro tanto* disenables itself from selling to them either.

He would also have had us remember that, let Imperial Preference be camouflaged as it may, to the extent that it makes articles of universal consumption like food dearer in this country, it is a tax levied on the community, and that the plan of subsidizing the Dominions in this way, and by the millions which are being spent in settling their empty spaces and marketing their produce, may become a hard drain upon a country impoverished by the war, and already taxed more heavily than any other in the world. Not the least objection to Imperial Preference in his view would have been his old and never yet controverted contention that whatever measures of law or policy act in restraint of international trade hold back the cause of international peace.

The answer to the conventional arguments of Free Traders is, of course, that circumstances alter cases, and that a policy good for one day may be less good or even bad for another. From the standpoint of equity a modern British Government . has no need to apologize for what it is doing, at a time of unparalleled industrial depression, to stimulate inter-Empire trade, in view of the fact that for eighty years Great Britain has offered the world a free run of her market, though so few nations have had the fairness to reciprocate the compliment. Nevertheless, attractive and appealing as is the cry " Buy only British," it would be unwise to forget the dangers inseparable from any drastic policy of exclusive trading. The idea that the Empire is self-contained is common, but it is fallacious ; there are important raw materials indispensable for our staple industries which can only be procured in sufficient quantities, or at all, by purchasing abroad. It would be our own fault if the countries which alone can supply such materials retaliated with export prohibitions. A far more serious danger, however, is lest the too great straining of the preference bow should, by increasing the cost of necessary commodities, make more difficult the life of the mass of our population. Such a result might bring about a deplorable reaction of imperial sentiment, and by one of those gyrations of public opinion which occur from time to time, both in internal and external policy, the nation might find itself carried back to the standpoint of Cobden and the " Manchester School " of his day, who were ready to cut the colonies adrift as costly encumbrances. Whether we shall expose ourselves to that danger or avoid it is a question which rests entirely in our own hands.

EPILOGUE

WITH the establishment of the League of Nations a new influence, a new leaven has entered the life of the world. We stand to-day upon the threshold of an epoch which will witness far-going and deep-plumbing transformations, readjustments and revaluations of all kinds in the social and political order. For that epoch and that order will be governed more and more by new moral equations, by standards and sanctions higher than those which have served in the past, by a greater regard for individuality in communal life, and by a more conscious striving after international harmony and unity of interest.

A future English historian will apply to the statesmanship of his period criteria altogether different from those which now are deemed sufficient. The questions which he will ask will not be " How much prestige did it gain for us ? Through how many wars did it bring us safely ? How much territory did it add to the Empire ? " but rather " Did its policy promote international peace ? What was its contribution to the world's common stock of good and happiness ? How far did it, by timely concessions, even renunciations, help other less fortunate nations to live a fuller life and realize their rightful destinies ? Did it make or lose friendships for us ? Did it leave the name of England, not more feared, but more trusted and more respected ? "

These latter were the questions by which, so long ago, Cobden tested the purpose of his own public life and the quality of his influence ; and how well the test was borne this book has tried to show. To-day, more personally and more imperiously than ever before, the same questions point the leaders of thought, in every sphere of national life, to the truest conception of patriotism and to its highest aim and duty in our modern world.

ABRIDGED BIBLIOGRAPHY

The Political Writings of Richard Cobden. 2 vols., 1867 and 1868. Popular edition of 1878, with Introductory Essay by Sir LOUIS MALLET.

Speeches on Questions of Public Policy by Richard Cobden, M.P., edited by JOHN BRIGHT and JAMES E. THOROLD ROGERS. 2 vols., 1870. Later edition in one volume.

JOHN (LORD) MORLEY, *The Life of Richard Cobden.* 2 vols., 1881.

Sir LOUIS MALLET, *The Political Opinions of Richard Cobden.* 1869.

HENRY ASHWORTH, *Recollections of Richard Cobden, M.P., and the Anti-Corn Law League,* 1877.

Mrs. S. SCHWABE, *Reminiscences of Richard Cobden,* with a Preface by Lord FARRER. 1895.

JOHN A. HOBSON, *Richard Cobden, the International Man.* 1919.

INDEX

GEORGE ALLEN & UNWIN LTD.
LONDON: 40 MUSEUM STREET, W.C.1
CAPE TOWN: 73 ST. GEORGE'S STREET
SYDNEY, N.S.W.: WYNYARD SQUARE
WELLINGTON, N.Z.: 4 WILLIS STREET

The Making of a State

By President T. G. MASARYK
Rendered into English by WICKHAM STEED

Demy 8vo.   About 21s.

"The book is, in reality, a detailed account of the movement for Czecho-slovak independence, and of Masaryk's work as leader of the movement. It is full of interesting historical facts and philosophical reflections ; and, if not dramatic in the ordinary sense of the word, is a monumental contribution to public knowledge of the world war, its causes, and its consequences, and of the essentials of democratic freedom. Years hence, when people are able to see the war in perspective, I am inclined to believe that Masaryk will stand out as one of the greatest, if not the greatest figure in it. He foresaw it, understood it from the beginning and, starting as a lonely exile, ended by redeeming his people from three centuries of servitude. As a positive and constructive achievement nothing in the war can compare with this ; for even President Wilson's part authorship of the League of Nations is hardly comparable to Masaryk's single-handed work. His book—written under great dis-advantages while he was engaged in actually building up his new State —is a book to be read and pondered, not to be glanced through in a search for sensations. I think it will hold one of the highest places in the literature upon the war."—WICKHAM STEED.

The World Policy of Germany, 1890-1912

By OTTO HAMMANN
Translated by MAUD A. HUTTMAN, Ph.D.

Demy 8vo.   10s. 6d.

The author was Chief of the Press Division of the German Foreign Office from 1891 to 1917. He played an important part behind the scenes of the diplomatic stage in Berlin, particularly during the Chancellorship of Prince Bülow. The book contains new and illuminating material on Germany's relations with England and the other Powers.

The International Anarchy, 1904-1914

By G. LOWES DICKINSON

Author of "The Choice Before Us," "War: Its Nature, Cause and Cure," etc
Demy 8vo.   17s. 6d.

"It is very much the best analysis of the international events leading to the Great War which has so far appeared. . . . His account is masterly. . . . It is absolutely clear and . . . extremely interesting."—Nation.

German Colonization, Past and Future

By Dr. HEINRICH SCHNEE
Late Governor of German East Africa
With an Introduction by W. H. DAWSON

Demy 8vo.   Illustrated   5s.

"The reader who is intelligently interested in world politics ought to acquaint himself with what is here said."—Star.

Paths to World Peace

Cr. 8vo. By BOLTON C. WALLER, B.A. 5*s.*

"Mr. Waller has written a thoughtful and in many ways original book."—*The Times.*

Information on the Problem of Security

By J. W. WHEELER-BENNETT, JUNR.

Author of "Information on the Reduction of Armaments"

Demy 8vo. 10*s.*

This book is a comprehensive history of the problem of security from the Peace Conference to the present day. It deals in detail with the predecessors, origin, and meaning of the Locarno Treaties; the Soviet efforts to achieve security by treaties of neutrality and non-aggression, and the attempt of the League of Nations to provide a general agreement for security in the Treaty of Mutual Assistance and the Geneva Protocol. The book is a work of useful information for all interested in this important feature of international affairs.

The Decline of the West

By OSWALD SPENGLER

TRANSLATED FROM THE GERMAN BY MAJOR C. F. ATKINSON

Royal 8vo. 21*s.*

"Highly original and backed by much learning. . . . Will doubtless excite a considerable interest in England."—*Manchester Guardian.*

"The most remarkable book that has appeared in my time."—J. MIDDLETON MURRY in the *Adelphi.*

Thirty Years of Modern History

Demy 8vo. By WILLIAM KAY WALLACE 10*s.* 6*d.*

"The book is of value because of its uncompromising challenge to the conventions of political discussion."—*The Times.*

All prices are net.

LONDON: GEORGE ALLEN & UNWIN LTD.
RUSKIN HOUSE, 40 MUSEUM STREET, W.C 1